trinawagnerbouu ʋ ʒ·············

Delbert McClinton

John and Robin Dickson Series in Texas Music
Sponsored by the Center for Texas Music History
Texas State University
Gary Hartman, General Editor

DELBERT McCLINTON

One of the Fortunate Few

DIANA FINLAY HENDRICKS

Foreword by Don Imus

TEXAS A&M UNIVERSITY PRESS   COLLEGE STATION

LIBRARY OF CONGRESS CATALOGING-IN-PUBLICATION DATA
Names: Hendricks, Diana Finlay, author.
Title: Delbert McClinton : one of the fortunate few.
Description: First edition. | College Station : Texas A&M University Press,
[2017] | Series: John and Robin Dickson series in Texas music | Includes
bibliographical references and index.
Identifiers: LCCN 2017023983 (print) | LCCN 2017025550 (ebook) | ISBN
9781623495893 (ebook) | ISBN 9781623495886 | ISBN 9781623495886q(cloth
: alk. paper)
Subjects: LCSH: McClinton, Delbert. | Blues musicians—Texas—Biography. |
Lyricists—Texas—Biography. | Country music—Texas—History and
criticism. | Blues-rock music—Texas—History and criticism.
Classification: LCC ML420.M3407 (ebook) | LCC ML420.M3407 H46 2017 (print) |
DDC 781.64092 [B] —dc23
LC record available at https://lccn.loc.gov/2017023983

Mark Hendricks
(1953–2017)

This book is dedicated
to the great love of my life,
for always believing in us,
and for encouraging me to tell this story
of history, love, heartbreak,
and damned good music.
I am truly
"One of the Fortunate Few."

I'm the best and the worst.
I'm the first and the last . . .
Just like you.

—Delbert McClinton
September 30, 2016

Contents

A gallery of photographs follows page 162.

Foreword

In Elmore Leonard's *10 Rules of Writing*, Number 10 is "Try to leave out the part that readers tend to skip."

For me that generally means forewords and introductions.

So, when Diana Hendricks asked if I'd write a foreword for the biography of Delbert McClinton she was working on, I said I would, figuring most people are like me and would ignore it, and go right to the parts where Delbert tells us a bunch of shit that probably isn't even close to being true. Or, on the remote chance it *is* true, it would be information he should have kept to himself.

I love Delbert. In a healthy way. Not like we were, say, cellmates doing life in Huntsville. Not like Rupert Pupkin either, prowling around stalking his ass leaving creepy notes in his mailbox.

When we have Delbert on *Imus in the Morning*, the crew loves Delbert. They love Delbert because he is not an asshole. Vince Gill and Dwight Yoakam are not assholes either. Levon Helm was a saint. Then there is Van Morrison. Van was on the show with the gospel group, The Blind Boys of Alabama. They were going to sing a duet but could not agree on a song. An argument ensued. You know who argues with blind people who are black and love Jesus? An asshole.

I first heard the album *Victim of Life's Circumstances* in the late 1970s. A cocaine dealer friend of mind played it for me in his apartment on the Upper East Side of Manhattan in New York City, not some hillbilly in a double wide in Nashville, Tennessee. Delbert had already caught a bunch of people's attention all over the country and now he'd caught mine. Having drug dealer fans does not make you a bad person, I should add.

Delbert is a great songwriter. God gave him a voice and phrasing as good as anyone who has ever made a record. He is funny and smart and doesn't make singing look like work. Or an exercise class. Lyle Lovett once said to me, "If we could all sing like we wanted to, we'd all sing like Delbert."

Now about this book. A biography. Why?

Why reveal a wealth of personal information that is frankly none of anybody's fucking business? And to a writer who is probably a Democrat. For example, in the song "Two More Bottles of Wine," Delbert announces that there really was a "Maggie," who after a couple months in Los Angeles moved out of wherever they were living.

Why tell us that? Now we want to know why she moved out? What happened? Where is she? Does she know Delbert used her name in a song that became a huge hit? Has she ever expressed any remorse for turning Delbert into a drunk? Ever asked Delbert for money? Did she get fat? See? Who needs this shit?

God knows what else Delbert told this Hendricks person, all stuff she has stuck in this book. Some of it he will have to explain to his wife, Wendy. A problem he could have easily avoided, though, frankly, it's not like Wendy was a nun when they met at the bar at The Lone Star Café. She just hasn't written a book about all of it.

Don Imus
Brenham, Texas

Acknowledgments

Don Imus tells me that no one reads this part of a book, but it's kind of like the credits of the movie. There are some people who made this book happen. And for whom I am grateful. So, read along or skip this part if you are in a hurry to get on with the book.

This story began in 2014, when Nancy Coplin recommended that Wendy Goldstein, Delbert McClinton's wife and manager, talk to me about writing a new biography for Delbert's website. I had no idea it would grow into this. Thank you, Nancy. You are the Great Connector in the music world. And Janice Williams Hays, thank you for tirelessly transcribing interviews, organizing the images, and climbing the McClinton family tree for stories, facts, and dates.

Two of my heroes, Joe Nick Patoski and Jan Reid, told me that I was the right person to take on this project. Nick Tosches and Peter Guralnick helped me understand the importance of the story. Gregg Andrews, Gary Hartman, and Jason Mellard at Texas State University's Center for Texas Music History filled in the historical significance of the music scenes. To Craig D. Hillis and Jonathan Hooper, who combed through the first manuscript; Richard Skanse, who reviewed the final edits; and Thom Lemmons at Texas A&M University Press, who believed I could do the story justice.

My ol' pal, Bill Mack, thank you for pushing me through those last few weeks, when I felt like a truck driver, marking those last miles toward home. You kept me between the lines, and on the right side of the road.

Thank you, Don Imus, for playing along. We are one step closer to your goal of making Delbert McClinton a household name.

Delaney McClinton, Clay and Brandy McClinton, Patty Worrell McClinton, Emellia Grace and Calvin Ross McClinton, Mary Bridwell, and Jack and Donna Bridwell, thank you for sharing your family with the rest of us, and opening your memories, photo albums, and hearts for this story.

To our children, I love you more: Jenni, Sterling and our Butterfly Annie, HalleyAnna and Dustin, Patrick, DeLynn and Paul, and Caitlin and Nora.

Wendy and Delbert, there are no words for your generosity in sharing the good and the bad, the joys and the heartbreaks. I am grateful for your blessing in letting me tell your story my way.

Once more, thanks to Wendy for your fact-checking eagle eye, and to Mark Hendricks, my first reader and most vigorous editor. Meanwhile, any inadvertent omissions or errors are mine, and will be corrected in future editions.

Diana Finlay Hendricks
September 30, 2016

Delbert McClinton

Prologue

Saturday, March 22, 2014
Nashville, Tennessee

The phone rang at 5:30 a.m. "Dad, wake up," said Delbert's eldest son, Monty. "I need to tell you something."

Delbert recalls, "I was already awake. A phone call at that hour of the morning never brings good news. Monty said, 'Clay has been in a bad car wreck and he's got a terrible head injury.' My world stopped."[1]

They were on the next flight to Austin out of Nashville.

Delbert McClinton and his wife, Wendy Goldstein, had arrived home late on the evening of March 21, after a three-week vacation tour of Thailand, Cambodia, and Laos. Suitcases could wait to be unpacked. After the long trip, Delbert had gone to bed early.

Delbert and Wendy's twenty-one-year-old daughter, Delaney, had come over to welcome her parents home. She and her mom had stayed up late talking about the trip and catching up.

Clay and Brandy McClinton were living in Spicewood, a rural community outside of Austin, on three acres of land. They were handcrafting the house when they were home, and traveling to support Clay's musical career most of the time. The couple had been in Arizona, visiting her parents. Brandy recalls, "We had played in Colorado, and gone out to visit my family for a change of pace. Our beloved dog, Sadie, had died suddenly about a week before. We were both taking it hard. But Clay was taking it harder."

Clay had recently turned thirty-nine. He was playing mainly in Texas, hoping for a break, and drinking a lot. Brandy's role as wife/manager had evolved into designated driver/caretaker. He was abusing himself, and she was growing weary of his antics.

"We had been in airports all day, from Prescott to El Paso, and then on to Austin. Clay had a few beers and a whiskey. By the time we got to Austin, he had basically blacked out. I was used to his drinking, but I was not used to his blacking out. We were able to get to the car, but he was not making much sense. As I was driving us home, he started talking about looking forward to seeing Sadie when we got home. I said, 'Baby, Sadie is dead, remember?'

"Clay was acting kind of weird. He wanted out of the car. He said he needed to pee. We were going fifty-five miles per hour. I said to give me a minute to slow down. He didn't wait for me to pull over. He took off his seatbelt and opened the car door. Before I could stop the car, he had stepped out, and hit his head on the pavement.

"I pulled over as quickly as I could and ran back to him, lying in the middle of the road. There was no blood. His eyes were closed. It was 10:30 at night, way out in the country, and I could see headlights coming. My only thought was to get him out of the road, and then deal with him. I had no idea how seriously he was injured. I was just mad that he was so drunk.

"Thankfully, those headlights belonged to an off-duty cop on her way home. She took one look at his eyes, and called for a helicopter. The helicopter was there within minutes, and took him directly to Brackenridge Hospital in Austin, and he was being operated on within the hour."[2]

As Clay was being transported, the off-duty officer got Brandy back into her car, and entered Brackenridge Hospital on her phone's GPS. She told Brandy to just follow the directions and drive slowly. "She said to take my time because I would not be able to see him for a long time, and I needed to get to the hospital safely," Brandy recalls.[3]

"I knew that Delbert and Wendy were in Thailand, and I wasn't sure when they were getting back. I called Clay's brother, Monty, in Fort Worth, who immediately came to Austin."

• • •

Delbert, Wendy, and Delaney arrived soon. Delbert recalls, "I walked into the most horrible scene you can imagine. It looked like thirty-five plugs and tubes on his head and up his nose and down his throat and he was all bandaged up. Clay had a closed head injury."[4]

He was in a medically induced coma and therapeutic hypothermia, which chemically paralyzed him to give his brain time to heal. For two weeks, Clay did not open his eyes, and no one knew if he would live, if he would be paralyzed, or if he would walk or talk again. There were so many unanswered questions, and none of the medical professionals could tell the family what the next day would bring.

Delbert still had some time off after the vacation. Brandy insisted that he go on and play a scheduled show in St. Augustine, Florida, scheduled for April 5, two weeks after the accident. With Clay still in the coma, and limited visitation time in the intensive care unit (ICU), Delbert reluctantly flew to Florida to meet up with the band, and Wendy flew home to Nashville, to regroup and come back.

Delbert met the band at the airport in Jacksonville, and rode the bus to the venue. "I wasn't feeling well, but figured it had to do with the stress of the last two weeks. We got to the venue. I thought I was having heartburn. I had some Zantac, so I took it but got no relief. It got worse. I knew something was not right, but didn't have any of the symptoms you hear about that are associated with heart attacks. They called the paramedics. They checked me out and told me that I was okay now, but recommended that I go to the hospital and find out if I had a heart event. They said the only way to know for sure if you're having a heart problem is to get your blood tested. If you get a heart 'bump,' the heart releases an enzyme that shows up in the tests.

"The paramedics recommended they take me to the hospital, and I said, 'Dang, that will probably cost $2,800. No thanks.' After they left, I felt it again. I turned around and had the promoter take me over to the hospital. I found out that yeah, I had a little 'nudge,' they called it. That was Saturday. The band played the show without me. They did a heart cath the next day and found that I had 95 percent blockage in the main artery. A 'Widow Maker,' they call it."[5]

Delbert was quickly scheduled for surgery the following day, Monday, April 7. Back home in Nashville, Wendy got the call that Delbert was in the hospital. She called Delaney and they were soon on a plane to Florida. The bypass went smoothly and Delbert says, "I went from 95 percent blockage to open road, and I could feel the difference."[6]

Clay also made progress. He gradually came out of the coma, looked around and asked, "What's going on?" Two days later, he was walking the halls assisted by only a walker.

He was on his way to recovery. After twenty days in ICU, he was transferred to a rehabilitation hospital for thirty-five days of therapy, before being released to go home in Brandy's care.

Clay has almost completely recovered from his head injury and is performing again. He is focused on his life and career. He no longer drinks, and smiles as he says, "I don't even want to write drinking songs anymore."[7]

"He's grateful," Delbert says. "His wife, Brandy, said, 'Clay has really taken advantage of his second chance.'"[8]

The same can be said for Delbert, who has also made a full recovery. He returned to the stage two months after his April 2014 heart bypass surgery. "I was melancholy. I felt kicked out of my own life for a while. I didn't know if I could sing. I didn't know if I could be me on stage," he said, "but I found that I had so much more energy and more stamina."[9]

Don Imus agrees. "Delbert was always good, but he sings better now. He looks a lot better than he has in years. He doesn't have bags under his eyes. He has energy. I think he is better than he ever was. He'll go forever. Sinatra worked for a long time — what, into his late eighties? And still had that great voice. Tony Bennett is what, like a hundred and fifty? They still wheel him out there and he knocks them out every single time. Generations like Delbert, his music, his style; it's ageless. All good art is. The song, 'Dreams to Remember'—my seventeen-year-old son came up to me the other day and told me that Delbert was better than Otis Redding, who had the original version of 'Dreams.' He was great when he was twenty-two and playing harmonica with Bruce Channel, and he's great now."[10]

As he reflects on his life, Delbert admits, "When Monty called and told me about Clay's accident, my first thought was, 'Where's the adult who can fix this?' I realized that I was the adult. There was no one to turn to. I was the guy. I instantly became aware of our mortality. All that 'I'm gonna live forever' shit went out the window. That's when I met me. That's when I met who I am. And realized what is important."[11]

CHAPTER 1
"I've Got Dreams to Remember"

Postwar Years–Lubbock, Texas

When the doctor came back into the back bedroom of our shotgun house, he asked my mother if she wanted to see her new baby boy, and she said, "No, I'll look at him later. Right now, I just want to rest." That was the first of many times I would exhaust my parents in their efforts to deal with me.
—DELBERT McCLINTON[1]

It was an unseasonably warm and dry Monday morning on November 4, 1940,[2] in Lubbock, Texas, when Delbert was born to Herman Louis McClinton and Vivian Fanny Dyer Bridwell McClinton. Born at home, at 2112 Ninth Street, he was his mother's third son, and his father's only offspring.

Vivian had married Jack Bridwell when she was sixteen. Jack and his good friend, Herman, were both drivers for Snyder Transfer, a large trucking company in West Texas. Vivian was widowed at the age of twenty, with a two-year-old son, Jack Jr., and pregnant with Randall when Jack Sr. died. Herman fell in love with Vivian and married her. Delbert was born two years later.

Vivian had been in long and difficult labor all weekend before Delbert finally made his debut. The doctor had given up hours before, and gone outside to sleep in his car in front of the house. Herman had to go out and wake him to help with the birth.

Lubbock and the surrounding area have given birth to more

than their share of talent over the last century: Buddy Holly; Mac Davis; Joe Ely; Terry Allen; Lloyd Maines and his daughter, Natalie Maines; Butch Hancock; Waylon Jennings; Tanya Tucker; Jimmy Dean . . . . The list goes on.

A longstanding question for music fans and musicologists is *what is it about Lubbock?* What has made it such fertile ground for musicians?

Lubbock natives speak with reverence about the natural formation on which this town was built. Delbert describes his birthplace: "The early Spaniards called it Llano Estacado, which means the Staked Plains. It's so flat that they would drive stakes into the ground or pile dried buffalo shit as a point of reference. There is a lot of history out there.

"There are two places in Lubbock where people can go to escape the monotony of the flat dusty landscape: Buffalo Lake and Mackenzie State Park. Mackenzie State Park was called Yellow House Canyon by the Comanches because the cliffs have a yellowish hue to them. This was a popular trading ground for the Comanche and Spaniards. The Spaniards called it Cañón de Rescates—The Canyon of Ransoms. There's no doubt, this place has seen a lot of suffering."[3]

In keeping with the stories of the badlands of the West, an article in the *Lubbock Avalanche-Journal* explains that the name of Ransom Canyon apparently came from the practice of real-world Comanches who kidnapped women and children in Texas, then sold them to Mexican traders—Comancheros—from New Mexico. In turn, some of the victims were offered for redemption by their families for a price. The Spanish name of Cañón de Rescates came to mean Rescue—or Ransom—Canyon.[4]

Lubbock's flatness is no exaggeration. Historian Art Leatherwood describes the Llano Estacado as the southern extension of the High Plains of North America, one of the largest tablelands on the continent, sloping approximately ten feet per linear mile.[5]

Lubbock was not yet a town during the heyday of the Wild West. Incorporated in 1909, the City of Lubbock was a mere thirty-one years old the year Delbert was born. Texas Tech University was established only seventeen years before his birth, and another Lubbock legend, Buddy Holly, was born four years before Delbert.

Between 1940 and 1950, Lubbock was the second-most rapidly growing city in the nation, lagging behind only Albuquerque.[6]

Delbert describes the Lubbock of his childhood: "I always heard that if you looked hard enough, you could see the back of your head. Flat and dry as far as you could see. Maybe a mesquite tree once in a while. There was nothing for hundreds of miles. And it was originally a buffalo slaughtering camp."[7]

How did such a gifted bunch of musicians and artists happen to hail from this stark place that has come to call itself "The Crossroads of the West?" Journalist Michael Hall has written the definitive oral history of Lubbock musicians and has come to the "one simple unsatisfying conclusion that all roads lead to Lubbock."[8]

Hall shares some of the commonalities among these Lubbock musical icons such as pianos in every house; radio stations from faraway places like Chicago and Dallas and Villa Acuña, Mexico; the options to practice music or plow fields; and just the fact that there was music *everywhere* — on the radio, in living rooms, on the streets, in stores, and of course, in legendary clubs.

But why did Lubbock become such a wellspring of talent?

Delbert shakes his head, "I don't know. Maybe it was the DDT trucks that drove down the alleys. They never said, 'Don't let your kids run in the fog of the poisonous mist,' so we did. It seems we all ran behind those trucks down the alleys as kids. Maybe they ought to do a study.

"I always loved music. It was everywhere out there. As a kid, Bob Wills was THE big deal. My parents would go dancing at the Cotton Club, and we kids would play in the cotton fields next to the parking lot — throwing clods at each other and such. Kids weren't allowed to go inside, so we'd hang in the windows at the Cotton Club, and listen to the music and watch the band, intrigued by the fiddler, the trumpet, and the drummer. Bob Wills, Milton Brown and the Brownies — that sound really made an impression on me. And you could hear Bob Wills everywhere. Downtown, the Halsey's Drug Store had speakers right over the door and they always played Bob Wills and Hank Williams music out onto the sidewalks. The radio stations were on all the time. Even walking down the street, we could just hear music everywhere. I don't know. There's nothing else to do out there. You either grow cotton, go crazy, or play music in Lubbock. There just wasn't a hell of a lot to do."[9]

Another Lubbock native, artist/songwriter Terry Allen says, "First look at the Llano Estacado. It is an amazing geographic anomaly in a sense. It spreads out for hundreds of miles in every direction, and Lubbock is in the center of it. When you are completely surrounded by a flat horizon, you miss a lot of things that are right in front of you. Your eye goes straight through to the edge. You have a different perception of how you look at things."

Allen continues, "So you are always in the center of this huge circle that goes on to the end of the world as you know it in all directions. You can very easily become an egomaniac. At the same time, you are surrounded by this huge circle, so you might become paranoid. I don't know. Maybe paranoid egomaniacs tend to become artists and songwriters and such."[10]

Blues rocker Angela Strehli, also from Lubbock, adds, "Lubbock was pretty desolate. You had to provide your own entertainment. We learned to entertain ourselves. And with some of us, as soon as we could, we moved away. But no matter where we went, we were different, and connected somehow."[11]

Music is useful in a sensible agricultural center. Unlike other forms of art, even dirt farmers can *use* music—to dance or listen, or just tap a foot. Premier Texas music and culture writer Joe Nick Patoski speaks of the usefulness of music as an art form as he speculates: "Lubbock has produced a disproportional number of music people. There is not much else going on. It is a rectangular, flat city. It's a big empty canvas that needs a lot of filling in with imagination. Music is the one form of creative expression that has not just been tolerated but in many cases, fostered in Lubbock. Certainly more than writing or filmmaking or other creative pursuits.

"Music is indigenous to Lubbock. It's isolated. It's the largest city in the Great Plains. It has a university presence and that brings a creative presence to a town. Even today, Texas Tech is isolated and remote, but for the Great Plains and even the Panhandle, Tech has always been The University. It's relative. If you grow up in Idalou or Floydada, Lubbock has always been the shining light. For that part of Texas, it has always served as a creative center. And music is the one creative form of expression that has been tolerated—more than others."[12]

Delbert absorbed the diverse musical styles that filled the air throughout the Texas Panhandle. His influences ran the gamut—whatever played on the radio—war songs and border tunes, western swing, and ragtime piano. It was as endless as the Lubbock horizon and became a part of his spirit.

Delbert offers his theory of the spirit of the Staked Plains, "I think you have to be from the Llano Estacado to be able to see the beauty of the place. I think it gave me a special sense of things being boundless."[13]

Delbert's father, Herman McClinton, grew up in Snyder in a large family with a fraternal twin brother, Howell; brothers, Joe, Bedford, and Rowen; and sisters, Atheline and Emily. Herman had the bug to work on the railroad, and Howell wanted to raise cattle. Herman left home to work for the Texas Pacific Railroad. The line ended in Toyah, which is now little more than a ghost town in Reeves County, Texas.

Howell bought some land, struck oil, and, as can happen, spent the rest of his life treating his family like second-class citizens. And yet young Delbert learned another lesson: money does not buy wealth.[14]

Among Delbert's earliest memories is traveling by train to Alexandria, Louisiana, to visit his father, who was injured in army boot camp and recovering in a military hospital. Cajun, country, and war songs were the soundtrack for that early memory.

Like so many other young men, Herman McClinton was drafted in 1942. He went to Alexandria for basic training. Delbert says, "My dad slipped on a loading dock and broke his back during basic training. He spent most of the next two years in army hospitals. I remember my mother and me taking a train to Alexandria to see him and sleeping in a tent on the base. My brothers, Jack and Randall, stayed behind in Lubbock with my aunts and uncles and grandparents. Armed guards patrolled through the night and German prisoners of war were held there. I found all of this to be the most exciting trip!"[15]

Music has been a continual soundtrack in Delbert's life. The artists, the subjects, and the styles may have changed, but he has held fast to all of the styles and genres that he was exposed to along the way. Among his earliest memories are the songs of this World War II era that he still loves: Johnny Mercer, Charles Brown, and Nat King Cole. He remembers, "Traveling on the train to Louisiana, I heard war songs, big band sounds. 'Comin' in on a Wing and a Prayer'. . . 'When the Lights Go on Again (All Over the World).' They were songs of troubled times with happy endings. Songs of hope and blue skies."[16]

The community of Delbert's early childhood was idyllic. He had the barefoot freedom to explore this relatively small town during America's most charming era. He writes in a journal: "When I was a boy in Lubbock, the milk man came down the street in a horse-drawn wagon. We used to laugh at those old horses pissing in the street. My grandmother was still using an ice box in 1949. There were old men who could tell you first hand stories about how the West was won, wild Indians, and things that would never be again.

After supper, people would sit out on their front porches or walk up and down the street and visit with their neighbors. They talked about their lives, their jobs, their families. They ate cold watermelon and homemade ice cream and listened to the radio. They played dominos and 42. They cared about each other—in a way that seems old fashioned and quaint today. Things changed more in the last fifty years than they had in the previous five hundred years. We were sitting in a cocked catapult that was about to be sprung."[17]

One day, Herman McClinton came home from the army. A 1946 army olive drab Ford pulled up in front of the house while Vivian and the boys were sitting at the dinner table, and he climbed out of the back seat with a duffle bag.

Aside from the trip to Louisiana, Delbert has few memories of his dad before that day because of the two years Herman spent in the hospital. He remembers looking at the framed picture of him on the table as his mother and grandmother told him that the man in the picture was his daddy. And he wondered why this daddy in the frame couldn't talk to him. But, on the day Herman McClinton came home from the army, Delbert's family routine changed significantly. Daddy was home.[18]

Herman got a job driving a Lubbock city bus. For the next five-and-a-half years, Delbert, Randall, and Jack had bus passes that allowed them to ride free all over town. "The parks, swimming, a movie—as long and as far as the bus ran, we could ride it," Delbert recalls. Perhaps this was yet another important influence for this musical road warrior. He has traveled countless miles on his own buses since those early days.

Delbert recalls his first paying job was walking over to a bus stop on Broadway, about three-and-a-half blocks from their home during the summer, and taking his father a sack lunch. His father would give him a nickel. "I would stop at the gumball machine and load up," he remembers. "It was hard to save that money. But, a nickel was a lot of money. It cost nine cents to get into a movie and I also saw a lot of matinees in those days."[19]

Being the youngest of three brothers is never a very advantageous position. Often, Vivian would insist that Jack and Randall take Delbert along on their adventures. Generally, that was not what they wanted to do. Delbert says, "So more often than not, they used me to their amusement."

Once, a new neighbor down the street brought in some goats and put them in a pen. Delbert had never seen goats and was not quite sure about them, but they looked interesting. Until Jack lifted his little brother over the fence into the pen and told him they were man-eating goats. Delbert scrambled out and over that fence with little help from anyone, and thankfully, was not "eaten" by the neighborhood livestock.[20]

Another time, he remembers going to a Boy Scout meeting with Jack and Randall: "It was dark when we started home. The moon was full. We had to cross a railyard and climb between the trains as part of our shortcut. There were few lights and nobody around when Jack and Randall stopped, and got this real scared look on their faces.

"They said, 'Oh, no!' I asked what was wrong, and they both pointed to the full moon. 'See that,' said Jack. 'It means the Ku Klux Klan [KKK] is out tonight!'

"Now I didn't know the KKK from cottage cheese, but I knew it couldn't be good. Bucking up my bravery, I said, 'So?' Randall said, 'We gotta run!' And off they went. Of course, I couldn't keep up with them and started crying. They finally stopped and said that the only way the KKK wouldn't get us was if the littlest one held his arms straight up in the air all the way home. So, not wanting to get got, I thrust my arms up and off we went. It didn't take long for my arms to get so tired that I had to drop them. And off they would run.

"This is how we went home—walk a while with my arms up, run a while, me crying and scared to death, wiping tears and snot off my face, and walk again. When we did get home, it was obvious to my dad that something was wrong. After getting the story from one terrified boy and two laughing older siblings, he took off his belt, gave them some licks, and made them stand in the dining room with their arms over their heads. Every time they dropped them, he popped them again."[21]

Despite those typical big-brother pranks, it was a good time for boys to be growing up. Delbert and his brothers were close and remained close until Randall died in 2008. Delbert and Jack remained close until Jack's death in 2016.

"I guess at some point, I realized that their last name was Bridwell and mine was McClinton, but it didn't matter. My dad was their father—and he was good to them. He treated us all well," he says.[22]

Growing up in West Texas in the 1940s was a pretty plain and simple life, Delbert recalls. "Everybody worked hard. Everybody was poor and everybody pitched in. There was a lot of common ground. But we were happy."

The McClintons always seemed to have someone living with them, which, Delbert explains, meant there were never enough beds to go around. "I think I spent the first ten years of my life sleeping on a pallet on the floor as often as I shared a bed," he says. "But my mother had a knack for making it all seem like a big party. She made it fun. When the blankets came out, we all wanted a spot on the floor."[23]

Vivian Fanny Dyer Bridwell McClinton was born in Fort Smith, Arkansas, and the family moved to East Texas when she was still a child. She was also from a large family, one of six girls. Vivian became a hairdresser by profession and worked in beauty salons throughout her life.

When Delbert was a child, his maternal grandparents moved to Lubbock and lived with them until his grandfather's death. "Pawpaw Dyer had been a barber in his younger years, but was blind as long as I knew him," Delbert said. But, that didn't stop him from getting up every morning and making his way downtown to sell razor blades and tweezers on a street corner. He would return home in the late afternoon.

"We still had boxes of his single-edged razor blades in the house when I moved out at nineteen. Years later, my mother gave me the last pair of tweezers and said, 'Now hold on to these, Honey. These are the good ones.' I lost 'em trying to get a tick off a dog."[24]

Delbert enjoys remembering those Lubbock days. "Kids were stronger back then. You had to participate in life. No cell phones. No one checking on you all day. You had to navigate and pay attention in life."

Stories of bus rides, bare feet, shortcuts, running in the cool mist of the "mosquito truck" that sprayed pesticides through the neighborhoods, and endless summer days bring back memories of a great, albeit sometimes dangerous, time to be growing up. "Around the Fourth of July, we had dangerous—real—fireworks. I was too little to be in control but old enough to get to tag along. Randall and Jack would get a piece of pipe and a tin can and put a TNT or Baby Giant or Cherry Bomb in it and shoot that can all the way down the street. You could go out and buy dynamite back then. I tagged along. They did stuff to me all the time. It's a wonder we survived those summers."[25]

Vivian's side of the family spent a lot of time with the McClintons. An aunt or a cousin—or more—were always coming to stay in the small house on Ninth Street. Delbert tells stories of the time that his cousin, Kenyan, and his wife, Gertie Banks, came to stay. "Gertie was a yodeler. She would yodel at the drop of a hat. Along with the radio. By herself. I guess she was pretty good. I think I would have known if she was bad. But it was really entertaining."[26]

Delbert says, "I think the first time I ever gave any thought to the fact that we were monetarily deprived was in about 1949, when my dad took a part-time job driving a Honey Dipper. A

Honey Dipper is one of those trucks that comes in with a long four-inch hose and sucks the shit out of your septic tank. I didn't have to be very smart to know that that's a lousy job. I felt sorry for my dad the night he took me with him on the job. But I never heard him complain about having to do whatever to keep the wolf away."[27]

Talking about his father, Delbert laughs as he recalls learning to swim. "The biggest deal in Lubbock was getting to go to Buffalo Lake down in *Cañón de Rescates*, just outside of town. The day I learned to swim, I rode on my daddy's shoulders as he swam out all the way to the dock in the middle of the lake. We climbed up on the dock and he grabbed me by an arm and a leg and threw me in. I learned to swim that day."[28]

Delbert likes to talk about his musical influences. "I listened to old 1940s country and pop. And there was *conjunto*. That has always been a part of Texas music with those popping horns and hot rhythm sections."

Herman and Vivian took in a few of those traveling tent shows in Lubbock, and Delbert tagged along. "Those Harley Sadler traveling tent shows came to town every year. Music, melodramas, entertainment. I remember they threw free candy into the crowds. It was the first time I ever got anything like that for free. Handfuls of free candy. Wow! They played, we went. And like I said, Lubbock being what it was, there wasn't a damned thing to do so we looked forward to it. It was kind of a big deal."[29]

In August and September 1951, the infamous Lubbock Lights appeared. The first publicized sighting of the lights occurred on August 25, 1951, at around 9:00 p.m. It was a Tuesday night, a couple of weeks before kids had to put on their shoes and go back to school. Everyone was taking advantage of the waning days of summer.

Songwriter, artist, and Lubbock native Terry Allen clearly remembers, "I was at a drive-in with my folks, laying in that shelf behind the back seat of an old 1950 Hudson when those things came in. They were like these V-shaped lights just sweeping out of the sky.

"I remember my dad saying, 'Don't pay any attention to them — it's just something they are doing out at the airbase.' The next day, the big headline in the *Avalanche-Journal* was, "WhatsIts [*sic*] Seen Over Lubbock." Some thought it was the reflection of streetlights catching the wings over low flying geese—which was one of the most preposterous of the ideas," Allen recalls.[30]

Coincidentally (or not?), Delbert and his oldest brother, Jack, were at the same drive-in when the lights went over. "We were going to see *Joan of Arc*. They were V-shaped, flying in a V formation—lots of them," he remembers, clearly. "Hell, yeah, we thought they were UFOs! I still think they were. I mean, what else could they be? I saw them go by!"[31]

Meredith McClain, professor emeritus of foreign languages at Texas Tech University, wrote the definitive article about the Lubbock Lights in the *Lubbock Avalanche-Journal*: "It began on Aug. 25, 1951, when three Texas Technological College (now Texas Tech University) professors sitting on the front patio of Dr. Wilbur I. Robinson's adobe home on Twenty-fourth Street observed an arc of green lights speeding soundlessly far overhead. Shortly afterward, the lights, or a second bank of them, came again.

"The unusual nocturnal displays, which others in the city witnessed and from time to time saw over several weeks, quickly became part of the UFO phenomenon sweeping the country.

"Numerous sightings of UFOs in the American Southwest had begun in 1947 and the Air Force responded by establishing a special 'Project Saucer,' to investigate all reports.

"In 1952, the Air Force downgraded the status of the special saucer project to a standard intelligence function, but it invited all citizens to report their sightings to the nearest Air Force installation. By then, the Air Force had dismissed as natural phenomena all but thirty-four of hundreds of such cases.

"Also in 1952, the then-popular and influential *LIFE* Magazine published a lead article on the flying saucers topic and titled it, 'There is a Case for Interplanetary Saucers.'

"After a year of sifting through many reports filed with the Air Force, *LIFE* went to press. Its long article focused on the essential details of what it considered ten of the most formidable UFO cases, starting with the Lubbock Lights.

"The strange lights of 1951 and the *LIFE* article in 1952 put Lubbock in the national consciousness. The three Tech professors were largely responsible. The men on the patio that August evening included Robinson, a geologist; William L. Ducker, head of petroleum engineering; and Dr. A. Gus Oberg, professor of chemical engineering. They had just settled in for their weekly Saturday Evening Seminar—and the only rule for their wide-ranging discussions was no talk of religion, politics or women.

"As darkness settled in, Ducker suddenly leapt from his chair, pointed wildly toward the sky and shouted, 'What the hell is that?' All three men observed the arc of green lights speeding sound-lessly high overhead. In the vague hope of a returning apparition, the professors snuffed out their pipes and cigar and trained their sharpened vision on the clear, night sky. Sure enough, it came over again—or, a second formation flew over.

"The LIFE article stated: 'The Lubbock Lights, flying in for-mation, are considered by the Air Force the most unexplainable phenomena yet observed.'" [32]

The credibility of observations of the three witnesses (all sci-entists) from the adobe house patio was an essential factor in the Air Force's judgment of the lights as a "most unexplainable" phenomenon. Also important were sightings by people through-out the city, all confirming what the professors had seen.

Because they could measure neither the size nor distance of the formations they saw in the sky, the professors could not determine the objects' speed. The best estimate they and others offered was that, considering the arc and silence of the objects, the lights were 50,000 feet in the air. In which case, they guessed, the lights were moving at 18,000 miles per hour. Or, perhaps, as some people have speculated, the arc of green lights represented nothing more than migrating birds reflecting a new lighting sys-tem installed along Nineteenth Street near Texas Technological College. [33]

Whether legend, theory, or scientific fact, the Lubbock Lights add to the mystique and magic of that Staked Plains city.

A few months after the Lubbock Lights came through town, the McClintons left Lubbock. The mysterious lights had nothing to do with the move. Herman's old back injury was causing him great pain as he sat in the bouncing bus driver's seat, day in and day out. He needed a job where he would not have to sit all day.

At the time, Herman had two brothers working for the railroad in Fort Worth, and he was quickly hired on as a brakeman. He later became a switchman, working for the Rock Island Railroad. It was December 1951. Delbert was eleven.[34]

No one could possibly have predicted how important this move would be for Delbert McClinton.

CHAPTER 2
Cost of Living

North Texas in the Early '50s

At recess on my first day at South Hi Mount Elementary
School in Fort Worth, this kid named Roger Lapham said,
"See this watch? If you can catch me, I'll give it to you."
   I really wanted that watch. I never had a watch. I never
even heard of a kid who had a watch. I never thought I would
ever own one, but knew that if I did, I would really move
up in the world. So he took off and I chased him, and I still
haven't caught him.
                        —DELBERT McCLINTON[1]

Delbert and Roger Lapham became good friends that year, and
even in their class picture, you see them on the front row. Delbert is the only kid not facing the camera, turned sideways talking to Roger in the picture.

   "Fort Worth was a new world for me. A big city. I did as well as
could be expected. An eleven-year old kid, uprooted from the only
town I'd ever known and taken 300 miles away. Before that, the
furthest I'd ever been was Snyder or Sweetwater to visit cousins.

   "We went through Muleshoe once, loaded in the back of a box
truck, to help my aunt and uncle move. My uncle was a genuine
Maytag repairman in Portales, New Mexico. I always thought that
was funny because of the old advertisement about the Maytag
repairman being the 'loneliest man in town.' But, we never really
took actual vacations just to see someplace new.

   "So, the move to Fort Worth was a big change. We even had to leave the dogs behind. We did wind up going back to get one of them, though," he recalls.[2]

Fort Worth was experiencing growing pains. The city had long been identified as a cattle drive stop called "Cowtown." The northern appetite for Texas cattle had originally required long drives up to Kansas City, Kansas, and points beyond. Fort Worth was a major stop on the old McCoy Trail, through to Missouri in the 1800s. When the railroad came to Fort Worth in 1876, it became the major hub for the Texas cattle industry, where the South Texas cowboys would herd their longhorns onto trains destined for the Midwest and Northeast.[3]

By 1951, Fort Worth was booming. The oil and military defense industries were changing the identity of Cowtown. Oil had been discovered in Corsicana in 1884. Beaumont's Old Spindletop hit in 1901, and the first gusher hit in Ranger, Texas, in 1917. Soon, more than twenty-five million acres were under lease across the state and every well was a potential gold mine. A new generation of "forty-niners" descended on Texas as "wildcatters," gamblers on oil speculation. By the 1920s, five of the nation's leading oil companies were operating in Fort Worth, handling 80 percent of all crude oil produced in Texas. Wildcatters-turned-oil tycoons built their mansions in Fort Worth as the longstanding cattle town grew in nouveau riche citizens.[4]

The wars had been good for Fort Worth industry. Military bases as well as defense plants built the city economy. Fort Worth established itself as a center of military aviation during World War I. In 1940, as the United States prepared for what would become World War II, the city donated 1,450 acres in White Settlement for a bomber plant—Air Force Plant No. 4.

According to Fort Worth historian Richard Selcer, "By 1942, Consolidated Aircraft Corporation was turning out B-24s like sausages. Ultimately, production went to three shifts a day, employing 30,000 workers. A total of 3,034 Liberators rolled off the assembly line during the next three years."[5]

A city built on cowboys, wildcatters, and war will be a little rough around the edges. In the '40s and '50s, the edges of town were where the gangsters, gamblers, and other characters could be found. And Fort Worth's infamous "Hell's Half Acre," suitably named during the days of the cattle drives, continued its wild streak.

In the foreword to *Gamblers and Gangsters: Fort Worth's Jacksboro Highway*, Quentin McGown writes, "From the earliest days of the cattle drives through town, Fort Worth embraced, if not with open arms, then certainly with an open palm, the profit and excitement of illegal entertainment. The crime and corruption which followed it were simply the costs of doing business."[6]

Fort Worth was finding itself in the early 1950s. It's common for outsiders to think of Dallas-Fort Worth as The Metroplex, Sister Cities, one big common ground. However, the cities have always been strikingly different. Delbert says, "Dallas has always been the big sister. She has fancy manners and nicer clothes, but she will never be as pretty as her little sister, Fort Worth."[7]

Fort Worth native Joe Nick Patoski explains: "Fort Worth has always been a 'second city,' like Oakland to San Francisco or Odessa to Midland. Dallas has always been more sophisticated and urbane. Dallas had a self-image that it was the New York of Texas, very image conscious. Houston was a boomtown that kept sprawling, San Antonio has always been a colorful fiesta city, but Dallas maintained that image of planned, cool, self-important sophistication. No matter what you do, no matter how good something is in Fort Worth, there's always Dallas. Dallas has always been newer and shinier, and has always had this real arrogant attitude that I never could figure out."

Patoski sums up the difference in the two cities: "If Fort Worth is where the West begins, Dallas is where the East peters out."[8]

The McClintons settled into their rented, shotgun duplex at 3809 Washburn Street on the west side of Fort Worth, the blue-collar little sister on the far side of the Metroplex. Herman worked the rail yard and Vivian worked as a hairdresser.

Once he adjusted to the move, Delbert settled in and grew comfortable with the freedom that Fort Worth allowed. Trains traveled farther than city buses. While they didn't have free passes on the freight trains, Delbert and his newfound friends did have free run of the Fort Worth rail yards by day. Their boundaries were as wide as the airwaves—with radio stations in the Dallas-Fort Worth area, Memphis, Chicago, Del Rio, Nashville and beyond—opening the world to these young boys at night.

Somewhere along that time, Delbert had traded a neighbor kid his authentic World War II SS dress dagger for a two-dollar crystal set, a very simple radio receiver. "I would put my head under the covers at night, tune in that crystal set, and listen to the world. It was God's own radio."[9]

"XERF Border Radio," he recalls, "Even today you can hear those Mexico border stations. They have always been a big part of Texas music—and you can hear it in my music. Tex-Mex is as good a word for it as any. Doug [Sahm] picked up on that as a kid in San Antonio, and he was the king of it. He is one unsung hero."[10]

Delbert continues, "Today, music industry people dominate a lot of what you get to hear, so you don't get to hear new sounds, real soul, and true spirit in the music. You don't get anything right from the source anymore. What do they call it, 'radio-friendly?' Music in Texas sounds like music in Tennessee or music in California. But back then, we got to listen to XERF in Villa Acuña, KNOK Radio, the all-Black station in Dallas, KFJZ Top 40, WLS out of Chicago."[11]

Delbert soaked it all in.

Imaginations ran wild with these preteens, camping out in the rail yard and spending long summer days exploring drainage pipes and shortcuts around the tracks. "After school, my friends and I would take off for the tracks and play out there till dark or later, like kids used to do," he said. "We always had a pile of old junk bicycles in our backyard, and we would use the parts to rebuild our bikes. Bikes were freedom. We would ride miles and miles every day. No one would steal your bike. You could leave it laying in the yard all night and it'd be there in the morning.

"We would ride our bikes to the edge of town, cross the tracks to the 'hump'—or the switching yard. Sometimes we'd camp out in the woods on the other side of the train yards—and go to sleep listening to the workers make up trains. We'd camp out like hobos and build campfires and shoot .410s. We could cut through this big drain tunnel without walking across the tracks or climbing between the trains, and get to the other side of the [rail] yard."[12]

He adds, "Music was always in the background. Radios or loud-speakers or your parents' record players. If you were around, and in the right places during that time, you were bombarded with some of the best music ever played."[13]

The summer of 1952, Delbert went to visit his mother's sister, Charlie Marie, and her family in Sweetwater, Texas. Her son, Walter Lee, was Delbert's favorite cousin. But, Uncle Earl was another story.

"He had always been the meanest old son of a bitch I'd ever known. He'd get drunk and terrorize the family and anybody else around. All of us kids were scared to death of him. But that summer—at least while I was there—he turned into a brand new man," recalls Delbert.

"Right after I got there, my cousin, Walter Lee, and I were out in the backyard. I was singing 'Hey, Joe,' a Carl Smith song. He threw the back door open and slammed the screen against the wall and hollered, 'Who's doing that singing?' We all stiffened up, and I said, 'That was me,' thinking I was really in for it," Delbert says.

"Uncle Earl went nuts. He thought I was great. He called Aunt Marie out back and made me sing it for her. He drove a Vandervoort Milk Truck at the time. He got Walter and me to get up early with him and go down to the milk plant. He'd pay us each fifty cents a day to help him.

"We'd get up at 3:30 in the morning to go down and help load the truck for the morning deliveries. Before starting the route, we would get donuts and coffee with the milkmen. Uncle Earl'd put me up on the counter at 5:30 in the morning in the donut shop in Sweetwater, Texas, and I'd sing Carl Smith, Lefty Frizzell, Hank Williams. Pretty soon, I was the biggest attraction—after the coffee and donuts—in Sweetwater, Texas, before 6:00 in the morning.

"Uncle Earl became a whole different guy for those two weeks when I was there. He started giving Walter and me money for the movies and stuff like that, and being a regular good guy. It was then that I thought I might be on to something. He was one of the first people who thought I had something.

"Aunt Marie and Uncle Earl ended up getting a divorce, and the last time I saw him was at Walter's funeral about twelve years later."[14]

Delbert speaks frequently about how important music was in his family. Hank Williams was considered country music's first superstar. His first hit, "Move It on Over," came out in April 1948, followed by a string of successes. Hank Williams was a regular on the *Louisiana Hayride* radio show out of Shreveport, Louisiana, which led to an invitation to become a member of the Grand Ole Opry in Nashville, Tennessee, "The Mother Church of Country Music."[15]

Like much of America, Delbert and his brothers were Hank Williams fans. What most fans didn't know was that the twenty-nine-year old country star was heavily abusing alcohol and morphine.

On New Year's Eve 1952, when Hank crawled into the back seat of his 1952 powder blue Cadillac and his driver took off for a concert venue in Canton, Ohio, his bad habits finally caught up with him. After not hearing from the singer in the back seat for several hours, the young chauffeur pulled the car over in a small town in West Virginia at 5:30 in the morning on New Year's Day 1953.

Williams was pronounced dead of a heart attack a short while later with only a rudimentary investigation. The coroner noted, as an aside that "there were needle marks on the arms and that Hank had recently been severely beaten and kicked in the groin." The official report remained that Hank died of a severe heart condition and hemorrhage," leaving conspiracy theorists much to ponder through the years.[16]

"No one in the country took Hank Williams's death harder than my brother, Randall," Delbert recalls. "I will never forget how much he cried. He was heartbroken. I thought he would never stop crying. It was as though Randall had lost a personal friend. It struck me how music can make a fan feel like a friend."[17]

The first time Delbert performed on a real stage in front of a crowd was in Fort Worth, later in 1953. It wasn't really a song, but a "call," as in square dancing. Herman and Vivian were avid square dancers, and Delbert enjoyed going to the dances with them.

"They would go every Wednesday night, and I would go along most of the time because there was always a band," he says. "My friends and I were in junior high and we had joined a square dance club in school, which met every Friday night at 6:00. I knew a lot of the calls, and my friends were raggin' on me to get up and do one, and I kept telling them, 'No way I'm gonna do that.'"

He finally agreed. "There wasn't a band on stage for this square dance, just a big 78 RPM record and me. I pretended like I was doing it with a big band, and it was great fun. The call I did was 'Oh, Johnny,' and I was shaking so hard, I thought I'd break something."

"When it was done, my ol' running buddies were just jumping through their hats, whooping and hollering like crazy. We always went from square dancing directly to the Heights movie theatre. That night I was a star! My friends talked about it all night, telling everybody we ran into about how 'ol' Delbo got up and *sang*!'"

Speaking of that old movie theatre, "We eventually got barred from the Heights Theatre because they caught us one night with water guns filled with Nair. Nair was a liquid hair remover that women used on their legs. We were sitting in the balcony shooting people on the head with this stuff and laughing our butts off. Today, they'd probably have arrested us," he says.[18]

Kicked out of chorus for not being serious enough; kicked out of theatres for having too much fun; running wild and free through the shortcuts, rail yards, and back alleys of Fort Worth. A pattern is developing. At thirteen, Delbert was already developing a strong, independent streak and a good sense of humor that would follow him throughout his career. He was not a follower. He loved to entertain a crowd. And it was downright fun to be a "star."

Delbert didn't know any professional musicians. He had never even seen anyone play a guitar up close, aside from hanging in the window at Lubbock's Cotton Club as a preteen, or watching the square dance band from back in the corner of the room. However, the year he turned fourteen, that changed. Two young men, casual friends of his brothers, wandered into his house, and changed Delbert McClinton's life forever.

Delbert says, "I was in junior high. Both of my brothers had friends who came into our house on a regular basis, carrying guitars. But, the magical day was one afternoon when I came in from school and heard someone singing a Hank Williams song, right there in our own house. We lived in a shotgun duplex. I came into the house, threw down my stuff, and headed straight to the sound. There, between the dining room and the kitchen, was my brother Jack [Bridwell]'s friend, Ray Harden.

"Ray was on the floor, leaning against the wall with his feet up on the door jam, like a human hammock, playing a little Martin guitar with a hole the size of a fist busted in it. He told me he stepped on it one night when he was drunk. Man. I even thought that was cool. I hung on every single word he said, and watched every move he made. I wanted to learn to play guitar and sing like that as bad as I'd ever wanted anything."[19]

Ray Harden was an oilfield roughneck, a hard-hat-wearing guy who drank a lot of beer and did as he pleased. Delbert describes him as "kind of a poor man's John Wayne gone to seed. And I soaked that up. He was the coolest cat I had ever met."[20]

The second time Delbert came face to face with his future was when his brother, Randall Bridwell, brought his friend, Joe Don Sanders, over with a guitar. Delbert remembers that Joe Don was a lot more dependable than Ray Harden was about coming around. "Joe Don taught me how to play a few chords. Then Randall and I decided we needed a guitar.

"Joe Don said he knew somebody who had an old Stella guitar for sale. It took every penny we had, but Randall and I bought it for three dollars and fifty cents. That old Stella was a piece of shit. It was the sorriest guitar ever made. The strings down by the hole were so far off. We couldn't tune that thing. But we practiced and learned chords and figured out songs. Our fingers bled. It was terrible, but man, I loved it. And before long, I was looking to put a band together."[21]

And soon, music would rock his world.

CHAPTER 3

"Never Been Rocked Enough"

The Birth of Rock and Roll

*I felt something that started in my ears and ran through me
like an electrical shock. That day, that moment, that song,
that voice, that music. It touched my soul. Until that day, I
didn't know music could do that to you.*
— DELBERT McCLINTON[1]

They had spent the night in the woods camping out and shooting guns. Delbert says that he and his friends were headed back home, coming across a big field.

"Across the way was a drive-in restaurant with trays on the car windows and big speakers blasting loud music. I heard 'Honey Hush,' by Big Joe Turner for the first time," Delbert recalls that hot summer afternoon like it was yesterday. "I just stopped in my tracks and stood there, soaking it all in."[2]

> *Ah let 'em roll like a big wheel*
> *In a Georgia cotton field*
> *Honey hush*
> *Come in this house, stop all that yackety yack*
> *Come in this house, stop all that yackety yack*
> *Come fix my supper, don't want no talkin' back.*
>   From "Honey Hush" — Big Joe Turner[3]

A quarter-century later, Delbert told *Rolling Stone* writer Gary Cartwright, "It was like falling in love. There's nothing like that first time."[4]

It was 1954, the summer before Delbert turned fifteen. It was also a pivotal time in American music history. He had cut his teeth on pop hits of the '40s and early '50s. But, "Honey Hush" was different. This was alive. This music moved. And it moved Delbert, the driving drums, the clean guitar, the pop of the horns. It was a sound that spoke to him. And that music still rings in his ears today, more than sixty years later.

"Big Joe Turner had it going. Songs like 'Honey Hush,' 'Lipstick, Powder and Paint,' I couldn't get enough of this music. He was a honker and shouter," recalls Delbert.[5]

Big Joe Turner was a Kansas City pioneer who mixed rhythm and blues with boogie-woogie. James Austin of Rhino Records said, "The result was jump blues, and Turner was its foremost practitioner." Legendary songwriter Doc Pomus said, "Rock and roll would have never happened without him."[6]

"Everybody was singing slow blues when I was young," Turner told James Austin, vice president of A&R for Rhino Records in Los Angeles. "And I thought I'd put a beat to it and sing it up-tempo."[7]

Delbert was getting calluses on his fingers from that old Stella, and listening and learning all he could from this wide array of music. "We had these teen canteen dances at the school once a month on Friday nights. Most of the time, the high school band would play music of the 1940s. But, one month in the fall of 1954, we were going to have a jukebox. So, every homeroom had to vote for an artist to put on the jukebox. We all had to write our choice down on a piece of paper and fold it up. I wrote down 'I Was the One,' by Elvis Presley and handed in my note. The girl picking up the ballots was unfolding and looking at every vote as she got them. She got to mine and looked, and turned up her nose and said, 'Elvis Presley? Who's THAT? I've never even heard of him.'"[8]

In the fall of 1954, few people had heard of the nineteen-year-old Memphis truck driver. With his first single on the Memphis Sun label, he recorded a new version of an old bluegrass standard, "Blue Moon of Kentucky," made famous by Bill Monroe eight years before. While history had not yet labeled Monroe "The Father of Bluegrass," he was certainly a no-foolishness traditionalist of the style. While Monroe's version was a beautiful slow waltz, the Elvis version featured a new sound filled with energy and attitude. Sun Studio's Sam Phillips had developed a "slapback," a homemade echo device for recording that he used liberally on this cut, adding to the high-energy excitement of the traditional song.[9]

Elvis had fallen flat in his debut performance at the Grand Ole Opry, where the traditionalists didn't approve of his upbeat rendition of the bluegrass standard, "Blue Moon of Kentucky." He had just made his debut on the *Louisiana Hayride*, a national radio show on Shreveport's KWKH. After only one appearance, this nineteen-year-old, rocking, hillbilly singer named Elvis Presley had signed a one-year contract with the *Louisiana Hayride*. His second record, "Good Rockin' Tonight," had risen to number 3 on the Memphis charts and was the first single showing up on charts throughout the South.[10]

Delbert was listening with great attention to this new style that sounded a lot like the jump blues he had been drawn to since first hearing "Honey Hush." Not surprisingly, in the early days of radio airplay, Elvis Presley was often mistaken as a black singer, when in fact he was a white kid from Memphis singing the songs he loved. Something was happening. American music was reaching a boiling point and the entire country was about to go through a major change. And Delbert was eager to be a part of this new musical magic.

In March 1955, Delbert was in the eighth grade. A new movie was the buzz with teens and parents alike. *Blackboard Jungle* was a hard-hitting social commentary film focusing on juvenile delinquency and violence in integrated urban schools, starring Glenn Ford, Vic Morrow, and Sidney Poitier. However, Delbert McClinton would be hard-pressed to tell you the plot or outcome of the movie. For him, it was all about this brand new sound. *Blackboard Jungle* helped to usher in the rock and roll revolution.

Musicologist James J. Mulay said, "From the opening strains of Bill Haley and His Comets' 'Rock Around the Clock' in *Blackboard Jungle*, the power of rock and roll on film was obvious."[11]

The film doesn't intend to glorify the potential of youth rebellion of the times. Rather, it portrays this uprising as a danger, threatening the American way of life. Journalist Jeremy Marks writes, "In case there was any confusion about this, a written introduction was added to the film which included the following scroll, as a primitive drum solo opens the movie: 'We are especially concerned when this delinquency boils over into our schools. . . . We believe that public awareness is a first step toward a remedy for any problem."[12]

However, the audience, mostly teens, saw something different in this movie. And in a time that predates social media, word spread quickly about the new sound. There were reports of riots at screenings. Teens went wild.

Marks adds that the "us versus them" mentality portrayed in the film has been attributed to the onset of the rock and roll attitude. He writes, "*Blackboard Jungle* provides its audience with only a taste, not a starter course in the sound of rock & roll. 'Rock Around the Clock' is the only rock song used in *Blackboard Jungle*."[13]

Delbert remembers the night he first heard the song: "That kind of music didn't really have a name yet, but [Haley's] song, 'Rock Around the Clock' opened the movie, *Blackboard Jungle*. My friends and I were fifteen. We went to the midnight showing. That was about the biggest show in town. The theatre was dark. The music started with those driving drums. And it changed me. It changed all of us. It wasn't about the movie. It was about the music. And about how music could get into your soul and make you feel different."[14]

> *One, two, three o'clock, four o'clock rock*
> *Five, six, seven o'clock, eight o'clock rock*
> *Nine, ten, eleven o'clock, twelve o'clock rock*
> *We're gonna rock around the clock tonight.*[15]

There was no doubt about the power of this music. The same year, Big Joe Turner had a hit with "Shake, Rattle and Roll." *Rolling Stone* would later include both of these songs in their "Greatest 500 Songs of All Time" list, with "Shake, Rattle and Roll" at number 127, and "Rock Around the Clock" at number 158.[16]

Delbert tells the story of his first real musical performance at the age of sixteen: "It was just me and a guitar, in February of 1957, at the Big V Jamboree in Liberator Village over by White Settlement.

"The Liberator was the nickname of the B-24 bomber built at General Dynamics in White Settlement. The war and the jobs it brought to Fort Worth had caused a housing shortage in the area, so in 1942, the government built a whole little town of houses near the plant on the northwest side of Fort Worth. The makeshift town was called Liberator Village, for the bombers built at the plant."

Delbert says, "The lobby of the Liberator Theatre had caught fire some years earlier and burned about halfway through the place. They found a new use for it. They still had a stage and half the seats, and everyone had to enter through the emergency exit doors on each side of the screen. About fifteen rows of seats had survived the fire, and people would file in and sit to watch the show in front of the burned out rubble from the fire. Can you imagine the liability nightmare of something like that today?

"Anyway, they had a Big V Jamboree on Saturdays and I heard about it. I went up there in February of 1957, and signed up and sang a Ray Price song, 'Crazy Arms,' just me and my guitar. Again, I shook so hard I could hardly play. But, it really didn't matter because you couldn't hear the guitar and the sound system was one of those little portable jobs with two ten-inch speakers and one microphone input. But, it felt good. The audience liked it. And I learned something."[17]

Delbert is quick to say that he was never much on formal education. "In fact, I got kicked out of choir in the fifth grade, for not taking it seriously. I left high school a half credit shy in English," admits the award-winning singer-songwriter.[18] But, his education was coming from a different kind of school.

The summer of 1957 came around. Delbert was almost seventeen. Rock and roll was fast becoming the heartbeat of America. Construction had begun on President Dwight Eisenhower's new Interstate Highway System, and talk was that car travel would never be the same. That summer, Delbert's aunt and uncle came to Fort Worth to visit and invited him to ride back to Florida with them.

"I'd have to say my Aunt Billie Rhea may have been the first person to really believe in me and think I could go somewhere professionally with my music. We got down to Cocoa Beach, and they took me out to the Starlight Bar-Motel on Cape Canaveral. Years later, that was the bar they used in the movie, *The Right Stuff*. It really was where all the astronauts and those people hung out. My aunt rented me a little Martin guitar from the local music store and dyed my hair jet black. Every Wednesday night, they had a talent show. The winner would get in the pot, and all four weekly winners of the month would compete on the final Saturday night of the month. The winner would get a hundred-dollar prize. That first Wednesday night, I got up and sang 'Going Steady,' the Tommy Sands hit, and 'That's All Right, Mama,' by Elvis. It went pretty good," Delbert recalls.[19]

It must have gone well, because he won the round, and went on to win the money in the finals.

Through his railroad job, Herman McClinton was supposed to be sending his son a free ticket home on the railroad, but it was going to take a couple of weeks.

Delbert remembers, "Back then, no one made long distance phone calls unless someone had died, but we had a way to beat the system by calling person to person through the operator. So, every few days, I would call home and ask the operator to let me speak with 'R. I. Ticket.' And they would not accept the call, which was code for 'There is no ticket here.' So, I kept playing that little guitar and going to the Starlight on Wednesday nights."[20]

It was Delbert's first big trip away from home, and he could see that the world was changing before his eyes. He even got to see an early space missile test. "Early one evening, we were fishing for blue crab," he says, "when my uncle said, 'See all those lights? Keep watching over there. Look way over there,' and pretty soon, we saw the rocket blast off into the sky."[21]

Before his long-awaited train ticket back to Fort Worth arrived, Delbert met his first "Big Shot in the Music Business." "I had played my songs and got off the stage and this woman came up. She said she was from Capitol Records and gave me her card. She liked what she heard and said 'send me a demo.' I thought that meant I was on my way," he says with a smile.[22]

The train ticket finally came through. Delbert got back to Fort Worth, and the first thing he did was walk into the T. H. Conn Music Store, and lay down one hundred dollars for a little mahogany Martin guitar. He was more serious than ever about playing music for the rest of his life.

He called his old buddies and put his first band together, the Mellow Fellows. Delbert shakes his head as he remembers: "We played our hearts out. Three guitars. No bass. We had a drummer, Ray Clark, who only had a snare and a ride cymbal. We could not play worth shit. So, we decided to add another guitar player. We added Joe Don's older brother, Gatemouth, who wasn't much better than we were.

"And we had called ourselves the Mellow Fellows for a while before changing the name a couple of times. The Mellow Fellows was just a bunch of us hanging out with guitars and spending more time thinking of a great band name than actually practicing and getting better.

"Ray Clark was a neighborhood friend whose father was a professional musician. Mr. Clark had been in the Lawrence Welk Orchestra. In those days, he was playing in a jazz trio. Ray had access to some drums and thought he was good enough. He probably was. None of us was very good on guitar, but we figured that if we had four guitars it would sound all right. We were willing to try."[23]

Ray's mother was a waitress at a local restaurant, the House of Molé, and it was somebody's birthday. They invited the Mellow Fellows to play a party after closing time. "They passed the hat after we played. We made about seven or eight dollars that night, which was probably a lot more than we were worth," Delbert says.[24]

He adds, "We played some restaurants and some parties, nothing special. Our first big gig was fronting Jerry Lee Lewis on a package show at the Sportatorium in Dallas, a big coliseum usually used for wrestling matches. It was going to be Jerry Lee's first time in Dallas. We were one of the three bands that played before Jerry Lee on the Big D Jamboree. We played a thirty-minute set, early rock and roll, rockabilly, Elvis stuff, Coasters, 'Goodnight, sweetheart, it's time to go' . . . I was playing rhythm guitar and I know now that we weren't any good. But, that day we didn't know any better. The sound was awful, of course, coming from those big horns hanging from the ceiling. And the crowd didn't know any better. We loved them and they loved us."[25]

Songwriting has been key to Delbert's unique brand. His songwriting is a patchwork quilt of American styles and genres and he was already learning to blend those influences into his own sounds. In an interview with Texas music historian Kathleen Hudson, he said, "I've probably been influenced by everybody I've heard because I like a little bit of everything. The only conscious direction that I believe I've ever taken is that I'm not trying to copy anybody else."[26]

Before writing songs, he began writing poetry in high school. In fact, his first published work was in the Arlington Heights school newspaper, the *Jacket Journal* (December 19, 1957). "Everyone in my English class had to write a Christmas poem for a contest. I won. It was published on the front page—'Christmas to the Blind,' and it described all of the things a blind person might see and smell, and the excitement surrounding Christmas without being able to see them." He recites from memory:[27]

> *If you've ever talked to a blind boy about Christmas on*
> * Christmas Eve*
> *You'd find he has a more beautiful Christmas than we*
> * could hope to see . . .*
> *The excited voices, the scent of the trees are visions of a*
> * story book rhyme.*
> *His heart will be filled with Christmas cheer, and we'll be*
> * the ones who are blind.*

Delbert writes in an old journal, "I was so obsessed with the music. I was trying to get an education because my parents wanted it so badly. I just about went nuts. My mother wrote me a long letter one time about how concerned she was that I would not get an education. I was living at home, and she went out and mailed it to our house. She said that mailing me a letter was the only way to get me to stand still long enough to listen to her."[28]

Delbert adds that he was twenty-one when he made his last failed attempt at a high school diploma. Still a half credit shy in English, he went back again to appease his father. "Over and over, my dad said, 'Son, without that high school diploma in your back pocket you won't amount to a hill of beans.'"[29]

Decades later, after Delbert had earned three Grammy Awards, a Carnegie Hall appearance, multiple television appearances, and a double-platinum songwriting credit for "B-Movie Boxcar Blues," an old high school friend went to the Arlington Heights school officials and asked if they would grant him a high school diploma, crediting his life's work for that half credit of English. Surely these accomplishments would allow him to "place out" of some of that half-credit of high school English. No. The school officials were willing to give him an *honorary* diploma, and they stood firm. Delbert McClinton had not completed their requirements to earn an actual diploma.[30]

But, a glance at the Arlington Heights Wikipedia page will show that they are quick to claim him among their "Notable Alumni," as a Grammy Award–winning singer-songwriter and musician.[31]

Diploma or not, at twenty-one, Delbert was intense. He had no great vision at the time. He was just working at what he loved. Little did he know that critics, fans, and musicians would all someday credit him with great accomplishments in American music.

But, not before he graduated from the school of hard knocks.

CHAPTER 4
"Right to Be Wrong"

Coming of Age in a Texas Roadhouse

*Down in Florida, that woman from Capitol Records told me
to send her a demo. Well, hell. This was it. I thought I had it
made. As soon as I got back to Fort Worth, I called some guys
together and we made a demo of "Mean Woman Blues," and I
sent it off to her. I never did hear back from her, but that was
where the fire got out of control.*
—DELBERT McCLINTON[1]

There was no turning back for Delbert and his musical career.
That first band, the Mellow Fellows, was proof that everybody
has to start somewhere.

The band changed names and personnel a few times, and the
talent improved tremendously. By February 1958, Delbert's band
was becoming well known around Fort Worth. The Straitjackets,
the band name, was spelled multiple ways through those years
in newspaper advertisements and on flyers and tickets, but one
thing was certain. However it was spelled, the Straitjackets had
something going on.[2] They started playing regular shows on Friday and Saturday nights at the Red Devil Lounge. Regular advertisements in the *Fort Worth Star Telegram* read
:

We have for your dancing and listening pleasure,
The STRAITJACKETS
New TV and Recording Stars
Featuring

Delbert McClinton, vocal artist
All Ladies Admitted Free
Gents: 50¢ Friday, $1.00 Saturday
2541 N.E. 28th St.
For Reservations, Call MA 4–0308[3]

They became one of the most popular bands in the area. When the Crystal Springs Ballroom held an elimination-style talent contest, it came down to the final two bands on February 28, 1958. Advertisements read, "Battle of the Bands: Straitjackets vs. Twisters—Help Select Fort Worth's Hottest Band." The Crystal Springs contest was the first of several talent show titles the Straitjackets would win. The Top Hat 7–11 Club on Pennsylvania Avenue also hosted regular talent shows. The bands would audition on Mondays and Tuesdays, and the finalists would vie for the big one-hundred-dollar cash prize on Saturday nights. The Straitjackets won that competition twice. This was a big deal. For the most part, the Straitjackets were playing wherever they could for whatever they could make; one hundred dollars cash for a Saturday night was more than fair.[4]

Eddie Miller was the first piano player for the Straitjackets. He says, "We were all kids, but here we were playing in strip clubs and road houses, because that's where people came to hear good music. We were good enough that we were in demand. The club owners always knew that we would draw a crowd. Our fans were gangsters and hookers and strippers. If there weren't two or three fights a night, we thought something was wrong. We didn't cater to them but it was our crowd.

"At that time, there were two kinds of live music, country music—and I mean real sawhorse country—and black music in the black clubs. So, we came along and were doing Jimmy Reed and Little Walter and Wilson Pickett and Otis Redding, and everybody loved it. We played white clubs and black clubs and backed up a lot of the great black artists who came through town. It didn't seem like a big deal then, but looking back, it really was."[5]

The Red Devil Lounge, Crystal Springs, the Bayou Club, the Covered Wagon Ballroom, and the 811 Club were just a few of the Fort Worth bars the Straitjackets called home during those

early days. Teen clubs, canteens, and parties all led to more rec-
ognition and a tighter sound.

By 1959, Delbert and the Straitjackets were the house band at
Jack's Place, a popular nightclub on the Mansfield Highway just
outside the Fort Worth city limits. Delbert was picking up the harmonica and learning from the headliners who came through.

He adds, "The first time I really focused on creating *my* sound
was on the way to rehearsal one afternoon. I was at the corner
of Sylvania and something. I was stopped at a red light, listening
to KNOK Radio. Jimmy Reed came on with 'Honest I Do.' From
that moment on, I was all about harmonica blues."[6]

Delbert describes Dallas' KNOK-AM radio as having played
a major role in his musical roots. "It's where I first heard Jimmy
Reed, Muddy Waters, Buster Brown. That was where I learned
that there was other music that was just as big as Bob (Wills),
Lefty (Frizzell), Hank (Williams), and Nat King Cole."[7]

Delbert describes Jack's as "the place where all the under-aged
people from Fort Worth went to drink and party. It was a Fort
Worth coming-of-age tradition, because the owner, Jack Padgett,
had a deal with the police. Basically, it went like this: There was
a neon mule out front on the sign. If the mule was kicking, all
was well, come on in. But, if the mule was not kicking, there was
going to be a raid. Everyone knew about the sign," he explains.[8]

"That was about when I got my first harmonica," Delbert recalls.
"I was hearing Jimmy Reed on the radio. Dallas' KNOK, a really
powerful, all-Black radio station had a slogan: 'Stacks of wax and
mounds of sounds for your listening pleasure.'"

He adds, "I was never that great on guitar. I learned just
enough—the pull and jerk method. But, I just took to the harmonica."[9]

Even in 1960, Fort Worth still had its share of gangsters. Dallas may have had organized crime, but Fort Worth had individual
colorful characters. The thirty-mile *hyphen* between Dallas and
Fort Worth kept the sister cities a world apart in the days that
Delbert was coming of age.

"I fell in love with Sandra Sue Riley when I was sixteen years
old," Delbert says. "She was part Choctaw Indian and looked it.
She was the prettiest thing I had ever seen. She had big brown

eyes and long dark hair. I met her at a Saturday matinee at the Ridglea Theatre. She was drop-dead gorgeous. She wore this mouton coat. It was a fake fur that all the girls were wearing, and no one wore it better than Sue Riley."[10]

Delbert adds, "I got so lost in loving her that it became another of those obsessions I was becoming an expert in acquiring. There was nothing that I wouldn't do—or didn't do for her. We were so much in love. Then we got married in April of 1959."[11]

1959 was still a time of innocence for American teens and theirs was a common enough story for the times. Sue thought she was pregnant. They told their parents. He was nineteen and she was seventeen. Everyone agreed that they should get married. Before the wedding date, she found that it was a false alarm. She was not pregnant after all.

"We went through with the wedding anyway," Delbert reflects. "I didn't know anything about relationships or responsibility. And hindsight is 20/20. We should have spent some time growing up, but it was nothing for kids to get married at that age with no clue back then. It was pretty dumb. But, if it hadn't been that, it would have been something else. We were both pretty clueless about life."[12]

While trying to adjust to home life, he continued to play music. It was his greatest passion. Not only were the Straitjackets drawing crowds as the house band at Jack's Place, they were backing big rhythm and blues stars who came through town: Buster Brown, Memphis Slim, Jimmy Reed, Al Smith, Big Joe Turner, and Bo Diddley. A glance through the 1960 *Fort Worth Star-Telegram* advertisements for Jack's Place shows these names as only a few of the musicians with whom the Straitjackets played. And if he wasn't leading the backup band, Delbert was sitting near the stage, watching and learning from this unaccredited but highly acclaimed honkytonk blues university.[13]

These were singers, songwriters, and musicians who had been Delbert's heroes, and would continue to be among his greatest influences throughout his career.

Joe Nick Patoski says, "Delbert was exposed to the two basic roots of Texas music—country and western and rhythm and blues, from an early age. He got to see both styles of music live and up close. As a teenager, he was a hepcat. He was hanging with black bands and being mentored by people like Jimmy Reed. The Strait-jackets were not just the opening act. They were the house band for those big artists. Most Chitlin' Circuit acts coming through town could not afford to travel with a full band, so they would use Delbert and his band. While Jack's Place had a predominately white crowd, Jimmy Reed had black and white gigs."[14]

Patoski adds, "Ultimately those 'salt and pepper' crowds had these white boys backing or opening for these black artists. The music world integrated long before the rest of the world. And they might play Jack's with Jimmy Reed on Saturday night, and then they'd go with Jimmy or whoever to Lawton, Oklahoma, or Wichita Falls to play black clubs on Sunday. Delbert got to travel with these R&B artists, and learn from them. This is the differ-ence that separates people like Delbert from, say, Bob Dylan, who grew up in Duluth, Minnesota. In his formative years, all Dylan had to listen to was recorded music."[15]

The live musical education Delbert was receiving in those clubs offered much more than recorded versions of these art-ists. Grammy award-winning producer and president of the his-toric jazz record label Blue Note, Don Was talks about the benefit of hearing music live and on stage versus on the radio or on a record: "Speaking to you as a musician, there are certain limita-tions to recording. Particularly the music we grew up listening to. Ultimately, it had to do with the limitations of how much music you could fit on a piece of vinyl before it started to sound shitty. If you had more than twenty minutes of music on a side, your record started sounding really bad. Go back even before LPs, and look at 78s, and guys like Charlie Parker. If you saw him live, he would play a twenty-minute solo but on the 78s, you couldn't get more than five minutes of music on a side. On record, you don't have time to capture the essence of these long extended, build-ing solos.

"If you look at the Charlie Parker records, they're like trailers for his live show, you know, like movie trailers. The physical lim-itations of lacquer prevented him from really practicing his art form to the fullest in the studio. But, if you saw him live, you got the real thing."[16]

Delbert was lucky enough to come of age surrounded by live music on those stages in Fort Worth in the mid-twentieth century. He was front and center, crossing lines and unpaved parking lots to play on stages in honkytonks and blues clubs on the "wrong side of town," during one of the most tumultuous periods in American history. Paying little mind to the racial tensions and conflicts making headlines across the country, Delbert was basking in the music, playing with, learning from, and backing some of the leading black artists in the nation.

Describing Fort Worth at that time, journalist Gary Cartwright writes in *Rolling Stone*, "Just below the surface of the white fundamentalist illusion was an enormous multiracial underbelly of outlaws, scammers, and downtrodden survivors."[17]

This is not a story about a white kid playing in a black club, or a black artist fronting a white band. This was simply good music transcending racial unrest and distrust. It was integrated bands and audiences and a time of bringing the best of all worlds together on smoky, dimly lit stages in county-line roadhouses.

Cartwright remembers, "By the late '50s, McClinton's band, the Straitjackets, were not just the house band at Jack's Place. I think they were the only white band that ever played at Jack's but they didn't sound white. They played backup for the stars who came through on weekends and were the house band the rest of the week. Delbert's first record, a cover of Sonny Boy Williamson's 'Wake Up Baby,' had so much soul, it was the first white single to be played on KNOK, Fort Worth's black radio station."[18]

Endnotes, footnotes, and stacks of research aside, who is the ultimate authority on Delbert McClinton and his career? Arguably, Delbert himself, as he has written fairly succinctly in "Victim of Life's Circumstances":

> *I'm a victim of life's circumstances*
> *I was raised around barrooms, Friday night dances*
> *Singin' them old country songs*
> *Half the time endin' up someplace I don't belong.*[19]

Delbert illustrates pure Texas music as his Heinz-57 musical pedigree includes a liberal amount of Texas country, Tejano, Cajun, zydeco, western swing, folk, rockabilly, swing, jazz, and a heavy dose of rhythm and blues.

Texas music writers have long established that the unique sound of Texas music is a blended, shared hybrid of sounds from around the world. Author Joe Nick Patoski describes the Big Three heritages that make up the state: "It's tri-ethnic, based on the Big Three heritages: African-, Mexican-, and Anglo-American. It welds a lot of different things together at odd angles to make a cohesive sound. It's stealing from the Germans and the Mexicans. A lot of people say it's crazy. And some people don't like it. But, it works here. And it is always evolving. No other state has the kind of region with the distinctive sounds we have in Texas. It's Texas Music."[20]

Historian Karl Hagstrom Miller writes in his book, *Segregating Sound*, that academic folklore and the music industry are rarely discussed in histories of segregation, yet they helped to orchestrate "a sonic demarcation on the road to desegregation."[21]

While Miller's book focuses primarily on the Jim Crow years, he lays some important groundwork for the true desegregation that was happening in the smoke-filled bars and honkytonks on the outskirts of cities across Texas and the South, as illustrated in the clubs Delbert and his band were performing in through those years.

Musicologist Mark Kurlansky writes, "There has never been an American generation that so identified with its music, regarded it as its own, the way the Americans who grew up in the 1950s and 1960s did."[22]

These descriptions accurately depict the middle of the twentieth century. However, as the United States moved into the postwar years of the 1950s and 1960s, Texas—and the entire country—climbed onto a wild roller coaster of change.

Delbert may have been among the first who successfully crossed those lines of color on stage, but he would be the first to tell you that, at the time, race relations were the last thing on his mind. He was building a unique sound that has carried him through more than sixty years on stage.

Gregg Andrews, historian and cofounder of the Center for Texas Music History at Texas State University, says, "It's important to remember that what we call 'Texas music' is not static. It's dynamic and constantly being reshaped, redefined, across ethnic, class, and generational, as well as geographical lines."[23]

Delbert has proven himself well versed in crossing those lines and making himself at home in a variety of Texas-rooted genres.

This Texas music history is important to the story, and Delbert was working through the nights trying to feed his musical hunger. Yet, he was soon to have a family to support. In reality, house band or not, the Straitjackets weren't making a living at this. Everyone had a day job. A good night brought in seventy-five dollars for the band.

Delbert says, "Hell, I didn't make any real money until the late 1980s. Up until then, we were just trying to keep playing. I'd get our cut of the door money and divide it five or six ways, depending on how many were in the band at the time. And maybe have enough money left to fill up the gas tank."[24]

Delbert's young wife, Sandra Sue, was working as a bookkeeper for the natural gas company in Fort Worth, bringing home most of the bacon. "She always had an amazing head for business," Delbert says. "She always had a good office job. She was so smart. Even in high school, she was in one of those vocational programs that let her out half a day to go work for the gas company."[25]

But as adept as Sue was in business, he is quick to admit that he was just not cut out for labor, skilled or unskilled: "We'd been married a year or so when we found out that we were going to have a baby. I realized that I had to do something to try to make more money and support the family. So I got a job at Stratoflex, a place in Fort Worth that made high-pressure hoses for jet aircraft. I was working two jobs. I was playing at Jack's and then going straight to work at Stratoflex on the graveyard shift till 7:30 in the morning.

"I hated that Stratoflex job with a passion. It was about as far from what I wanted to be doing as anything I could make up. But Stratoflex had plenty of dirty, stinking jobs, literally, for uneducated fools like me. So there I was, punching a clock.

"On the nights I wasn't playing at Jack's, I rode to work with a guy that lived across the street from us. We worked from 11:30 p.m. to 7:30 a.m. He always liked to stop for a beer in the morning on the way home from work. The Bungalow was one of those sleazy little bars that opened for business at that time of day. And that's where I was at 8:00 in the morning when my dad found me with the news that Sue had gone into labor.

"So off we went to the hospital, with me stinking of machine oil and metal shavings clinging to my clothes. Sue had a long, hard labor. And my guess is, so did those who had to put up with the way I smelled all day."[26]

And late in the day on August 20, 1961, Sandra Sue gave birth to a beautiful, blond-headed boy. They named him Monty Michael McClinton. Delbert spent his first night as a father at his parents' house, and remembers that he was the first one up the next morning. "I wasn't much of a coffee drinker at the time, but my folks were, so I made my first pot of coffee that morning. I remember my dad saying that it was 'a little bit stiff.'"[27]

Showered and in clean clothes, Delbert was back at the hospital early that morning to check on his young wife of two years, and their baby boy. "I was so happy and so scared at the same time. I didn't know which way to jump!"[28]

Not having a real talent for making money, and having no skill other than playing music, put Delbert in a frustrating position. He admits that being a bar band musician in 1961 didn't pay much — nor does it today. "And it didn't get you much respect beyond those who came to hear the music, and they—for the most part—were not what you might call the Spartans of the Community."[29]

Yet, Delbert continued to work the wee hours—graveyard shifts at Stratoflex, a company owned by T. Cullen Davis and his brother, Ken, oil heirs and Fort Worth royalty.

Delbert writes about that job with clarity: "One night at Stratoflex, the foreman put me on a job that finally sent me over the edge. I had to sit next to this god-awful, loud automatic screw machine and check the threads on the brass fittings that this thing was spitting out. I had a six-inch piece of hardened machine steel with the exact threads cut into it.

"I had to screw every one of those damned bolts on and off of that six-inch piece of steel. The good ones went into one box and the bad ones in another. This process redefined monotony beyond words. That hateful machine spit out about six bolts to every one I could check, with a grotesque syncopation lacking any kind of rhythm at all. I fell asleep at some point in defense of my sanity.

"I was awakened at about 7:00 a.m. by the big boss man. That condescending son of a bitch woke me up by kicking the chair I was sitting on and hollering, 'Hey! Is this the way you work?'

"I wanted to shove that piece of machine steel up his ass. But I needed that job, at least until I could find another one. So I suffered the humiliation and started looking."[30]

Soon enough, he found another job—at Montgomery Ward Department Store. Delbert shakes his head as he describes it: "I got a job working on the third floor of the main store in Receiving. We had to open these huge boxes of crap that came back from smaller Montgomery Ward stores in the outlying towns around Fort Worth. This was all broken stuff and pieces of things that were no longer of any use or discontinued.

"At first, the volume of things in those boxes fascinated me, but that fascination didn't last very long. My job was to catalog every single piece of this broken crap. It was like going to the dump and sorting everything into piles and writing down how many of each thing there was, and what state of disrepair it was in. Then they would compare my list to the list that the small store had submitted when they sent all that broken crap back.

"It was insane. Again, I knew I had to find a way out. I decided that maybe I needed a job with less on-site supervision."[31]

Delbert's next job was working the counter and driving a hot-shot truck for a foreign car parts house. A friend was working there and he helped Delbert get the job. "It was something a smart monkey could have done but I was not good at it. I couldn't learn catalog numbers and didn't know a clutch plate from a brake lining. Finally, the boss told my friend that they probably didn't need me. We all agreed that he was probably right."[32]

Delbert could not catch a break when it came to finding a day job. However, the loan company gig was probably the worst of the bunch, as Delbert says, "So, I went to work for a finance company. I have never worked for such a sorry bunch of people in my life, before or since. They preyed on poor people, especially black people. I worked for the devil and his brother. They had me skip chasing, looking for people who had defaulted on their shady loans. I would get a list of the last known addresses. And I was supposed to go check to see if they still lived there. I would go home and take a nap on the couch and then come back and say, 'No. They don't live there no more.'

"For a while, it was the perfect job. Until I realized what assholes they were. They had put the wrong date on the paperwork for the final payment for this poor guy's car loan. He had paid on time on the usual date all along, but the final date was not usual. They took me to where he was working, and told me to ride with him back to the office, supposedly to straighten everything out.

"This guy was working at a job and paying for his car. And they had messed with him on the paperwork. And they were going to repo his car.

"We got over to this guy's job, and I realized how wrong that was. It was one of those rare, remarkable moments in human perception. This guy was working his ass off and trying to do everything right. And there I was, working for the devil and his brother. I got in the car with him, and we headed toward the office and I looked at that poor guy and said, 'Let me tell you what's about to happen.'

"I told him and said, 'So when I step out of this car, you haul ass.' I got out and he hauled ass. And I quit."[33]

Delbert has celebrated most of his rites of passage in bars. "On my twenty-first birthday," he remembers, "we were playing Jack's Place. On the way to the gig, I stopped at a liquor store and bought a pint of Wild Turkey. My first legal purchase. I didn't drink back then, so I didn't know much but from all I knew, it was the coolest brand of liquor. I wanted to show my ID to somebody, and I bought it because I could, and I suffered because I did. Bo Diddley was playing that night and my band was backing him up. But I missed the show. Yeah, I took two or three shots, I passed out on stage and someone hauled me off into Jack Padgett's office. I learned a big lesson that night. But not before I did it again," he admits, with a shake of a head.[34]

A week or so later, he recalls sitting backstage with Buster Brown and Sonny Boy with a fifth of Old Grand-Dad. "I was sitting in between them on the couch there, and double-shooting it. Every time the bottle passed by back and forth, I took a shot. I missed that show, too," he says.[35]

Three weeks after Delbert's twenty-first birthday, on November 28, 1961, Jack's Place burned to the ground. According to news reports, firefighters from Fort Worth and four surrounding towns came to try to stop the flames, but to no avail. Jack's was a total loss. Because the building had no windows, the only way to access the flames was to go up on ladders and spray water down through the roof. Newspaper reports said it was a fifty-thousand-dollar loss. It was the end of an era for Fort Worth. Jack's neon mule would kick no more.

And it was the end of a chapter for the Straitjackets. However, they quickly found a new home at the Westmore and then the Skyliner Ballroom on the Jacksboro Highway.

Historian Mike Nichols describes the Jacksboro Highway in his book, *Lost Fort Worth*: "For much of America, the 1950s were a time of 'I Like Ike' and 'I Love Lucy.' But out on the Jacksboro Highway, the boys in the backrooms liked gambling, they liked prostitution and they *loved* cops who looked the other way."[36]

Historian Ann Arnold writes in her definitive Jacksboro highway chronicle, *Gamblers and Gangsters*, that between 1943 and 1959, nineteen gangland killings took place in Fort Worth. Most of the victims were regular customers or employees out on the Jacksboro Highway. Most of the murders were never solved. She writes that these murders were generally committed by knife fights, gunshots, or car bombings, and this number does not include the usual casualties of typical Saturday night bar brawls on Jacksboro Highway.[37]

The Straitjackets were gaining regional traction. The band was now made up of Delbert, Ronny Kelly, Jim "Prairie Dog" Dinsmore, Billy Cox, and Bob Jones. Talentsville USA was a major talent show sponsored by Coca-Cola that held regional competitions and state finals. In white dinner jackets and peg-legged slacks, the Straitjackets won the Fort Worth competition easily, leading a field of more than two hundred contestants. They went on to win the regional competition and placed second in the state finals.[38]

When the Straitjackets made the Jacksboro Highway clubs their home—specifically the Skyliner Ballroom—much of the gangster activity had slowed down in the badlands of Fort Worth.

Prohibition had long since been repealed and with the advent of the 1960s, illicit activities weren't quite the commodity they had been in earlier years.

The Skyliner Ballroom continued to be one of the wildest and most colorful clubs on the strip, according to historian Ann Arnold. Delbert and the Straitjackets played Blue Mondays, as well as backing up Reed, Howlin' Wolf, Sonny Boy Williamson, and many other national acts. When they first started playing the Skyliner, the club still featured strippers, who would perform on the same nights the Straitjackets would play.

"The band would play a while and then the girls would come out and dance. I had to go back to the dressing room and ask them what music they would want to dance to that night. They liked 'Peter Gunn,' 'Tequila,' 'Watermelon Man,' songs with a little drama," he recalls.

Delbert says, "I was at the right place at the right time, and I knew it."[39]

He adds, "We would play a lot with Jimmy Reed, Sonny Boy, and Buster Brown and often, they would hire us to go with them up to Mother's Place, a popular black club in Lawton, Oklahoma, and other places along the way to play with them for a few days. Jimmy Reed had a one-eyed bass player he would bring along, who was also his manager. We played a lot of little towns with them. Every trip, I'd learn something. Sometimes about music. Sometimes about life. The first joint I ever smoked was in the bathroom at Mother's Place with Sonny Boy."[40]

Today, one of Delbert's prize possessions is locked in a curio case in his Nashville living room, opposite the ebony black grand piano. "We were going to be playing with Jimmy Reed. And we had a really shitty microphone that had come with a little tape recorder. I had a new Shure 55SW microphone on layaway, but I needed to get it out that day for that show. I managed to scrape enough money together to pay off that microphone so Jimmy Reed could use it that night. That very night, he threw up on it. And I still have it," he says, as he takes the vintage silver microphone from the case. "Now that's history," he smiles.[41]

Legendary stripper Candy Barr, once a regular featured attraction at the Skyliner, had been sentenced to prison for fifteen years for possession of marijuana in the mid-1950s, but would be released after a much shorter stay. She was close friends with Dallas and Fort Worth club owner and low-level mobster, Jack Ruby, who gained national fame when he shot and killed Lee Harvey Oswald, President John F. Kennedy's alleged killer, two days after Kennedy's assassination.

Ruby frequented the Jacksboro Highway clubs and owned or had part interest in a couple of them. He would occasionally hire Delbert and the Straitjackets to perform at his clubs in Dallas and Fort Worth.

Delbert says, "Fort Worth had a pretty solid crime world. And I knew a lot of those guys. Hell, I knew most of the gangsters, and every whore and stripper in town. They were friends. Coworkers, I guess. We all worked the same places trying to make a living."[42]

He recalls one night when the vice squad come out to the Tropicana. "One of the guys had just gotten out of the joint. Eight or ten of his friends were celebrating his release. These were all characters that I knew. We had this little ledge right at the front of the stage, where in bygone days, they used to have footlights.

"The people celebrating the release were carrying guns, which was illegal in bars, of course. The plain-clothes vice squad came in to check out the gathering. These guys would come dancing by the stage with their women, and drop their pistols at my feet while I was singing. I would just slide the guns under that ledge with my foot, and keep singing. The cops never checked the stage, and when they left, my friends came and got their guns back."[43]

There were two kinds of establishments on the edge of town: "The clubs on the highway were classified as divas and dives. In the diva clubs, well-dressed couples were ushered to their tables with deference by men in tuxedos. In the dives, drunks were tossed out the back door by bouncers in Levi's jackets."[44]

The Straitjackets's typical set list was heavy on rhythm and blues with some funky country mixed in. "We played music that people would dance to. Most people came out to dance. And we were good at getting them on the floor," Delbert says.[45]

"We'd play those clubs five nights a week till midnight, and then pack up and go play at the East Side Club till five in the morning," Delbert recalls.[46]

He remembers many wild stories of those after-hour gigs, but a couple in particular stand out: "Carroll Hall was a friend of mine who owned the East Side Club, and was well-connected with the local outlaws. The East Side Club was common ground. All the different characters were welcome, but no bullshit was allowed. If you had a problem with someone, you had to take it somewhere else. This worked pretty well for the most part, but there were always crazies who didn't follow anyone's rules.

"Fort Worth, from the mid-1950s to the late 1960s, had an unusual number of gangland style killings, and an abundance of gun-carrying individuals. Some were friends. Some were acquaintances. They were all dangerous. And most people in an after-hours joint at 4:00 in the morning are a demented lot.

"So, I was playing the piano and Ronny [Kelly] was standing up singing. It was a spinet piano, so Carroll could lean over and talk right in my ear. It was still pretty loud and I wasn't sure I had heard him right, so I said, 'What?'

"He said it again: 'Some asshole called and said there's a bomb in the club, but I think it's bullshit. But just to be on the safe side, stay close to the front door.'

"Today, I'm thinking, *What the fuck does that mean? If you stay close to the front door you won't get killed by a bomb?* But that night, I just nodded and kept playing like what he said made perfectly good sense."[47]

Another night, at the Tropicana, while the band was on break, a woman Delbert knew to be the main squeeze of one of those characters, came over and asked if he would go talk to her man before there was trouble. "He might listen to you," she pled.

"By the time we got back to the bar, my friend, Bill, had a pistol stuck up some guy's nose. I walked up to within about three feet of them and stopped. Bill never took his eyes off the guy. I said, 'Man, don't do this. It's gonna fuck up everybody's night. Please?'

"After a long minute, he slowly let the hammer down and relaxed his stare just a little. I said, 'Maybe this guy should find another place to drink, huh Bill?'

"Bill lowered the pistol to where it was laying on the bar, but still in his grip, and leaned back just a little. I felt like things had become a little less tense. I guess the guy did too, because he slid off the stool and disappeared."[48]

While the world may wonder what ever happened to the guy who slid off the Tropicana Club bar stool, there is little question about the power and persuasion of Delbert's voice, on or off the stage.

Nashville Tennessean music writer Michael McCall said, "McClinton's raspy, ferocious voice carries in it the history of American popular music. There's the down-home rhythm and testifying punch of gospel-based R&B, the aggressive snarl of the blues, the mournful rumination of honkytonk, the jaunty spirit of swing, and the up-front sexuality of early rock 'n' roll." McCall added, "Texas in general and Fort Worth in particular have long been a major source of the music that binds us all—blues, jazz, Western swing, rock 'n' roll, R&B, country—and musicians there were expected to play most of it and make people dance to all of it."[49]

"You had to know Fort Worth in the 1950s to understand McClinton's unquestioning obedience to his obsession," writes Gary Cartwright. "It was a unique city experiencing a unique age—an adolescent, slightly schizophrenic, bawdy brawling cow town looking for a quick ride and celebrating its rites of passage."[50]

The year Delbert turned twenty-one, Robert Weston Smith, better known as Wolfman Jack, debuted on the 100,000-watt XERF in Ciudad Acuña, Mexico, which claimed to be the most powerful radio station in North America. Most domestic radio stations were running at about 1,000 watts. When the weather was right, the 100,000-watt station could be heard from the Texas-Mexico border all the way to Canada. A Virginia native, Wolfman Jack had done some radio time in Shreveport, Louisiana, before hitting the waves on the Texas-Mexico border. Wolfman Jack was following in his mentor's footsteps, and like Alan "Moondog" Freed, Wolfman played a role in the transformation of black rhythm and blues into rock and roll music. In fact, Wolfman Jack attributed his stage name in part to bluesman Howlin' Wolf. [51]

Beyond the geographical range, XERF knew no musical boundaries. Delbert's musical style took root in that format: a little Tejano, a little Hank Williams. Throw in some Jimmy Reed harmonica. Add a liberal splash of Big Joe Turner, and a dash of

Frank Sinatra. He was developing a style that would continue to serve him well, well into the twenty-first century.

Delbert and his band, under several names, had started playing in clubs long before they reached the legal drinking age. Club management would rope off an area and tell the under-aged band members that they had to sit there on breaks lest they be tempted to drink. "Somehow," Delbert says, "we wound up getting more than our share of alcohol anyway."[52]

While these drinking incidents may have been rites of passage, drinking didn't keep Delbert from garnering the attention of music businessmen. Chief among them was Major Bill Smith, a Fort Worth record producer.

CHAPTER 5
"Honky Tonkin' (I Guess I Done Me Some)"

The Straitjackets

Major Bill was the only guy in town producing music. He fancied himself as a bargain basement Colonel Tom Parker. He was really a lot more like Houston's big promoter/producer, Huey Meaux. Both of them were just trying to get something going. It was hit or miss.

— DELBERT McCLINTON[1]

Major Bill Smith was a former Army Air Corps bomber pilot, shot down and wounded over Germany. After the war, he became a public relations officer at Carswell Air Force Base near Fort Worth, and quickly got involved in the budding Texas music industry. On Sundays, he would go down to the missions to preach. Major Bill was described as a "relentless self-promoter who was disinclined to let the facts get in the way of a good story."[2]

Major Bill used a recording studio in the basement of the old KFJZ radio station in Fort Worth. The radio station had started in the early 1940s as a country station but by the early '60s, KFJZ was broadcasting a more sophisticated "beautiful music format." That elevator music didn't quite jibe with the music being created in the basement.[3]

The promoter owned several record labels during that era. His first big success came in 1956 with Sonny James's "Twenty Feet of Muddy Water." He followed that with several regional and local hits, and spent a lot of time searching for talent in the Dallas–Fort Worth area.[4]

Major Bill would hire Delbert and the band as the session musicians for the studio every time he needed a backup band. "And if there was any time left on the clock after they finished, he would give it to me and let it roll. We did a few covers, like Sonny Boy Williamson's 'Don't Start Me Talking.'"[5]

However, one Saturday afternoon recording session in that basement studio paid off pretty well in the end.

Marvin "Smokey" Montgomery found a kid in Grapevine named Bruce Channel. Montgomery had long since made a name in the music business. Montgomery had played with Bob Wills, and was leading a reincarnation of the Light Crust Dough Boys for Burrus Mills Flour Company. Bruce Channel (born Bruce McMeans in Jacksonville, Texas) grew up in the suburbs between Dallas and Fort Worth, wanting to be a songwriter. He was only twenty-one, but by this time, he had his share of musical street credibility.[6]

Though the two men were born twenty-four days apart, and grew up twenty-four miles apart, neither Delbert McClinton nor Bruce Channel had any idea of what their future held, or that it would lead to a lifelong friendship.

Bruce says, "From early on, I would hear songs that I liked, and look up the people who wrote them and learn their other songs. I wanted to be a songwriter. I was always more influenced by the writers than the singers. But, you have to get out there and play those songs for someone." So, he put together a little band and played local dances and sock hops, and landed on the Big D Jamboree.

When Bruce was about fourteen, Elvis Presley became popular. Bruce says, "That changed everything. I knew I wanted to do music. But, mostly, I wanted to write songs. I had a summer job at a company that made butane tanks and containers, where I met a guy named Buddy Combs. He wanted me to meet his sister, Margaret Cobb, who knew how to write songs."

Bruce and Margaret Cobb wrote several songs together. "Hey Baby" was one of them. Marvin Montgomery was a friend of Margaret's, and she told him about Bruce.[7]

Bruce's performances on the Big D Jamboree had attracted

the attention of the music producer of the *Louisiana Hayride*. Broadcast live on KWKH every Saturday night from the Shreveport Municipal Memorial Auditorium, the *Louisiana Hayride* was second only to Nashville's Grand Ole Opry in popularity, and was even broadcast overseas on the Armed Forces Network.

Soon, Marvin Montgomery added Bruce to his Light Crust Doughboys show. Bruce was getting into the swing of writing, and wanted to record. Marvin told him about a music promoter/record producer he knew in downtown Fort Worth, Major Bill Smith.

Bruce says, "We went to see Major Bill and he agreed to work with me, so we went into the studio, on West Seventh Street in Fort Worth, with Marvin as the coproducer on the session."[8]

Delbert recalls, "He could sing his ass off. He could sound more like Roy Orbison than Roy Orbison did. Major Bill called me to get some guys together to record a few demos on Bruce. I remember that session like yesterday—or the day before yesterday. Jimmy Gordie played guitar; Bruce (Channel) played rhythm; my drummer, Jerry Foster, played drums; and I played harmonica. 'Hey Baby' was the B side and the A side was another of Bruce's songs, 'Dream Girl.'"[9]

Bruce remembers the day clearly. "I walked into the studio with Marvin Montgomery and played through my songs, just me and the guitar, while Delbert and the other guys listened.

"Then, just like that, Delbert kicked off 'Hey Baby' with his harmonica—with that intro you know so well. He is just a virtuoso with that thing—all he has to do is hear what you are doing and he will find the key and play it. He just kicked it off with that harmonica—and the band jumped in and knew just what to do. We recorded it once, twice, and then Marvin came in and put some piano on it the third time through, and that was history. Delbert's harmonica intro was so true. It was what identified the song. It was different. Everyone knew the song with that first harmonica riff. And I guess you'd have to agree that little song has stood the test of time."[10]

Delbert says, "We recorded about four songs that night. We realized 'Hey Baby' was a hit on the first or second playback. Major Bill put it out on his independent label, Le Cam, in Texas, Oklahoma,

Arkansas, and Louisiana. Within weeks, it had topped the charts in all four states. Major Bill made a deal with Mercury Records for national distribution. They put it out on Smash, a new startup part of Mercury, and before we knew it, 'Hey Baby' was a hit."[11]

"We each made five dollars for that session, as usual. It was just 'roll and play' recording—no overdubs, nothing fancy," Delbert recalls.[12]

"Hey Baby" became a huge hit single, and landed at number 1 in *Billboard Magazine* in March 1962, staying there for three weeks. The week after "Hey Baby" hit number 1 on *Billboard*, Bruce Channel went on a national tour with Fats Domino, Brook Benton, Don and Juan, the Impressions, and the Duke of Earl. "We started in New York and went down the East Coast and then across and up to Denver and ended in Houston," Bruce says. "They had one tour band for the whole show, so I went out as a single, and they tried to replicate Delbert's harmonica part with horns, and it just didn't work."[13]

"Hey Baby" soon blasted across the Atlantic, and concert promoters wanted Bruce Channel in England. Bruce recalls, "They had a British band, The Barons, ready to back me up. I told Major Bill that I just could not do it without Delbert. I could not have done it with just that British band. And boy, Delbert saved our bacon over there. Everyone loved that harmonica. Everybody loved Delbert."[14]

"And because Bruce wanted that harmonica on the tour, that started a whole new life for me," Delbert reflects.[15]

In the fall of 1962, Delbert traveled with Major Bill to London, the day before Bruce was to arrive. "I had loved all of those historic British movies, stories, and history, and World War I and World War II. All of those names and places had an intangible magic to them. It was as though I was going to be shown the secret to life.

"It was the second time I had ever flown. The first time was the day before when I took a midnight flight out of Dallas–Fort Worth Airport to New York.

"We were above the snowy, white clouds in the clear, blue sky when we started our descent. The clouds started getting darker, and misty with a sense of suspense. A cloak and dagger exhilaration overcame me. It was the London of my dreams. It was more than I could have imagined. To say I was overwhelmed would not be adequate. I was transported into another time with castles and ladies in distress, and royalty. It was the oldest civilization I had ever experienced. It was so incredibly exciting.

"After we landed in London, we grabbed a cab, and went to the hotel.

"And I left my bag of harmonicas in the cab.

"That was all I was there for. To play harmonica. And before I even got into the hotel, I had already lost my tools."[16]

Delbert says that there was no doubt Major Bill was good at getting things done. "It happened that there was a Hohner harmonica manufacturing plant in the city. We made immediate plans and got that taken care of, and were on to the next plan, when the cab driver walked into the hotel and asked if I had left my harmonicas in the car. He had come to them."[17]

Once again, Delbert illustrates that he has always been "One of the Fortunate Few."

"I was twenty-two years old and as green as grass, and had never felt more alive. Bruce would not be arriving till the next day, so I took off walking. It was all I could do to keep from telling people, 'Hey, look at me. I'm here in London, England!'

"I didn't want to miss a moment. I was focused on the most ordinary things: the candy with the liqueur center was certainly not something I'd ever seen in Texas. They had potato chips with little bags of salt separate, that you could add or not, and most of the coffee was a squirt of concentrate with hot water added. I smoked every kind of cigarette available and tried some really funky cheese. Milk over there was served at room temperature, and ice was pretty much nonexistent. I bought my mother a string of pearls, and a pocket watch for my dad. I felt like the king.

"When Bruce arrived the next day, we were scheduled to rehearse with the band that was going to back us for the tour, The Barons. We were picked up and driven to the venue where the tour would open that night.

"We arrived at the theatre about two in the afternoon for the sound check, and two young girls were already at the stage door. When they saw Bruce, they went nuts. I had never seen anyone starstruck. We found it quite amusing.

"We spent the afternoon working out the show with the band. There were about seven acts on the bill, and Bruce and I were to close the show. I would go out and sing a few songs and then introduce Bruce, and stay and play harmonica with him.

"When we kicked into 'Hey Baby,' the crowd went crazy. At the end of the show, people were pressed hard against the front of the stage and reaching for Bruce. He took off his guitar and walked to the edge to shake some hands and they grabbed him. I saw what was happening and grabbed him by the back of his belt and pulled him back, but not before they damn near tore his coat off.

"As we were leaving the theatre after the show, those two girls from the stage door earlier that day were running alongside the bus, screaming and holding up their arms and pointing at them. They had cut Bruce's name into their arms with a razor blade."[18]

"The bus was an old World War II British Army ambulance with big old knobby tires, and it had a hole cut out in the back where you could go pee. That was all just part of the experience. There were no precedents. We thought it was fantastic," Delbert said.

On that tour, Delbert and John Lennon spent time together over a period of several days. The two twenty-two-year-old musician/singers had a lot in common. Delbert explains, "The Beatles were opening for us on a couple of the shows, in Liverpool and New Brighton. They would open the show, then I would play three songs or so, and then Bruce would come out and we would do the headliner set. John wanted me to give him some tips on harmonica. The story's been romanticized to more than it was. I didn't *teach* him. I showed him what I did. When to suck and when to blow. Nothing really more than that."

He continues, "But it was a great moment in time. I did hang out with John a few nights when we were off. The Beatles were playing regular gigs at the time at the Cavern, a cellar in an old building. The club was completely empty when we got there. It was the middle of the afternoon. I sort of looked at John and thought, 'What the hell?' Then, in a matter of minutes, a herd of people came in and the place filled up, body to body. On another of our nights off, John came by the hotel with a friend of his, and they took me out and showed me things I never imagined. Beatnik joints, beanbag chairs, and people just laying over in the corner [having sex], you know? I mean, they sure didn't do that in Fort Worth. It was that European intensity in the '60s. It was most unusual, but it was something to see."[19]

You can take the boy out of Texas but . . . . One night when they were not playing, Delbert and Bruce wanted to go to a fancy restaurant. They were seated at a formal table with full service of flatware and dishes. The waiters, in tuxedos, were formal. Delbert says, "It was all real la-de-dah. We were minding our Ps and Qs, and just trying our best not to be hillbillies."

The two Texans were seated and had ordered their dinner when Bruce saw something else of interest. "Give me an order of that Yorkshire Pudding, too," he said. Delbert recalls that they ate all of their food, most of which they recognized but could not name. They were about done when Bruce politely asked, "Excuse me, when are you going to bring that pudding?" to which the waiter leaned forward, and looked down his nose at the table and announced, "You've eaten it, sir!"

Delbert adds, "It got to be every night on the (six-week) tour, somebody from another band would come to the dressing room because there wasn't that much harmonica going on in anything but blues music. It wasn't going on in rock and roll yet. And they wanted me to teach them how I did it. It's hard to show somebody anything on the harmonica. It's a lot like masturbation. You fool around with it. You figure it out.

"Years later, somewhere along the line, Lennon mentioned to some reporter that he was influenced by the harmonica on 'Hey Baby,' and it's grown into 'I've taught him everything he knew.' It's been romanticized a great deal, as those stories are, but that's exactly what it was. We were the same age. We hung out. We were on common ground. We were just two guys who couldn't get enough of it. Wanting to learn everything we could. And believing we could change the world."[20]

Delbert returned to Texas and continued playing with legendary blues musicians in Fort Worth, hitting the road when he could, and recording for Major Bill.

Looking back, Delbert admits that his life does take on sort of a Forrest Gump storyline, as he bumps into history, wandering through the twentieth century. Along the way, he was on the front row of several headline-making moments in history.

Delbert was one of the last people to see President John F. Kennedy alive, less than an hour before the assassination. "I was working at a men's clothing store, the Stag Shop. Stuart, my boss, was reading the Radio Shack circular and saw this Big Ear advertised. It was a dish thing that you could put up to your ear and hold to the wall and eavesdrop. We decided that it was the funniest damned thing in the world. So he sent me out to get one at the Radio Shack store."

This was November 22, 1963. President Kennedy had just spoken to the Fort Worth Chamber of Commerce, and was traveling to Carswell Air Force Base for the short jaunt to Dallas' Love Field on Air Force One. Delbert was on his way to Radio Shack, on a narrow two-lane highway. Motorcycle police officers were coming through directing traffic to pull over to the sides of the road to make way for the presidential motorcade as it made its way to the Air Force Base for the thirteen-minute flight to Dallas.[21]

The motorcade took up both lanes, traveling very slowly through the most congested area, as Texas Governor John Connally and President Kennedy waved at the spectators in this impromptu parade. Delbert was standing beside his car.

"President Kennedy and I locked eyes. We smiled at each other," Delbert recalls. "I went on over to Radio Shack and got the Big Ear. When I got back to the store, I told my boss I had just seen President Kennedy up close. Stuart was standing in front of the radio. He said, 'The president was just shot in Dallas. Listen!' It was unreal."[22]

Later that day, Lee Harvey Oswald was arrested for the president's assassination and the murder of a Dallas police officer. The following day, as Oswald was being transported from the Dallas police holding facility to the Dallas County Jail, Jack Ruby entered the basement of the police station and shot Oswald dead on live television.

Delbert recalls, "The nation was stunned in disbelief in this unprecedented horror. Conspiracy theories and unresolved justice was the common current of our lives."[23]

Months later, Delbert had gone to pick up a pizza. He arrived home to see an unfamiliar, but obviously unmarked government sedan parked in front of his house. Two Federal Bureau of Investigation (FBI) agents were standing in his living room, wanting to know about Delbert's relationship with Jack Ruby.

The FBI had discovered Delbert's phone number in Ruby's address book. He could think of no connection, except that he had played in some of Ruby's low-end clubs. "I had played a couple of his beer joints—it was in the last days of burlesque and his strip club-beer joints were pretty terrible places to play. So, I didn't have anything to tell the feds, but they were checking every name and number they came across."[24]

The agents were satisfied that Delbert had no viable connection with Jack Ruby beyond club bookings, and soon left. However, like all Americans, he still holds vivid memories of the tragedy in Dallas.

Aside from a trip to Florida at seventeen and the British tour with Bruce Channel, Delbert hadn't traveled much beyond the Fort Worth area. And as Delbert says about his first marriage, "It wasn't quite the hell that it soon became. It was not good, but it wasn't dangerous yet."[25]

Music continued to be the center of his world. Already a fan of Ray Price, Delbert remembers the first time he heard Jerry Lee Lewis's version of "Crazy Arms." Hearing Jerry Lee Lewis rock that traditional country shuffle, made Delbert realize that he too, could take a song and put his own brand, rhythm, phrasing and style on it—to make it his own. Rhythm and blues (R&B) and blues had opened the door, but with the advent of rock and roll, even mainstream radio recognized that rules could be broken and songs could be altered. They did not have to be copied note for note to be covered. Delbert says, "We learned that we could tear that tag off the pillow, and not go to jail."[26]

National radio host Don Imus identifies Delbert's authenticity as one of the keys to his success in building those bridges. "One thing that helped at that time," Imus says, "was that Delbert was a blue-eyed, white guy singing the blues and singing well and authentically, as opposed to the white artist ripping off black artists, like Pat Boone ripping off Little Richard and Chuck

Berry. I heard Pat Boone when I was in high school and was deeply offended by it. White people like Delbert and Elvis were embracing black blues and performing it well. And they became accepted by the African American community—no bigotry and no racism."[27]

By 1965, rock and roll had established a strong foothold on America's youth. R&B was holding its own. And country music still held forth. In Cowtown, Bob Wills was still the king.

Fort Worth continued to boom with another war to support and more military contracts. Subdivisions were springing up everywhere and many homes were built with garages instead of carports. With those garages came garage bands—neighborhood kids on every block were learning to play music, dreaming big, and reaching for the stars.

By now, the Straitjackets were at the top of the heap—at least in the Dallas–Fort Worth metroplex. But, as the song goes, "Nothing Lasts Forever."

CHAPTER 6
"If You Really Want Me To, I'll Go"

The Rondels

My close friend and cousin, Walter Lee, died on June 8, 1965. I had to go be a pallbearer. I got back to town and the band had fired me. So one of the other Straitjackets, Ronnie Kelly, and our guitar player friend, Billy Sanders, and I just put together another band, the Rondels, named for Ronny and me, and started over.

—DELBERT McCLINTON[1]

No blues story comes without some tragedy. And Delbert's is no exception. Walter Lee Connell III was Delbert's favorite cousin and lifelong friend. His death was a somber beginning for the next chapter of Delbert's career.

Walter, twenty-three, died on June 8, 1965, of asphyxiation. He and a friend, Joel Lee Searcy, twenty-two, were found slumped in the seats of an English-made sports car, according to news reports. Witnesses said the sports car's engine was running and a hose was attached to its exhaust pipe and funneled into the window of the car. Both men were dead when they were discovered. It was reported that a brief note of affection for a woman was found in the car, which belonged to Connell.[2]

Describing the shift in bands, Bruce Nixon wrote a feature on Delbert's longtime guitar player, Billy Wade Sanders, in *Guitar Player* magazine in December 1983. Billy explained, "Delbert had started the Straitjackets, a band on Fort Worth's west side that is still pretty well remembered by older fans and players around the city. At the same time, Ronnie Kelly and I were playing on the south side. I hooked up with the Straitjackets, and pretty soon Ronnie came along. When the Straitjackets split up, Ronnie and I went with Delbert and we started the Rondels."[3]

It was a natural progression. Ronnie Kelly and Billy Sanders were popular on the south side, and they believed in Delbert. As Howard DeWitt and Lee Cotten write in a 1992 issue of *DISCoveries,* "As the 1960s dawned, Delbert McClinton was recognized as the leader of the best bar band in Fort Worth."[4]

Billy Wade Sanders played most of his career with Delbert. He and Delbert remained lifelong friends until Billy died of cancer in September 2003.

Billy's strong upbringing in country music ("My daddy always wanted to see me play bluegrass at the Cowtown Jamboree here in Fort Worth," he told Nixon) helped to mold the personality and character of Delbert's sound. He said, "Hillbilly, country and blues are not that far apart. They all go back to the roots."[5]

Sanders had come from the same roots of country, swing, and blues as Delbert and Ronnie Kelly. They added Jimmy Rogers on bass, and Jim Dinsmore on drums. The Rondels went through a few drummers, just the beginning of Delbert's revolving door of drummers.

Soon, the Rondels brought on Jerry Foster on drums. With the acclaim from their former band, the Straitjackets, the Rondels quickly rose to the top in Fort Worth bar band popularity. And the Straitjackets became a blurred memory.

Music was changing. Peter Guralnick writes, "Back in the '50s, you could catch Ray Price, Ornette Coleman, King Curtis, Roger Miller, Bob Wills, T. Bone Walker and Doc Severinsen, all comfortably existing within the same musical setting. C. L. Dupree was the reigning guitarist, and as Billy Wade Sanders said, 'All the guitarists worth a shit had to go out to the White Sands to hear him play.'

"One Ray Price bandleader said, 'You could play hillbilly one night, swing the next, jazz the next, and if you had enough coke, play the blues till dawn on every one of them. There wasn't any division. Music was music, until the radio jocks and record guys got scared of rock 'n' roll.'"[6]

Guralnick adds, "Delbert McClinton, it is obvious, never got scared of rock 'n' roll nor of the blues, nor of country music either."[7]

Delbert describes the music the Rondels played at the time, "We would play some rockabilly and some blues and rock and roll and we would throw in some country. Good songs are good songs. We would play songs that we thought were good no matter where they came from—and we would do our best to do them justice. We never tried to sound like the record. We would shape the songs into our own style. But, we never really thought a lot about what our *sound* was. We gave ourselves some freedom to explore and play our way."[8]

As the Rondels were experimenting with their approach to popular music, the top tracks on the radio were changing more dramatically than ever before. The record labels were drawing lines in the sand. People who were established in pop or country were hesitant to move into rock and roll. Unlike the clubs and musicians themselves, the music industry was still slow to integrate their rosters, and for the most part, radio stations were still staying in their traditional programming lanes.[9]

Guralick, in *Lost Highways,* writes about Delbert and the Straitjackets/Rondels years: "They were local celebrities. They were the band around Fort Worth, much like Doug Sahm's group in San Antonio, and the legendary Boogie Kings of Bossier City [Louisiana]."[10]

The Rondels attracted the attention of young Fort Worth car dealer Jerry Conditt. Born and raised in Fort Worth, Jerry graduated from the University of North Texas,[11] and became a captain in the Air Force. "I was in the military for as little time as I could be," Jerry says. "I came back to Fort Worth as soon as I could."[12]

Back home, Jerry put that business degree to good use. He bought the Stork Club in Fort Worth, and soon owned seven or eight clubs in the Fort Worth area. His father had been in the car business since 1937, and encouraged Jerry to get into car sales. Jerry opened a used car lot right behind his dad's business.

"That's where I was when the Rondels came to talk to me.

Ronnie Kelly did the talking. He said, 'I understand you invest in different things sometimes. We wonder if you could be our manager and we would give you 10 percent of everything.' They needed an investor—or a manager—immediately. They had a gig with the Beach Boys in Florida, and didn't have a car or money to get there. And that's how I got into the music management business," he says with a laugh. "I guess I kept them in cars and managed to help them make a little money for a while."

Jerry gave the Rondels a Cadillac to drive to Florida, and a credit card to cover expenses. "I took them to J. C. Penney's to buy them some clothes. At that time, all the good bands dressed alike. We got them dressed up nice, and they made it to Florida and back. I decided that if I wanted to recoup my investment, I'd best be their booking agent and manager. So, I started booking them into my clubs and other clubs around town. It didn't take long. No matter where they'd play around town, we could guarantee that at least one hundred people would come out."

Jerry talks about the "telephone clubs" that were popular in the day: the Tracer and the Party Line. The Rondels were a regular draw at both clubs. In this day of cell phones, text messages, Twitter, and even online dating sites, it might be hard to fathom the low-tech notion of these telephone clubs, but they were hot spots for the young adults of the day. Jerry described the concept: "Everybody's table had a phone. There was a board on the wall that had a map that showed you the table numbers. So, you would see a couple of pretty girls at Table 24, and call them up and ask them to dance. Or say, 'You sure are pretty,' or 'Can I buy you a drink?' Then, they'd look around and try to figure out who was calling them. It was a fun way to meet people—and depending on how good a talker you were, you might wind up dancing to the Rondels with the prettiest girl in the room!"[13]

"The Tracer was a popular young white club," Jerry recalls. "It was one of the best clubs in town that had bands. I went in and talked to the owner, Garland Holcomb. I told him he could have the Rondels for three hundred dollars a week. He said, 'I can't pay that much. I don't run that much money.' So, I told him I would just rent the club for three nights a week—Friday, Saturday, and Sunday—and I will take the door and half the liquor. We made a

lot of money, or thought so at the time. And we got the ball rolling for the Rondels."[14]

Jerry took his job as manager seriously. He created professional
press packets, promotional pictures, and even started a popular
Rondels Fan Club.

For three dollars (check, cash, or money order), fans would
receive "An attractive membership card, the latest 45 rpm record,
a personalized, autographed photo of the Rondels, and All Special Privileges Unique to Rondel Fan Club Members."[15] Neither
Delbert nor Jerry Conditt recalls exactly what the "special privileges" were, but the fan club caught on with members from as
far away as New York and Florida.

A personalized letter that accompanied the Rondels swag in
the fan club packet spoke to the times. From the greeting: "Now
You're Swinging! Welcome to the Rondels Fan Club" to the "Clo-
sin' with a beat; like we gotta go-go," Delbert and Ronnie, along
with Billy Wade Sanders, Jimmy Rogers, and drummer *du jour*
Dahrel Norris had a loyal fan base.

Jerry Conditt says, "I opened a building across the street from
my car lot and named it Rondel Enterprises. I told the boys, 'Look,
I stay up as late as you do. I'm in the clubs promoting them and
all. You're going to have to work an eight-hour day like I do.' I put
in some phones. They had to man the phones. I told them if a fan
calls, you have to answer and talk to them. They had to answer the
fan mail, writing back, sending photos, and if things were slow,
I think one time, I wanted them to just call people in the phone
book and tell them where they were playing. I don't know that
they ever did that. They were probably over there sleeping. But,
I had them make special appearances at my car lot and other
places, just go build the audience base. It seemed to work. And
the press loved them."[16]

Major Bill stayed in the picture as well. With Delbert's long
popularity with the Straitjackets, Major Bill immediately signed
the Rondels to an exclusive record contract. He released the first
Rondels single, "Mathilda/Tina," on his Shalimar label. DeWitt
and Cotten write, "The A side was a rock and roll remake of a
Cookie and the Cupcakes 1958 hit, 'Mathilda,' complete with the
heavy-handed influence of both Cajun and New Orleans rhythm

and blues. It was an immediate local jukebox hit. However, it was the flipside that Major Bill tried to break nationally. 'Tina' had a garage band sound with an infectious vocal, which has made it a much sought-after collector's item."[17]

When DeWitt and Cotten interviewed Major Bill Smith for their 1992 feature in *DISCoveries,* Major Bill maintained that "Tina" could still be a hit record, nearly thirty years after it was released. Described as a "1950s style song with a Beatles 1960s listening quality," it was not a jukebox hit, but it got a great deal of airplay on the radio. "That boy [Delbert McClinton] could still have a hit with 'Tina,'" Major Bill remarked.[18]

It didn't take long for the Rondels to build on their Straitjackets fan base with the help of Jerry Conditt. In September 1965, the Rondels had been playing together for less than three months, but their single, "If You Really Want Me To, I'll Go," had already reached the top twenty in regional radio charts, when Jerry issued his first promotional blast:

> The Rondels are as contagious as measles; but unlike measles, you keep wanting more of the five-some. At a time when mop hair is covering up for lack of talent for some groups, this fresh, strikingly clean-cut Quintet holds a unique position! The Rondels are rocketing to prominence throughout the South and Midwest with scores of radio, TV and nightclub engagements, yet they continue to lace together songs and rhythm with the same freshness and youthful enthusiasm that spring-boarded them to fame several years ago.[19]

Jerry could sense success. "We started booking outside of Fort Worth. By 1965, the Rondels were playing private events and fraternity parties at TCU, the University of Texas, and other colleges. By 1966, they were playing regularly around the Texas bar circuit, as well as Tennessee, Louisiana, Arkansas, and other states along the way."[20]

It wasn't easy to break into the touring circuit. "I set up one of the first tours in Sherman, Weatherford, and some of the other little towns around Fort Worth," recalls Jerry. "I sent out a guy to sell presale tickets. He said it was looking good and that everyone was coming to the show. So, we went up to Sherman and about three people showed up. Billy Sanders walks outside and says, 'Hey! Here come a bunch of cars!' We go outside and look and they drive right past, honking and cheering. Turns out, they were all heading to the high school basketball championship game. Nobody was left in town to listen to the band," he adds. "Yes. We had a few failures along the way."[21]

However, the Rondels also had a lot of success. Jerry was quite a promoter and a businessman, traits that Delbert admits he has always lacked. "We always traveled well. Most of the time, Jerry had us in a Cadillac convertible or a Lincoln Continental with a little trailer to pull behind," Delbert says. "Jerry always had us dressed sharp, and in nice cars."[22]

Jerry recalls the Rondels's first trip to Chicago. "Delbert would set up the equipment. They got up there to the club and started setting everything up and they didn't have union cards." Jerry says, "We didn't even know what unions were!"[23]

Jerry says that might have been one of the worst gigs they ever played. However, there were others. "One place, the band had to set up behind the bar to play. It was in a loud bowling alley, and several clubs featured go-go girls dancing in cages on each side of the stage," he recalls.[24]

Delbert remembers another road trip the Rondels played up in the Midwest: "We had a gig in Duluth, Minnesota. It was as ugly as all get out. We got one hotel room with extra rollaway beds. You had to walk across the beds to get to the bathroom. The hotel backed up to a big drop off, and down below the hotel was a trash dump. We went out and bought some fish sticks and frozen French fries. We drove down to that dump and built a fire. We had pulled the car up—and had the doors open and the radio on while we cooked the fish sticks and fries on an open fire, like hobos. All of a sudden, an ad came on the radio for the club we were playing in that night. It said, 'The *Hondells* are appearing tonight!'

"We just looked at each other over our fish stick supper and thought, 'Oh shit! They thought they hired the *Hondells!*"[25]

The Hondells were a very popular surf band from Los Angeles at the time. They had a couple of national hits with "Big Red

Rubber Ball" and "Go Little Honda." They had been featured in the Frankie Avalon and Annette Funicello blockbuster hit movie, *Beach Blanket Bingo*.

The Rondels finished their fish sticks, put out the campfire at the dump, and headed for the club to put out a fire of a different kind.

"We told them that we were the Rondels—not the Hondells. We were from Fort Worth, not Los Angeles," Delbert remembers. "But it was okay. Nobody seemed to care. We decided that they had probably never heard the Hondells's hit anyway. But those go-go dancers in cages sure were a big draw!"[26]

As the Rondels continued to record, their regional success continued to grow. Delbert's original song, and the biggest hit in the Rondels's catalog, "If You Really Want Me To, I'll Go," was released on Smash and rocketed to number 1 on Dallas–Fort Worth's fifty-thousand-watt radio station, Countrypolitan KCUL 1540.

The Rondels were at the top of the heap, the top of their game, and the top of the local charts. With packed clubs, fan clubs, headlines, and recording contracts, there was no place to go but up.

CHAPTER 7
"Livin' It Down"

Learning the Business of Music

Major Bill thought "If You Really Want Me To, I'll Go" might have potential. He called up Huey Meaux in Houston, and played it for him. Huey offered Bill five hundred dollars for the song on the spot. That's when Major Bill knew he had something.

—DELBERT McCLINTON[1]

With the regional success of "If You Really Want Me To, I'll Go" along with the Rondels's broadening base of popularity, Major Bill believed it could draw national attention. He sent the single to Smash Records. Riding on jukebox success, Smash hurried to release the record, with "Walk About," as the B-side. It quickly became a jukebox hit as well. However, the record had no distribution, so fans could not buy it.

According to *DISCoveries,* the record debuted into the pop singles chart at number 97—for one week. Smash was interested in other Rondels sides. Then "almost overnight, the song was pulled off the air."[2]

This was the first of many business dead-ends in Delbert's career. He says, "It's a complicated story, but basically, the song's publishing was clouded. Someone claimed to own part of the publishing, as part of a business deal with Major Bill, and didn't think Major Bill had the right to sell the record to Smash. It didn't have anything to do with the band or the music. And I wasn't paying attention to the business side of things," he admits.[3]

Ultimately, Big State Distributors, the Southwest's largest

record wholesaler, stopped shipment of the Smash single. Cases of the single were left in the warehouse, stacked in the back to make room for the next hit record that would come along. Delbert says, "That record ended up dying on the floor of the Big State warehouse because Smash couldn't get a straight answer from anyone."[4]

DeWitt and Cotten write, "Radio stations had the record and were playing it. But consumers couldn't buy the record. The irony here is that the song became a country hit for Waylon Jennings in 1967."[5]

And so began a long string of music business disappointments for Delbert McClinton. But, like so many others that would come later, he took it in stride, and kept playing for the music.

Legendary radio personality Bill Mack was the number one drive-time disc jockey for KCUL back in the mid-1960s. Just about any country music fan who has listened to music on the radio in the second half of the twentieth century is familiar with Bill Mack. Nobody in radio has a more recognizable voice. Some are quick to identify him as the writer of LeAnn Rimes's breakout hit, "Blue," or George Strait's hit, "Drinkin' Champagne," or a multitude of other songs recorded by everyone from Dean Martin to Jerry Lee Lewis. Bill has taken home a truckload of awards, from a Grammy for Country Song of the Year for "Blue," and several platinum albums for his songwriting prowess, to more radio awards than any other country music DJ in the world.[6]

Starting in radio at a small station in Shamrock, Texas, Bill bounced around the West Texas airwaves, and even did a stint on Villa Acuna/Del Rio's famous Border Blaster radio station XERF, before landing at KCUL in Fort Worth. He moved over to WBAP, the Fort Worth–Dallas mega radio station where his popular program grew into the syndicated *Midnight Trucking Radio Network* in 1969. Soon after, he began his syndicated weekly radio show, *Country Crossroads*, with coast-to-coast coverage of the latest interviews with the top country stars in the nation. He pioneered country music on satellite radio with his XM Open Road channel and later with Willie's Place, and continues to be one of the leading authorities on country music from its early days of Bob Wills and Milton Brown playing clubs in Fort Worth, to the artists topping the charts today.

Through his seven decades of exposure to artists in all stages of their careers, Bill still speaks fondly of Delbert, saying, "Delbert was pretty much established here in Fort Worth even before the Rondels, but that band really put him on the map and got him out of town on tour. When I met him, Delbert was struggling, beginning his career, but he set—and continues to set—the best example of professionalism I have ever seen in the business. He had a better-than-average attitude when everyone was struggling, and he was always willing to do what he had to do to get his music out there.

"Talk about being a major player in the game. Delbert always deserved more than he got. He still does. I put him up there with the best of the best. I am not exaggerating. He has always been a hero of mine.

"Those Major Bill recordings on all of those old labels got great airplay, but looking back, Major Bill had a racket going. He—and others in the business—were signing songwriters and artists and recording good songs so they could own the publishing. That was where the money was. There was no money in records for the artist or the songwriter back then. I'd venture to guess Delbert never saw a dime from any of those records.

"The records played on the radio well, but were not really distributed. The publisher was hoping that maybe the song would be heard by a more established artist who would record it. That was—and still is—where the money was. And the investment in the songwriter/original artist was never too much.

"Songwriters like Delbert McClinton would sign away their songs for the opportunity to record a few songs. Maybe the label would press five hundred copies of a record and push them out. If the song did well enough, they might press another five hundred or so. The songwriters or recording artists who worked for people like Major Bill—or even some of the big labels back then—never saw any money from records. But, they all thought of it as promotion that helped bring people out to the clubs to hear them play live. And for people like Delbert, playing music for an audience is what it is all about.

"I don't think Delbert even knows today what an example he has set for others to follow. I will say this without reservation. No one will ever exceed him in value. Not only is he a tremendous musician and a wonderful songwriter, he is also a good friend to everyone he meets.

"Delbert has never been about the money. As long as I have known him, he's wanted to get out and play and be heard. He wanted to share his music. And if it cost as much getting there as he made that night on the stage, he was breaking even and that was good enough. Delbert set an example, sincere and dedicated to his music and his art at whatever the cost.

"He has established an image that would be very hard to duplicate. He is at the top of the league, and has always been a bigger star than he would admit. Delbert has paved great roads and never had that superstar attitude, never become cynical. From those early days on the Jacksboro Highway in Fort Worth to the big shows he does today, he has never given a bad performance."[7]

Coming from a man who has come to know virtually every country star and most of the pop stars who have topped the charts in the last seventy years, Bill Mack admits that it sounds like he is exaggerating his praise for Delbert, but he says, "It's true. And you can ask anyone in the business and they will agree. Delbert is the kind of musician that other musicians aspire to be. He does it all, no matter the pay. And you can tell he truly loves what he is doing. I hope he realizes how good he is."[8]

As the Rondels continued to gain popularity, Jerry Conditt realized that marketing the band was becoming a full-time job. He hired Georgia Lapping as the administrative assistant for his management company. In the Conditt archives are reams of correspondence, clippings, and other memorabilia from the Rondels's heyday.

Among the archives is a copy of a letter Georgia wrote to Congressman Jim Wright of Fort Worth, on November 4, 1965. Wright had been a state representative for two terms in the late 1940s, and was elected to the US House of Representatives in 1955, a seat he held continually until 1989. Wright followed Tip O'Neill as the speaker of the house from 1987 to 1989. Georgia describes the band and makes a big pitch:

The time is right for the pendulum to swing away from the "mop-head" look to the clean-cut, barbered look with TALENT. [We] have ordered deep red blazers and grey slacks for them, which should be sharp. I think it would be a wonderful tie-in for the All American Gift from our All-American City to have our clean-cut All American-looking "Rondels" to present shows for the servicemen in Viet Nam. They're also very anxious to do this, and of course, we're anxious for this also. We will work out the details some way, I am confident of this, for transportation for the gifts, as well as for the boys to go over to present the gifts and to entertain. And I will certainly appreciate any assistance you can give.[9]

The opportunity never arose for the Rondels to travel to Vietnam to entertain the troops, but other—not so voluntary—opportunities were hitting mailboxes around the country. By August 1965, thirty-five thousand young men were being drafted—called up each month to serve in what journalist Reid Orvedahl calls, "America's longest and most divisive war."[10] President Lyndon Johnson was determined to defeat communism and escalated the United States involvement in the Vietnam War

Orvedahl writes, "The marriage deferment was no longer going to be enough. To find more soldiers, the Defense Department advised the president to change an old policy: Let them draft married men without children."[11]

On August 26, 1965, without any advanced notice, President Johnson signed an executive order. Anyone who was married before midnight would still be eligible for marriage deferment. However, men who married after midnight would not be able to avoid or postpone serving just because they were married.

Orvedahl explains, "So now many men faced one of the most important decisions of their lives: Should they rush to the altar, or risk fighting in Vietnam?"[12]

There was another way to avoid the draft. Rondels drummer Jerry Foster was about to be drafted, so he joined the navy. A December 22, 1965, clipping from the *Fort Worth Star-Telegram* announces Jerry Foster's completion of basic training and new rank as a Fireman Apprentice. His music days were over.[13]

Delbert had the marriage and child deferment. By now, Monty was four, and Sandra Sue Riley McClinton was unhappy. Delbert says, "And I was miserable. It was 1965. Sue was on my ass to start making some regular money. I took a job at General Dynamics where they were making planes for the war. The first thing they did was put me in a three-week program referred to as Riveting School.

"A rivet is a metal pin that passes through holes in two or more pieces of metal to hold them together, and when you get the rivet through the metal, someone on the other side of the metal (or in this case, inside the plane) has to hammer or 'buck' the rivet back flat so it won't come loose. They teach you to use the rivet gun and a bucking bar.

"When you finish the school, you are set to go on the assembly line and build airplanes. Pretty absurd, thinking that three weeks of school is going to teach you enough to build war jets, but that was the deal.

"A day of riveting school went like this: you pair up with someone and you drive rivets for a while and trade places and then buck rivets for a while from the other side. This goes on for eight hours, and then you clock out and go home. A monkey could be trained to do this job.

"But at the end of three weeks, I graduated and got a certificate saying I had successfully completed the course. With one hand we received our certificates, and with the other hand, our pink slips. Our entire class was laid off. I've never been on a bad acid trip, but it's got to be similar to working at a government aircraft manufacturing plant."[14]

Delbert goes on to say that a few months later, General Dynamics started a modification program to install spoilers on the wings of the F-111 Bomber. The last people laid off were the first ones hired back. And so began his second stint into the surreal complexities of bureaucracy. He continues the story: "The work we were rehired to do was all good on paper and in theory, but soon it was evident that the modification program needed to go back to the drawing board. A good example of how bad this idea was, was when a single dropped rivet required taking off an entire wing of a completed aircraft to retrieve the lost rivet. So all work on that project was stopped.

"Needless to say, the shit hit the fan. Now they had a group of people who had been rehired, and had nothing to do. There was a rule that a person could not be laid off twice in one year. So now, we were supposed to show up for work and be farmed out to supervisors who had nothing for us to do because the union had a probationary period before we could join, and we had not worked long enough to fulfill that probation.

"So the supervisors hated us because it was their job to make us look like we were doing something. If we didn't look busy, their supervisors chewed them out. The pecking order in a place like this illustrates the most concentrated prejudice I think I have ever seen.

"So, the first day, this other guy and I were told to check out blueprints regarding some part of an aircraft, find a spot to lay them out on the floor, and look like we were busy looking at them. We made that job last a while.

"Then a supervisor handed me a small fastener and told me to go to every tool bin in the plant and find a hundred thousand of them. Then he told me that there weren't any of them in the plant but to go look anyway and get signed off at each bin by the person in charge.

"General Dynamics covered an area of several city blocks and there were God knows how many tool bins. This went on for weeks and I felt like a bad actor in a lousy movie that wouldn't end. Finally, I completed that job and a few days before my probation period was up, on a Friday, I was inside the fuselage of an F-111, bucking rivets, when two guards and a guy in a suit showed up and called out my name.

I climbed out of the fuselage and walked over to them. 'I'm McClinton,' I said.

"The guy in the suit handed me a green piece of paper. I asked what it was.

"'You've been terminated,' he said. I stood there letting that soak in for a minute, and asked, 'Why?'

"'Unsatisfactory performance,' he said. I asked who had determined that. 'Your supervisor,' the Suit replied. I asked, 'Which one? I have had a new supervisor every day since I've been here.'

"At this point the guards stepped forward and told me to get my toolbox and they would escort me out. By now, I was being very loud and sharing my opinion liberally. I was so mad I could have twisted a tree. Not about the job. The job was a joke. I just hated being treated with so little respect. But I learned a very important thing that day. I learned that you better cover your ass because nobody's gonna cover it for you."[15]

Thus ended Delbert's efforts for finding a day job for a while. But, the Rondels were gaining traction and making headlines. They closed out 1965 with their biggest show of the year. The heavily advertised New Year's Eve Blast headlined Chuck Berry and featured the Rondels. Opening the six-hour long show were Louis Howard and the Red Hearts with Little Gary Ferguson. The show was held at the Amon Carter Exhibit Hall and tickets were five dollars and fifty cents per person in advance or six dollars and fifty cents at the door. Only five or six dollars for Chuck Berry, the Rondels, and Little Gary Ferguson, a talented preteen precursor to Michael Jackson and Dallas's answer to Little Stevie Wonder.[16]

Anne Miller Tinsley, a society writer for the *Star-Telegram,* advanced the show with this column: "All I said was 'Show me a rock 'n' roll group that is entertaining for someone past 16 and I'll eat my hat.' I heard the Rondels. Munch. Munch."

She went on to write: "The Rondels, who will be featured at the New Years Eve dance at the Exhibit Hall on Amon Carter Square, gave a press preview Tuesday of the kind of music they will play to close out the year. I went in saying, 'I don't like rock 'n' roll,' and I came out saying, 'I'm beginning to like rock 'n' roll.'

"Five young men—but not as young as they look—make up the group. And guess what. Not a single one of them sports a page-boy. . . . Their biggest selling record so far has been 'If You Really Want Me To, I'll Go.' First time I ever heard the record was in a pizza parlor. Somebody played it on the jukebox and after the first four bars, every teenager in the place was singing along. At the press party, the group sang their latest release, 'Lose Your Money,' but I bet they don't. It's sure to be a best seller too."[17]

Jerry Conditt had a golden touch when it came to publicity. The *Star-Telegram* mentioned the Rondels regularly in various columns and news stories. One clip in Jerry's archives is a paragraph from Tony Slaughter's "The Fort Worth Scene," a popular column:

> Off to Muncie, Indiana: The Rondels are off for an engagement at Club 67, in far away Muncie, Indiana. Roger Miller, whose mother is a Fort Worth department store employee, has a Las Vegas debut tomorrow night at the Sahara Hotel. The Fort Worth Lions Club will hear Viet Nam correspondent [Star-Telegram] Bob Schieffer tomorrow noon at Hotel Texas.[18]

Proof again that Conditt's publicity savvy had the Rondels at the tip of everyone's tongue, and the lead story in the news of the day. The clean-cut, sweater-wearing, five-piece band looked more like college fraternity lettermen than a cutting edge blues band. Conditt says, "We were able to cross over the lines. We could play a society event one weekend, a fraternity party the next, and fill in the week in some of the best clubs in Fort Worth, black or white." He added, "There was no doubt that Delbert and Ronnie favored the clubs. The audiences were more appreciative. They were also regulars at the afterhours East Side Club, playing from midnight till four in the morning. Those boys just loved to play."[19]

And when they weren't playing in clubs, Delbert and members of the band spent a lot of time hanging out over at a club that featured Ray Sharpe, who had a hit with "Linda Lu," a song that has been covered by Delbert, the Rolling Stones, the Flying Burrito Brothers, Doug Sahm, and even Tom Jones. Sharpe was another Fort Worth native and one of Major Bill Smith's acts. Major Bill described Sharpe as the "greatest white-sounding black dude ever."[20]

Bill Mack says, "Major Bill continued signing everyone who had a song with potential to his label, and then taking all the publishing, and sometimes some of the writing credit, in the deal."[21]

Major Bill was not the only one doing this. It was general practice for Houston record promoter Huey Meaux and others in major music spots. One of his biggest successes, Doug Sahm (the Sir Douglas Quintet) once said, "Back then, we didn't understand—or care about—the money. We'd tell Huey, 'Just take what you want off the top and if there's any left over, we'll split it up.'"[22]

Bill Mack explains, "You have to know that this was accepted practice. I'm not saying it was limited to Major Bill or Huey Meaux. It was how the business works. Acuff-Rose in Nashville did this to Hank Williams. They wanted him for his writing, more than his ability to sing. They would sign artists for their publishing, and sometimes writer credit. I was right there. Delbert can look back like I did at various labels he recorded on. We were all so innocent. Songwriters just wanted their songs played. And publishers profited. But, as Hank Williams used to say, 'It is the songwriter who makes the song. Not the singer.'"[23]

The Rondels continued to record for Major Bill. He was the biggest game in town. They were opening shows for the Beach Boys throughout Texas and the South, and headlining most of the major venues in Dallas and Fort Worth.

Music journalist Peter Guralnick writes in *Westward,* the Sunday magazine of the *Dallas Times Herald,* that Fort Worth club goers had a unique style of dancing that started way back in the heyday of Jack's Place and in the prime of the Jacksboro Highway bars. Delbert's music was—and continues to be—a perfect sound for the Fort Worth Push.

"It was not a dance. It was *the* dance," Delbert explains. "Done behind a real good strong shuffle beat. That was the reason I think the blues got to be so popular in Fort Worth. It was the kind of music all those people liked to dance to. In fact, they still do. They've still got Push Clubs in Fort Worth."[24]

The Rondels's personnel changed but Delbert, Ronnie Kelly, and Billy Wade Sanders were the constants through the years. They had the groove. Major Bill released at least eighteen singles of the Rondels from 1963 through 1970, including four different label versions of "Mathilda," reaching for a hit.

According to DeWitt and Cotten, "The late 1960s were bittersweet for Delbert. Mainstream commercial success continued to elude him, but his songwriting skills were honed to a high level. The hundreds of clubs, bars, and small concert venues he played each year also molded him into a consummate performer."[25]

The band members' home lives were in constant turmoil, according to Delbert. The band families didn't understand the loyalty the Rondels had for their music and for each other. Between

1967 and 1969, the band had frequent personnel changes and struggles to get in harmony with one another. Finally, in 1969, what may have been America's finest bar band called it quits.[26]

Life had finally taken precedence over the music for the Rondels. They may have been paying their dues in the clubs, but they all had bills to pay at home. Delbert says, "My marriage was shot to hell. Nothing was going right. The way I saw it, I was still doing what I was doing ten or twelve years before. I wasn't getting anywhere. The Rondels broke up. My marriage broke up. I was nearly thirty years old, singing in bars, trying to get a divorce, with not much of anything to my name, and not even living at home."[27]

Delbert continued to play. He formed several bands: the Bright Side, the Acme Music Company, and the Losers. He was honing his sound, playing a now-familiar blend of old rock 'n' roll, rhythm and blues, and the new country/rock genre that was just coming to light. Delbert was not recording though, and considers these years wasted as far as his musical career goes.[28]

"There was so much wrong with my life right then. I was getting tired of barely getting by. I was holding on to whatever I could. The passion for playing never went away, but I was starting to see that I was nearly thirty, and going nowhere. This was as good as it was going to get in Fort Worth unless I did something or went somewhere," he said.[29]

By 1969, Fort Worth was embedded in the drug culture of the times. The city had a long history of not overreacting to bootleggers, gamblers, gangsters, and other illegal activities. It was not necessarily looser than other towns in Texas, but the culture was as embedded in the bars and bands of Cowtown as just about anywhere else in the country.

Though he can't remember the name of the bar, there's one night on the honkytonk trail that Delbert will never forget. An old friend walked in. He had known Margaret Knight in high school. "She was beautiful, wild, and free," Delbert recalls with a shake of his head. "She came into the club where I was singing the night she got her divorce. She had already been married a couple of times. She was a woman of her time. She had a shiny 1966 Chrysler Imperial, and we were destined to take some wild trips together."[30]

CHAPTER 8

"Two More Bottles of Wine"

The Los Angeles Years

Maggie came to town, and we were a bright shining light for a few weeks in Fort Worth. But, I still wasn't getting anywhere. I was thirty years old, and I wanted out of everything—and most of all, out of Fort Worth. Glen [Clark] and Ray [Clark] were writing and telling me how great Los Angeles was. Maggie had a Chrysler Imperial, a sack full of cash from her divorce settlement, and a sense of adventure. So, we loaded up and drove nonstop to Topanga Canyon.

      —DELBERT McCLINTON[1]

It was late winter of 1970 when they loaded the car. Driving to California brought Delbert a sense of freedom he had never experienced. Although it would be a difficult time for him personally, it also was a productive time in terms of evolving as a songwriter and performer. Delbert's move to the West Coast was encouraged by his longtime friend and musical partner, Glen Clark, another Fort Worth musician who had played keyboard off and on in Delbert's bands for years. Glen made the move to Los Angeles in 1969, and wrote several letters encouraging Delbert to head west and join him.

Glen's father was a song leader in a Fort Worth area Church of Christ congregation. Music had a constant presence in the Clark household. Everyone in the family played piano and sang, and Glen was somewhat of a child prodigy. He successfully auditioned for the Texas Boys Choir when he was ten years old and within weeks, he was touring with the group. "It was a pretty big deal at the time," Glen says.[2]

However, he believes his greatest early influence happened outside of church and the regimented music studies of the Texas Boys Choir. Glen was about seven years old when he first heard secular music being performed live, and there was no turning back.

Glen was spending the night with his friend, Vaughn Clark (no relation). Vaughn's father had been a drummer for Lawrence Welk and had long cultivated an interest in music among his children. Vaughn's fifteen-year-old brother, Ray Clark, was playing drums in a band with some of his high school friends. Delbert McClinton was the bandleader.

"Delbert was already rocking. Man, I wanted to be just like that guy," Glen recalls. "I did everything I could to learn that kind of music. My parents encouraged me in a proper way, with music lessons and voice training. But the Texas Boys Choir was a little too regimented," he admits. "I got out of it pretty quick. Here I was singing Latin masses with the Texas Boys Choir. I discovered black radio stations and country radio stations, and I hear high school kids, *that I know personally*, playing this great stuff that made my hair stand up on end. I went to my classical piano teacher and asked her to teach me that. She just couldn't teach me to play with soul. So, I made the switch from classical to rock and blues and country."[3]

Glen started performing in bands regularly at the age of sixteen, playing piano with the popular Bobby Crown and the Capers, a blues and R&B group in Fort Worth. Bobby Crown, McClinton, and Bruce Channel all were inspired by that same Texas blues shuffle that became an integral part of what some were calling the Fort Worth sound.

Glen says, "Everyone wanted to do that music, but Delbert made it his own. Even back then, he had his own spin on the music. He respected the styles, learned from them, and built on them. Delbert has always been a master of that. He can take a combination of sounds from different bands and styles and make it his own. He has always kept that edge that made you know you were listening to something you wouldn't forget."[4]

Glen started performing on keyboards regularly with McClinton in 1968, playing a few regular gigs and an after-hours weekly show at Fort Worth's Colonial Club, near the General Motors plant. "It was plain awful. We thought it was going to be great, because the show started at 2:00 a.m. We figured that we could play our original music and kick back and just get in the groove, but the factory shift workers would get off work about that time and come in and want to be rowdy and drink and listen to Top 40 country. I think it was probably one of the roughest regular gigs Delbert and I ever played, and that's saying a lot. That was the last band Delbert and I were in together in Texas. We called ourselves the Losers," Glen recalls.[5]

Glen finished high school and went to the University of North Texas (North Texas State University at the time) to continue his education. "I got busted for pot in Denton. The cop felt sorry for me, and the charges were dismissed, but it was reported to the dean. It was mid-semester. The dean called me in and said, 'Son, you have to come into my office once a month and verify that you are not smoking pot.' I said, 'I don't think I will be able to do that, sir. But I appreciate your offer.'"[6]

Glen loaded his Volkswagen bus with a chest of drawers from his mother's house with all of his clothes in it, a Hammond C3 organ, twenty dollars, and a plan.

Glen moved to Los Angeles in 1969. "I was wanting to do original music. Around Fort Worth and Denton, everyone wanted to hear the songs they heard on the radio. Top 40 hits. Our friend, Ray Clark (Delbert's former drummer), had moved out to Topanga Canyon, and had been writing to me. Back then, you didn't call on the phone. You wrote letters."[7]

Glen says, "Ray had been out there for several years. When I went out there, he had a place for me to stay. He had been writing to me for a while, telling me that it was where I needed to be if I was serious about music. I had been trying to write songs and playing in North Texas where no one wanted to hear original music. Ray said, 'They'll love your original stuff out here,' and he was right. The climate was different. They wanted to hear original music. Playing music was like performing a play, with people coming out to really listen to what you were singing. It was a great place to be."[8]

Ray had been on the road with Arlin Harmon and the Big Beats, and was tired of traveling. He had moved into a cabin in Topanga Canyon in Western Los Angeles County.

Topanga Canyon had become a magnet for free spirits, counter culture, and original artists. Wallace Berman, who has been credited as the father of assemblage art, had attained comfortable success by this time, and opened his Topanga Canyon home to an array of artists and musicians who needed a place to develop their art. Neil Young lived in Topanga and would record most of his *After the Gold Rush* album in his home basement studio in 1970. Topanga Canyon property was easy to come by and rent was dirt cheap.[9]

Drugs played a big part in the culture of the West Coast at the time. The criminal element was far different from the gamblers and gangsters of Fort Worth. Charles Manson was building his "family" at the Spahn Movie Ranch, not far from Topanga Canyon, where he had briefly befriended both Neil Young and Dennis Wilson of the Beach Boys.[10]

California had beckoned Texas songwriters and musicians for decades. If New York was the traditional home to the American music industry, and Nashville had come into its own as the country capital, Los Angeles welcomed the contemporary artists, undiscovered actors, original musicians, and creative writers with little money and big dreams.

Bill Mack says, "Bob Wills finally became a national success when he left Texas for the West Coast. The Bakersfield Sound, created by Buck Owens and Merle Haggard, as a reaction to the sophisticated string-orchestra sounds coming out of Nashville, was taking country music by a storm."[11]

San Antonio's Doug Sahm, who had risen to international fame with the Sir Douglas Quintet under the direction of Houston's Huey Meaux, had made the trek west in 1965, after a marijuana bust in Texas. He settled his family in the Salinas Valley as soon as his probation officer assured him that he would not be reported as a fugitive from Texas. Several of his band members went with him, but his best friend, Augie Meyers, didn't catch up with the band until 1969. Augie admitted that he couldn't go at first because his probation officer would not let him leave Texas. He told Sahm biographer Jan Reid, "I was married and had a family myself, a boy in school. But, one day, Clay came home and said their new teacher used to be a policeman. They asked him what he ever did, who he had put in jail, and he said, 'Well, I helped arrest the Sir Douglas Quintet.'"[12]

Augie managed to fulfill his legal obligations to the State of Texas, and move his family out to the West Coast, joining Doug in the San Francisco scene, trading their British-style suits and Beatle boots for more comfortable Texas cowboy boots and hats.

This new West Coast music scene was becoming heavily populated with talented Texas expatriate songwriters and musicians, looking for a place to hone their art into success.

Glen adds, "The climate was so different. People wanted to hear original music. I only had about four or five original songs good enough to play when I got there, but I played them a lot and wrote some more. Delbert was going through a hard time back in Fort Worth. I wrote him a letter and told him to come on out. We had a place for him to stay. I forgot to mention that housekeeping was not a priority."[13]

Delbert was still playing around Fort Worth, and had taken up with Maggie. His divorce was pending, and Sue was so angry. He was not getting time to spend with his son, Monty, anyway, so he decided that this might be a good move, professionally and mentally.

The early 1970s were prime time for living on love and cheap beer. Hippies were coming into their own. The counterculture was booming everywhere, but the West Coast was ground zero.

The Los Angles music scene was developing its own voice and growing into a strong country-folk-rock movement. This rhythm and blues and country influence on rock focused on the songwriter and the lyrics. Gram Parsons and the Byrds, the Nitty Gritty Dirt Band, and Pure Prairie League were adding steel guitars and fiddles to rock and rhythm and blues mixes. The scene was open to new and experimental sounds and was a good fit for artists like Delbert seeking to create new sounds.

Delbert and Maggie piled what they could carry in the back of her car and headed west together. They moved in with Glen Clark and Ray Clark and Ray's girlfriend, Monique. As Delbert describes it, "And just like that, we became hippies."[14]

"The night we got there, after driving straight through from Fort Worth, we were hot and tired and sweaty. Ray came down the hill and led us up to the house. He had long curly hair below his shoulders. He and his girlfriend lived in this cabin with a dirt floor, on the side of the mountain," We wanted to take showers. Ray said something about being careful with the water because of the septic tank or something. And we said, 'Okay, yeah.' Ray had set Maggie and me up with a mattress on the floor of this room with a dirt floor. I got up in the middle of the night to go pee and the floor all around the mattress is flooded—soaking, fucking wet, and stinks with raw sewage," he adds.

"We had a Fort Worth guitar player friend of mine and his girl-friend who had just wanted to ride out there with us, and Maggie and me, and we had all come in and taken showers and no one listened to Ray talking about the possibility of the old septic tank overflowing. Maggie and I were sleeping in that shit. Crazy. But we were, well, I wasn't that young, but I was young enough, and I was hungry. So hungry to do something. And I knew that if I worked hard enough, I'd get something to eat. It was okay, the way we lived. It was an adventure."[15]

Glen adds, "Southern California really was a different world for Delbert and me. Everyone was smoking pot and doing some kind of drugs. There was this whole open sex scene going on. It was just the way it was. Ray was working, and got us that job at the veterinary supply warehouse. We rode to work with him every day. His wife didn't do anything. Monique stayed home. The deal at Ray's was that we would all work and Monique would stay home and take care of the house and cook. She talked about being friends with some of the Manson girls, but I don't know. Everybody kind of knew everybody else in the Canyon. She sure didn't clean house. That was the filthiest place you ever saw. She wasn't much of a cook either, but we didn't expect much."[16]

After a few weeks of living with Ray and his girlfriend, Glen, Delbert, and Maggie rented their own apartment together. Delbert remembers: "We got this place in Venice, with a bedroom and middle room with a mattress on the floor and a kitchen and a bathroom. The whole place was painted black—floor, ceiling, sink, everything—and it had four locks on the front door. I don't remember the real name of the apartments, but they were better known as 'Methedrine Manor.' The only thing that came through the windows were the police lights on the street every night. They'd fill the room with red and blue light.

"Glen and I were working with Ray at a veterinary supply warehouse in West L.A. A lot of days I'd be sweeping out my corner of the warehouse, wondering, what the hell I was doing here. We were hungry, but, man, we were living the dream, or working toward it."[17]

Delbert's relationship with Maggie did not last long. The West Coast quickly lost its gleam for her. The day she left, Delbert was heartbroken. He sat on the mattress in that dank, black apartment and wrote a song about sweeping out a warehouse in West Los Angeles. In 1978, "Two More Bottles of Wine" became a number 1 hit on the country charts for singer Emmylou Harris and marked a major milestone in Delbert's evolution as a songwriter.

We came out west together with a common desire
The fever we had might'a set the West Coast on fire
Two months later got a troublin' mind
'Cause Maggie moved out and left me behind
But it's all right 'cause it's midnight and I got two more bottles of wine.
Well, the way she left sure turned my head around
Seemed like overnight she just up and put me down
Ain't gonna let it bother me today
'Cause I've been workin' and I'm too tired anyway
But it's all right 'cause it's midnight and I got two more bottles of wine.
Well, I'm sixteen-hundred miles from the people I know
I've been doin' all I can but opportunity sure comes slow
Thought I'd be a big star by today
But I've been sweepin' out a warehouse in West L.A.
But it's all right 'cause it's midnight and I got two more bottles of wine
Yes, it's all right 'cause it's midnight and I got two more bottles of wine.[18]

Delbert says, "Emmylou cut that song in 1978, I didn't even know until someone called and told me about it. I don't think I ever made any money off of that cut because I was pretty much fucked out of all of the publishing back then. I didn't know any better."[19]

Less than ten years after writing those lines, Delbert talked to journalist Gary Cartwright for an interview in *Rolling Stone* magazine. Delbert recalled that he felt better after the song was finished. "'I'd hate to think I have to suffer like that every time I wrote a song,'" he said. "'I don't ever want to be that depressed again, but I want to be an interpreter of those feelings . . . a teller of the things I've done, not the things I do.'"[20]

CHAPTER 9
"California Livin'"

Clean Records

Maggie was the only woman who ever broke my heart. The warehouse work was hard. Glen and I were struggling. I was sending all but twenty dollars of my pay back home every week to support my son. But, I finally felt like I was really doing something with my music.
—DELBERT McCLINTON[1]

Delbert McClinton and Glen Clark stayed active writing songs, but they kept their day jobs. Glen recalls, "We would go to work at the veterinary supply house, Sharpe and Vejar, and sweep and pack boxes, and unload one-hundred-pound sacks of dog food from boxcars like a fire brigade when the trains would come through. It was hard work, but the bosses and everyone there knew that Delbert and I were trying to make music, and they were real supportive.

"We made minimum wage but we also made a lot of good friends. Even the bosses would support our music. We'd get off around 3:30 or 4:00, and take the Pacific Coast Highway leaving West L.A., driving back to Topanga Canyon. We'd light up a joint and look out at the ocean and say, 'Oh, yeah. We don't have to be back at work till 8:00 tomorrow.' Every day was a new day."[2]

Delbert and Glen loved the song "Gimme Little Sign" by Brenton Wood. They went to his record label and met with the guy behind the desk. They told Hal Wynn at Medallion Records that they wanted to be on his label. He reached into a drawer and pulled out a contract and signed Delbert and Glen as "McClinton and Clark," promising that if they thought about it, and wanted out of the contract, he would simply tear it up.[3]

The two men left Wynn's office and immediately began having second thoughts about signing the contract. Glen remembers: "We stopped at the restroom on the way out and I said to Delbert, 'I still think we ought to go see Daniel Moore.' Wynn was with Medallion Records, but Moore was an independent producer I had met a year before. If he liked our demo, as an independent producer, he would sign us, shop the demo to several record companies, and get us the best deal out there. So, we went to see Daniel.

"We told him, 'We signed with this other guy, but we really like you,' and Daniel said for us to try to get out of the other contract if we could. We called Hal and said we were thinking about going in a different direction, and as he had promised, he tore up the contract. We went in with Daniel. He was a straight-shooting guy. He had long hair and a beard and smoked pot. He was like us, so we really liked him. We made a three-song demo with Daniel and another Fort Worth guy, T Bone Burnett, which led to a showcase and a record deal as Delbert and Glen, with Clean Records, a subsidiary of Atlantic. Looking back, it seems like it was overnight, but it wasn't really."[4]

T Bone Burnett and Darrell Leonard (a friend of Glen's from the University of North Texas, who went on to become a Grammy and W. C. Handy Award–winning trumpet player) were renting a hunting lodge in Tujunga Canyon. They set up a recording studio. Glen says, "A bunch of musicians were living out at that lodge, just hanging around and playing music and recording."[5]

Today, songwriter, producer, performer, and artist advocate T Bone Burnett is a thirteen-time Grammy award winner. He was one of those loosely-related groups of Fort Worth musicians who grew up in the Brutons' Record Town, and snuck out of their homes and into the Jacksboro Highway clubs as teenagers, earning an organic education in country and rhythm and blues music. In 1971, T Bone was among the Fort Worth musicians who migrated to Los Angeles to break into this burgeoning music scene.

He says, "I didn't really know Delbert in Fort Worth. I was good friends with Stephen and Sumter Bruton, and they were friends with Delbert. I guess Bing Crosby was the first cool white person I ever heard, and Delbert was the first cool white person I ever *met*.

"Delbert has the best of all worlds. He grew up with that mix of country and blues, and metabolized black culture with first-hand tutorials from some of the best. With that voice, he has always been able to croon like crazy. He has always had that tone, and that ability to blend it into his own sound."[6]

T Bone adds that the late '50s and early '60s were a good time to grow up in Fort Worth: "Those Jacksboro Highway places would have Ike and Tina Turner, Bobby Bland, Little Jimmy Parker, and we had the regulars to learn from like Cornell Dupree, Ornette Coleman, Charlie Christian. And Bob Wills, Willie Nelson, and everyone that was playing out at Panther Hall.

"Those musical styles have always blended. Stephen Bruton told me that even way back in 1938, when (Mississippi blues legend) Robert Johnson died, he and Milton Brown [and the Brownies] had a session planned."[7]

T Bone explains that so much true integration came through music, starting with the blending of sounds and rhythms and beats, and moving on to the stage with live shows.

T Bone points out that this unique Fort Worth sound brought attention to Delbert and Glen after that Tujunga Canyon session.

T Bone had started producing records in Fort Worth when he was seventeen. In 1970, when he was twenty-two, he produced Robert Ealey's *Live at the New Bluebird Nightclub*. Shortly thereafter, he moved to Los Angeles. "We had that place in the canyon, but I really don't remember a lot of details about that time. I know Glen and Delbert crashed out there for a while, and we had epic jam sessions day and night. We all wanted to do something. We had come unstuck in time. Everyone was loose and free."[8]

That first self-titled *Delbert and Glen* album on Clean Records is the first of T Bone's production efforts listed in his impressive discography. Delbert and Glen are in good company on that list, with artists ranging from Alison Krauss and Elvis Costello to Elton John and Tony Bennett.[9]

Glen says, "T Bone was working at Sound City Studios, and I

had gone in there a few times. I didn't really know him before we were all staying at the lodge. Daniel was kind of the driving force that everyone gravitated to, and T Bone was in the right place at the right time. Daniel got a lot of the credit, but T Bone did a lot of the behind the scenes work that we didn't even know about.

"Once we had a demo, Daniel shopped it around. Earl McGrath and David Geffen said they wanted to come see us. Earl McGrath was a Big Deal. In the early 1960s, Earl had met Ahmet Ertegun, who would change his life forever."[10]

Ertegun was the cofounder and chairman of Atlantic Records, the label of Ray Charles, Led Zeppelin, and the Rolling Stones.[11]

Delbert explains, "By the time we knew him, Earl McGrath was best friends with Ahmet Ertegun, the head of Atlantic. Earl had wanted his own record label so Ahmet helped him put together Clean Records. We made that demo at the lodge, and Daniel started pitching it."[12]

Glen Clark remembers, "Earl and David Geffen [who had just created Asylum Records] came out to Tujunga Canyon to see us. The hunting lodge had this long, winding, low driveway. They could not get the limo up to the lodge. They climbed out of the car and hiked up there. And we played for them. They both liked us. And we liked Earl. We were anything but conformists, and Earl was a wildcard like us. We signed with his Clean Records, which was going to be distributed by Atlantic."[13]

Delbert and Glen each got one thousand dollars for signing with Clean Records. "I was thirty-one years old and that was the most money I had ever held in my hand at one time that was all mine," Delbert says. "The first thing I did was get my teeth fixed. I had really bad stained teeth, brown, West Texas teeth. And I had pretty low self-esteem. Every time I would smile, I'd cover my mouth. It really was terrible. I knew that the music was magic, and that sustained me, but in every other place, I felt like a low life."[14]

He reminisces about some of the painful self-truths he came to understand, looking back on that time in his life: "I wasn't smart. I didn't hurt anyone intentionally, but I lied a lot, especially to Sue. I was just kind of a dumbass. I was just that poor, pitiful son of a bitch that doesn't even know his ass from a hole in the ground. I remember the first time I had a real, genuine, important thought. I promised myself that I would never lie to myself again. Of course, I did, but at least I realized the only thing, the most important thing that I had ever learned was that I didn't know anything. I just bumped around like a pinball. On payday, I'd buy a large box of Velveeta cheese and a box of saltine crackers. Sometimes, I'd splurge on a can of chicken noodle soup. I rolled my own cigarettes with one of those old rolling machines because I couldn't afford ready-rolls.

"Somewhere along the way I hit a milestone. Of course, it took me another twelve or so years to stop lying to myself, and that would have been in my mid-forties, actually. I probably got worse about lying to myself in my early forties than I did in my thirties.

"I wasn't a good husband. I wasn't a good father. I was a pretty sorry son, but my parents loved me no matter what. I knew better, but I was doing it anyway. That's the personal psyche part of who I was in those days.

"But I wasn't lying when I told myself I had to do this. I had to live in Los Angeles and make music and make these records. I had to do all I could in this music business. It was all I really knew how to do. It was survival. I rationalized it. For me to deny what I had to do was as futile as a tear in a glass eye. There was just no other way."[15]

Despite the turmoil in Delbert's personal life, he and Glen ultimately made two albums for Clean Records, blending all of those Texas sounds that they had grown up with.

Both albums generated a lot of interest, Glen says. "We didn't get a lot of airplay. I think we hit the Top 40 with 'The Letter,' and we got a lot of good press and some respect for what we were doing. I was trying to be a songwriter, so that was encouraging to me. It did nothing in terms of financial success, but getting credibility and industry respect was important. We were treated well by everyone we met in the music industry."[16]

Los Angeles music critic Richie Unterberger reviewed Delbert and Glen's 1972 self-titled debut album, describing it as "very much a Texas record, despite their California transplantation, blending blues, country, soul, gospel, and rock & roll. The feel of the album is very much that of a seasoned bar band, albeit a bar band with mostly original material."[17]

Those Texas roots would continue to shine through McClinton

and Clark's music, despite their transformation from Fort Worth blues prodigies to West Los Angeles hippies.

Fellow Texan Doug Sahm was earning similar accolades four hundred miles up the Pacific Coast in San Francisco. He maintained his San Antonio roots through his California transplantation as well. While Delbert's Texas roots leaned heavily toward the blues shuffle, Doug's Tex-Mex sound continued to surge through his music. Doug was beginning his Atlantic recording career as well, bringing those organic, original sounds from Texas to the California coast—and to the national stage.

Writer Joe Nick Patoski talks about the Texas migration to California in search of audiences for their unique music: "Doug went to San Francisco to be a hippie. James Pennebaker, Daniel Moore, Stephen Bruton, Delbert and Glen all went to Southern California. They could be hippies out there, but that was where the music business was. These guys were all getting a foothold in that scene, playing on sessions, connecting with people, and developing their own sounds."[18]

Delbert and Glen's self-titled debut album serves as a Fort Worth music primer. Delbert's harmonica and Glen's keyboards bring that smooth shuffle and blues roots to vinyl, with rough-edged arrangements.

Rising Storm, a short-lived vintage music blog in the early 2000s, shared this review of *Delbert and Glen*: "Songwriting credits are split evenly between the two artists but McClinton's harmonica playing and hoarse, soulful vocals were the highlight of this LP. Delbert and Glen differentiated themselves from the twangy country-rock crowd by crafting a unique mixture of ballsy, intimate Texas music: greasy blues, hillbilly country music, gospel, raucous rock n roll, and funky Southern-style jive. The 1972–1973 era was a prolific time for both musicians as they served up a handful of original Americana classics. [Original] songs such as 'Old Standby,' 'I Received a Letter,' 'Here Come the Blues,' 'I Feel the Burden,' 'Everyday Will Be Like a Holiday,' and 'Ain't What You Eat But the Way That You Chew It' are wonderful examples of the early incarnation of this new genre."[19]

Glen Clark says, "When we recorded that first album at Paramount Recording Studios in Hollywood, we were all as green as we could be."[20]

From the debut album, Glen's "I Received a Letter" was the first single and charted at number 90 in the Top 100 on *Billboard*'s charts, where it stayed for three weeks. The second single from that album, "Old Standby," another Clark composition, was released and failed to chart. Howard DeWitt and Lee Cotten write, "Although Clean Records released two well-produced albums, Delbert and Glen had little chance for success."[21]

Delbert and Glen had signed a two-record deal with Earl McGrath. Glen recalls, "The act was beginning to dissipate before we made the second record. We were—well—we were not very self-disciplined. Our habits were bad, and our work ethic was not really that good." He adds, "We just kind of ran out of gas."[22]

Delbert moved back to Fort Worth to decide what to do about that long-suffering relationship with Sandra Sue. Glen stayed in Los Angeles. Glen's childhood friend, Stephen Bruton, became his roommate, and they continued to try to make headway in the business.

The second Delbert and Glen Clean album was called *Subject to Change*. Glen says, "Delbert was already back in Fort Worth. We started the basic tracks in Birmingham [Alabama] and did overdubs in New York and some in Dallas. Stephen [Bruton] came along with us to play guitar on the sessions."[23]

Although *Subject to Change* did not receive the raves that their debut had, the title was a foresight for what would come to be the next chapter in both Delbert's and Glen's careers.

CHAPTER 10
"Victim of Life's Circumstances"
Going Solo

Glen and I both wound up back in Fort Worth after the first [Clean] record came out. We're playing beer joints—the same shit we always did—and she comes in one night. On the break, I go to the bathroom and when I come out, she's blocking the doorway. I put my hands on her waist to move her out of the way and that electric spark hits me. Whatever the fuck happens that makes people do crazy shit. That feeling you feel when all reason jumps out of your body.

—DELBERT McCLINTON[1]

Delbert recognized Donna Sue Cowden. Since the late 1960s, she had come out to the Fort Worth clubs where he played and about once a year, they would catch themselves stealing glances at one another. That night, in 1973, Delbert was still married to Sandra Sue. He didn't want to stay married, but she didn't want a divorce. Delbert says, "I was miserable. Sandra Sue was, too. We both wanted something else. But, she wouldn't cooperate. She didn't believe in divorce, no matter what. We were pretty hopeless. About nine or ten of the twelve years we were married were horrible. It did a number on all of us. I had a very bad temper and she had a worse one.

"From the time I left for California, she went crazy. I finally realized that Monty's life was in danger. I wasn't making any money. We were living off help from the record company, and I was still working at the warehouse with Glen and sending most of my money home.

"But let's back up. This story starts back in the Rondels days before I went to L.A., when I was still living with Sandra Sue, and playing that after-hours gig at the East Side Club. It was a pretty rough crowd and I was out in the middle of the madness all night long, so I decided I needed a pistol.

"I bought a .25 automatic pistol from a Forest Hill cop who was a regular at the East Side Club. It was a piece of shit. I shot it a few times, and it would just jam. Sometimes the cartridge wouldn't go into the chamber, and sometimes you would shoot it and it would eject the shell and then jam before the second shot. I just stuck it in the back of my sock drawer and forgot about it.

"Glen and I had gotten the Clean record deal, and I decided to try again to make our marriage work. It was such a horrible time for all of us, Sue, Monty, and me. I wasn't so young. I was thirty, but still didn't know my ass from a hole in the ground. I don't blame it on her. I was no fucking Prince Charming. I was a cheater and a liar. And we were young and didn't know what we were doing. I figured all I could do was try to make it work.

"I had rented an apartment in Reseda. I flew Sue and Monty out to L.A., and picked them up at the airport and took them home. She hadn't been there for thirty minutes, when the fur started flying. She reached in her suitcase and pulled that .25 out. She went to put a cartridge in the chamber and it jammed."[2]

He adds, philosophically, "Everyone has someone try to shoot 'em sometime, and that time it happened to me."[3]

Seriously, he adds, "By this time, she had an intensity I had never seen. She would scream and hit. And she had such a violent, angry personality. She died of a brain aneurysm in 1988, and I have wondered if she already had it back then."[4]

Sandra Sue took Monty and moved back to Fort Worth, as the animosity continued to grow. "It wasn't healthy for either of us, and I know Monty took a large part of the brunt of it," he adds.

From that point on, Sandra Sue refused to let Delbert see Monty. He talks about going back to Fort Worth to play, and parking down the street from the house, late at night after a gig, when the world was asleep, and sneaking over to the hedges and look-ing at Monty through the window while he was sleeping.

"I was not very bright. I'd been stuck in one place most of my life. All I ever did was play in beer joints. And you don't get to learn about good relationships in beer joints. Finally, I got a law-yer. The last thing I wanted to do was humiliate Sandra Sue more than she had humiliated herself. I was a good guy in some ways, but I was a real shit in some ways, too." he says.[5]

"She finally agreed to the divorce. I had taken up with Donna Sue while we were still married. Sandra Sue had completely cut me off from seeing Monty. For a while, he was afraid of me. She had told him all kinds of stuff about me. And some of it was prob-ably true. The divorce was eventually granted, citing irreconcil-able differences.

"She was crazy. I was crazy. She was crazier. But, I loved Monty and knew he was going through some hard times. I did little things to try to stay connected. My mother made the best homemade fudge when I was growing up. It was the first thing I learned to cook. I would make that fudge for Monty. I remember going over to their house late at night and tying a little bag of that fudge to his bicycle seat so he would find it in the morning."[6]

Donna Sue and Delbert had quickly become an item. She was a trust-fund baby. Her family had oil money, and that helped Del-bert and Donna as he continued to try to gain traction with his career. The second Clean record, *Subject to Change*, barely made a ripple, and Delbert's relationship with Clean, as well as "Del-bert and Glen," faded away.

DeWitt and Cotten write in *DISCoveries*: "The albums failed to garner sales because of improper packaging and uninspired promotion. The music was strong and the songs should have appealed to either country/rock or the traditional country music listeners. But *Delbert and Glen* and *Subject to Change* were rel-egated to the bargain bins.

"In the midst of a soft rock sound favoring bands like Bread, Delbert and Glen failed to find an audience. Musically, however, they were ahead of their time. They had a definite country direc-tion but it had a rock and roll feel."[7]

After the second Delbert and Glen LP, "Clean Records just

dissolved," Delbert says. "I think the label was just a whim at the time. It was fun while it lasted for Earl, and when it stopped being fun, he went on to something else. But, Earl McGrath was good to me and Glen as long as he lived. [McGrath died in January 2016.] He even said that for his part, we could have all of our material back, but try to dig that out of Atlantic's vaults. That would take the rest of my life and yours. And that's not the way I want to live."[8]

More than forty years later, Glen says, "Delbert and I have stayed good friends. We've been through a lot together. We were poor as church mice, but we both put our hearts into music and chased those dreams. To this day, Delbert is my reference point through all the ups and downs. If I need to talk to someone, or have a weight I need to share, he is one of the first people I will call. And he always will be. He can count on me and I can count on him. I don't know how you describe that kind of friendship."[9]

Before his divorce from Sandra Sue was final, Delbert and Donna Sue were living together. By the end of 1973, she was pregnant. In September 1974, Donna Sue gave birth to a son, Clayton Ross McClinton, the spitting image of Delbert. Donna Sue, at twenty-eight, was six years younger than Delbert, and reveled in the musician lifestyle. She enjoyed partying and being a band wife. But, says Delbert, she wasn't ever really happy.

As soon as he returned from California to Fort Worth, Delbert had set about putting together a band. From the Straitjackets and Rondels days, Billy Wade Sanders was selling used cars, and Robert Harwell was a mailman. In what could have been a scene right out of the *Blues Brothers* movie, Delbert found each of them and told them that he was getting the old band back together.

Billy Sanders told music writer Peter Guralnick: "I had a family and was making pretty good money in the car business when Delbert came by. I wasn't going to do it. But then I agreed to help him out a week here and a week there, and before I knew it, I was right back in the mainstream again, riding around in the back of an old pickup truck with the equipment."[10]

Billy would continue to play with Delbert well into the 1990s, before leaving the band for health reasons. Delbert says, "Billy was the best friend ever. We grew into our fifties playing together.

We were good friends for more than thirty-five years. He was one of those guys who could walk into a room and within thirty seconds everyone in the room was trying to get around him. I really miss him. Back in the early days, when we were opening shows for Willie [Nelson], he was kind of my Paul [English]. In fact, he and Paul could go toe to toe with their bullshit. Both of them had been used car dealers. And they were both silver-tongued devils."[11]

Playing the old familiar club circuit, the Clean record deal had come and gone. Delbert was right back in the place he had tried so desperately to leave: playing for the door in bars around Texas every night. Then, out of the blue, Delbert got a call from an old friend who had become a branch manager for ABC Records. Charles Stewart had a studio in Pantego, a small town between Dallas and Fort Worth.

Delbert recalls, "He said, 'If you have some songs, why don't you come out to the studio and we'll demo them, and I will get them to Don Gant, [the top record producer and talent scout at ABC in Nashville].' And that's what we did."[12]

Don Gant liked the demo and worked up a recording contract for Delbert with ABC.

"Clay was a baby. I had a record deal. I got a twenty-three-foot travel trailer and we moved to Nashville. I figured that was what we ought to do," he shrugs. "But, the ink was still wet on the contract when everything blew up at ABC."[13]

In a corporate turnover that was common in the industry at the time, the entire Nashville staff was fired and replaced, and the new people had no idea who Delbert McClinton was, or how to market his music. Rock? Country? Folk? Blues? None of the new people at ABC knew quite where he would fit in the record stores, or what to do with him.[14]

Critics say that despite these difficulties, the ABC period chronicled some of Delbert's best music. DeWitt and Cotten write, "These three LPs represent a window into his artistic mind."[15]

The first ABC album, *Victim of Life's Circumstances*, was released in 1975. With *Victim*, ABC decided to promote Delbert as a country act, sending a mailer to country music stations around the nation with a picture of Delbert wearing jeans and a checkered shirt. Artists topping *Billboard*'s country charts were Cal Smith, Tom T. Hall, Conway Twitty, and Charlie Pride, all traditional acts steeped in the Grand Ole Opry sounds of country music. Even in a checkered shirt, Delbert was steeped in that Jacksboro Highway blues.

Even then, fiddles and steel guitars were moving over and making room for orchestrated strings and smooth sophistication on country music radio. Delbert was playing his signature harmonica, bluesy, hard-driving original sound. Staying true to his art and writing from the heart, the title song and first single on Delbert's debut solo album, "Victim of Life's Circumstances," remains one of his most popular today, but failed to chart.

Six-O-Five A.M. on Sunday Mornin'
I was supposed to've left for Memphis late last night
I stopped at one of them old highway places
And because of it I'll sleep in the Tarrant County Jail tonight
I started out the night with good intentions
But I ended up gettin' sideways drinkin' wine
The last thing I remember we was roarin'
Then somethin' hit my head and knocked me from my conscious mind

I'm a victim of life's circumstances
I was raised around barrooms, Friday night dances
Singin' them old country songs
Half the time endin' up someplace I don't belong

I said, Jailer, what y'all got me charged with
He looked at me and he half-way closed one eye
He said you mean to say you don't remember
Cuttin' up some honky with that bone-handled knife

I'm a victim of life's circumstances
I was raised around barrooms, Friday night dances
Singin' them old country songs
Half the time endin' up someplace I don't belong.[16]

Top 40 country radio stations weren't looking for bar songs. They were trying to elevate country music to a more contemporary sound. But this rough-edged theme of playing too many bars, growing up in honkytonks, and just being "a victim of life's circumstances" made the song a natural for a new format of music that was rising on the horizon: "progressive country."

Delbert decided to do the second ABC album on his own terms. He collected some of his favorite songs, including some rock 'n' roll and rhythm and blues (R&B), classics for *Genuine Cowhide*. In addition to several of Delbert's original songs, the album included covers of Bo Diddley, Fats Domino, and others. Forty years later, songwriter Joe Ely would remark that *Genuine Cowhide* was one of his greatest influences.[17] While the album is well remembered for the music, the artwork featured an embossed cover of a leather wallet bearing a ringed imprint of a never-used but always-ready condom stored inside, which garnered "hoots of appreciation from men of his generation," according to one of them, music writer Jan Reid.[18] *Genuine Cowhide* was another personal success, but commercial failure for Delbert.

1977 brought Delbert's third and final project for ABC Records, *Love Rustler*. Even the liner notes appeared to make excuses for this artist who just didn't want to color inside the lines of traditional country music. Music writer Bob Kirsh attempts to explain Delbert even before the shrink-wrap is broken on the album cover: "Delbert McClinton is a rarity, an artist who sings for the love of singing, sticks to his roots without being afraid to try something new, and passes on costumes and glitter and formula songs and sound effects and all the other bandwagons that roll into fashion and roll out just as fast in today's often confusing pop music world. It's that simple. Or is it? With all the fuss currently surrounding Texas music, it's a pleasure to listen to one of this so-called 'sound's' pioneers. A Delbert album, like a Delbert show, is a lesson in rock 'n' roll."[19]

Delbert says, "They never knew what to do with me. I never really had anyone to deal with at ABC. They didn't seem to know who I was. I think, toward the end, they had decided that I was going to be their progressive country artist, but by the time *Love Rustler* came out, ABC was out of business."[20]

The ABC marketing department may not have known what to do with Delbert McClinton, but critics still agree that those three releases represent some of the best blues and R&B music of the time.[21]

Despite two record deals and five albums, Delbert would continue to play small clubs and honkytonks, traveling in a pickup with a camper shell, pulling a trailer. "We had the mattress that I was born on in the back of the pickup. We'd take turns riding in the cab, driving, and sleeping in the back of the truck on the way to gigs," Delbert says.[22]

CHAPTER 11

"It Ain't Whatcha Eat but the Way How You Chew It"

Progressive Country

In the mid-1970s, Austin was happening. I was playing down there a lot, and we were tired of Nashville. We packed up and moved. Austin had this scene going that worked for us. People wanted to hear original music. Hippies and cowboys came out to hear the same bands. And everyone got along.

—DELBERT McCLINTON[1]

Progressive country. Redneck rock. Rhythm and blues. The 1970s were a coming of age for the Austin music scene. It wasn't just about the music. Everyone was feeling a new sense of freedom. Texas politicians were hanging out backstage at concerts. A startup magazine called *Texas Monthly* was seeking young, hungry contributing writers. With new art, music, and literature, Austin was being called the Paris of the 1970s. Newspaper hacks were stretching their boundaries from journalism to literature, and gathering at such iconic Austin landmarks as Soap Creek Saloon, the Texas Chili Parlor, and of course, the Armadillo World Headquarters.

In November 1973, Jan Reid's "The Coming of Redneck Hip" marked his first major feature in the pages of *Texas Monthly*. He chronicled this new country-rock hybrid sound that was coming out of Austin, and wrote of the migration of seasoned musicians into the capitol city. As he told the story of the first financial music festival disaster that was the Dripping Springs Reunion music festival in 1972, he knew the people behind this new movement were on to something more. He introduced Armadillo World

Headquarters owner Eddie Wilson to a broader audience than the young hippies and old cowboys who stood side by side in the old armory building-turned-music hall in Austin. Reid writes, "[Eddie] Wilson and his music business colleagues stress that any Austin music boom must remain localized.

"The creation of a music center in Austin would bring millions of dollars into the local economy, millions that would wind up in the pockets of Austin musicians, technicians, artists and publicists struggling to get by now. Even the environment would benefit. According to Wilson the music industry, unlike others that a growing Austin might attract, 'doesn't pollute and it doesn't get in the way visually; about fifty million dollars could be put into the Austin music business and remain invisible.' The stage has been set very nicely, so why not continue? Thus the music businessmen proceed, caution thrown to the winds."[2]

In *The Improbable Rise of Redneck Rock,* a book that grew from that magazine article, Reid writes, "A number of musicians who were already battered and bruised by the major music centers began to settle in Austin. They were songwriters and singers of varied experience and potential, but they were good enough to land recording contracts with major companies." Reid adds that the newly established Armadillo World Headquarters, a counter-culture honkytonk with adequate floor space but almost no furnishings became a community center for artistic expression, hosting legendary acts, and new bands from around the country.[3]

The originators of the Armadillo World Headquarters were a young beer distributor, Eddie Wilson; an entertainment lawyer, Mike Tolleson; and a graphic artist named Jim Franklin. They rented an old airplane hangar-like armory building that had been sitting vacant for nearly a decade, and the Armadillo was soon in a league with San Francisco and New York music venues. Jan Reid writes, "Suddenly, Austin swarmed with singer-songwriters who looked like bearded hippies but wore cowboy hats and recruited fiddle and steel guitar players."[4]

Delbert and Donna Sue didn't live in Austin for long, but their time in Austin coincided with a major shift in commercial music. Nashville, Tennessee, the traditional home of the country music industry, had become too confining for artists who wanted to do more than copy the hits of the day. This was not the first time differing opinions had threatened the Nashville dominance of the genre.

In the mid- to late-1950s, Buck Owens and Merle Haggard had established a new country scene on the West Coast that came to be known as the "Bakersfield Sound." Renowned radio personality Bill Mack says, "This was a direct reaction to the slick, orchestrated Nashville sounds of the time. While Nashville producers were muting rhythm sections and smoothing vocals into an easy listening mode, Buck Owens teamed with Don Rich and brought that twangy Fender guitar sound to the front of the record mix. Merle Haggard was celebrating his rough voice, and singing of prisons and swinging doors, while in Nashville, Ray Price was crooning 'Danny Boy.'"[5]

Commonly referred to as the "Nashville Sound" and "California Country," these two music scenes would compete head-on for audiences, even hosting competing national awards shows, "The Country Music Awards" in Nashville and "The Academy of Country Music Awards" in California. Bill Mack continues, "The Nashville country music industry had worked long and hard to develop a legitimate genre. They were not going to allow it to be taken over by rock and roll drums and rowdy bands. The new sophistication that had finally found its way into country music allowed orchestrated country hits to cross-over into the pop charts, but the Nashville country music industry was very protective of its newly created sound, and did not welcome organic music that sounded untrained and unpolished."[6]

Fast-forward ten years and fifteen hundred miles from Bakersfield to Austin. Another group of rebels had grown tired of—or been kicked to the curb in—Nashville. They want the freedom to create their own sounds and focus on original music. Willie Nelson has often been credited for starting this new culture in Austin, and it quickly caught on.

This new Austin music scene will be vital to the Delbert McClinton story because Austin was not only a melting pot for "outlaw" musicians but also a revival for singer-songwriters and a renaissance for blues music. While Delbert is quick to say he wasn't really a part of that progressive country scene, his time in Austin was not to be overlooked.

Texas writer Joe Nick Patoski says, "Delbert was a minor player in the progressive country scene, but a major piece of the blues awakening that was happening in Austin. He was playing that Texas circuit: Houston, Lubbock, Dallas, Fort Worth, Austin, and he had a sound that was working for him. His music showed me that the thin line separating R&B from country and western was real fuzzy. Most people can't pull that off. However, a good artist can mix that up. And Delbert was doing that. He was mixing up sound stereotypes with that hard driving blues beat and a fiddle, doing good songs his way. Delbert was making something that hippies elsewhere would consider uncool. But, where he was coming from, it was more than cool. It was authentic."[7]

Another Texas native, Willie Nelson, was tired of the limitations of the Nashville music industry expectations, and hungry to stretch his creativity. In the definitive biography, *An Epic Life: Willie Nelson,* Patoski writes, "His first concept album, *Yesterday's Wine,* marked the beginning of the end of Willie's relationship with RCA. The label pressed up the standard ten thousand copies and let nature take its course. Promotion behind Willie Nelson's albums had historically been non-existent. Nothing had changed, and the situation would remain the same for the three RCA albums that followed, before his ties with RCA were severed."

This was business as usual in Nashville. As Patoski writes, "Chet Atkins [guitar virtuoso and head of RCA Records] may have been a picker's picker. But as a producer and label chief, he stuck to a formula."[8]

This was an all-too-familiar story for Delbert McClinton, and other singer-songwriters who sought to be more than craftsmen cranking out a product in the Nashville music factories.

While Patoski credits Atkins with keeping country music alive when rock 'n' roll took over the sales bins, "There was no way he was going to have hits on all the acts he produced, and Willie was proof," he said.

Songwriter Hank Cochran said, "The thing with Willie is they wanted him to tell them what he was gonna do in the studio; and he didn't know what he was gonna do until he got into the studio."[9]

Delbert echoes that characteristic. He says, "I am hell-bent on getting live vocals. I want that sound. You lose the spontaneity, which is the *truth in music*. A mistake doesn't matter. There's a southwestern Indian tribe that purposely puts a flaw in every blanket they make to show the imperfection of mankind. I feel the same way about music. You know, you can polish something till it don't shine."[10]

Austin welcomed originality, and this new genre reveled in spontaneity and the rough edges of live music. Joe Ely talks about Austin in the mid-1970s: "Everyone was talking about progressive country. The word got out that Austin was a good place to live, with lots of places to play. Rent was cheap and old houses were plentiful. You didn't have to hustle to make a living. Musicians could pitch in and get a house together and start a band and make a little money. And, if you had a girlfriend, you could actually sometimes pay the rent."[11]

Joe adds, "There were about twenty clubs in Austin that featured live music. There was a happening blues scene on the east side. And a strong conjunto, Tex-Mex scene, and cowboy bars like the Broken Spoke and the Split Rail."[12]

Today, many of the people who were at the center of the progressive country scene still consider the title deceptive. "Progressive country was the silliest name," Joe says. "It was much bigger than country. But, I think the people who were trying to figure out how to market it decided that they had to call it something so they could herd it up and sell it. And Delbert and I both got lumped into that for a while."[13]

What was actually happening in Austin in the 1970s was bigger than one genre. It was blues, rock, country, Tex-Mex, zydeco, and folk. While music writers were trying to get their heads around this new free-for-all genre, and debating what to call it, an undercurrent of the blues was making a huge impact.

Delbert explains, "Everyone was putting on a cowboy hat or a bandana around their neck. Willie brought it on in 1972 with the Dripping Springs Reunion. And that scene was all about the musicians. The musicians were getting the perks. It was a real coming together. It wasn't about the business, it was about the music. Artists were starting to sing the songs that they wrote. It was an exciting time for me."[14]

He adds, "The blues scene was not as much of a coming

together. It was a completely different atmospheric situation. It was something that you either are or you aren't. I remember going on a blues cruise early on, and all the musicians had *The Look*. They were wearing black pants, black shoes, black ties, black hats, and I thought it comical to see these guys dressed like that, walking on the beaches of St. Thomas. And they were finding a groove. But it was not as flamboyant, or as much of a scene as progressive country. Stevie [Ray Vaughan] made it happen. The Thunderbirds certainly did. At that time in Austin, all of a sudden this new music was exploding. The Thunderbirds were a white band playing blues as well as anybody ever did. It was a time of spreading good, new music every which way."[15]

Musicologist Travis Stimeling writes, "a generation of young Texans redefined what it mean to be Texan in a countercultural age by claiming ownership of distinctly Texan forms of expressive culture, including not only music, but also fashion, language and art."[16]

Joe Ely says, "All of these Texas organic musical styles were coming together. In other towns, musics were not mixing a lot. Mexican bands were in certain places, and honkytonk bands were playing somewhere else, and blues bands were in another club. But in Austin, all of this music came together.

"Something happened in the 1970s. You would walk into a bar and see San Antonio's West Side Horns jamming with the blues guys from Dallas. Soap Creek Saloon was a good example. They booked as much great blues as they did great country. They would have Doug Sahm and Delbert McClinton and Jimmie and Stevie Ray Vaughan, and Paul Ray and the Cobras, and Freda and the Firedogs and Asleep at the Wheel. It was like heaven.

"Delbert played this perfect combination of blues and country. It was a natural blend of the kind of music that started in Texas with such a rich history of Blind Lemon Jefferson, Mance Lipscomb, and Lightnin' [Hopkins]. Delbert was mixing up rocking blues and adding a fiddle and hitting those harmonica solos. Something this interesting had not been done before. Anything goes. No rules. And we were in the middle of it."[17]

Students from the University of Texas were mingling with South Austin hippies, and honky-tonk cowboys. The names were as varied as the description of the music: western beat, outlaw music, redneck rock, progressive country, cosmic cowboys. By any name, it was new and different and didn't quite fit in any of the standard record bins.

Delbert adds, "Those days in Austin were such an awakening for me. The whole integration thing was going on, and people were getting it. It was a time of no precedents, you did what you felt, and it's still exciting to talk about."[18]

Joe Nick Patoski explains, "Delbert was a big part of the birth of Americana music. He could take that old country R&B that he loved most, and modernize it, paying loyal attention to the original intent. Doug [Sahm] did it too. They took that traditional American, traditional Texas music and did not bastardize it. They stayed faithful and true to the roots as they built on that foundation."[19]

Texas electric blues singer and music historian Angela Strehli went to Austin to attend the University of Texas. She earned a degree in sociology and Spanish, and immediately began to play music around town. "Out on the east side edge of town, a little bar called Alexander's Place had these great Sunday afternoon outdoor concerts with barbecue. It was one of the best gigs a person could ever have. Clifford Antone was a big blues fan who had come to UT from Port Arthur, and was on a mission to introduce the world to blues music," she said.[20]

She added, "We had a lot of support from black people who loved blues music and saw it disappearing from the radio. For young people, blues was the past, the older generation. They wanted to do their own thing—disco, soul, rock. It was completely understandable. As it turned out, we were filling a gap and this important music stayed relevant and was passed down."[21]

At the time, blues was way underground, according to Angela. "It wasn't hip, but we knew it was important. Radio wasn't interested. But Clifford Antone was."

Angela added, "Clifford wanted to open a blues club in Austin on the west side of Interstate 35. He was convinced that if the university students and other people who didn't have access to the east side clubs could hear the blues masters, it would catch on, and they would understand what we were trying to do.

"As a musician, I wanted to do it. We would have a chance to be on a big stage, opening for our heroes. So, we opened Antone's in 1975. It was one of the first music clubs on Sixth Street. This was Sixth Street long before it became a tourist attraction. There were a bunch of winos wandering the streets and old empty buildings. Jimmie Vaughan and the Fabulous Thunderbirds were sort of the house band. And we could get these legendary blues players to come down from Chicago and play with the house band, saving the expense of having to pay for their bands to come to town. And of course we had a regular rotation of Paul Ray, Stevie Ray, Delbert, Marcia Ball, and others. We had a couple of exceptions to the 'seven nights a week blues club,' with Asleep at the Wheel and Joe Ely, but it worked. A lot of people who had never heard blues before came out and loved what they heard, and loved Antone's."[22]

Grammy winner Marcia Ball had graduated from her Freda and the Firedogs band to a solo career in 1974. She says, "We had good clubs in Austin then: the One-Knight, Alexander's, Soap Creek Saloon, the Armadillo World Headquarters. And we could play somewhere just about every night. I called that time the progressive country *scare,* as people were trying to dissect and define what we were doing. We didn't even know, ourselves.

"But blues was coming on strong to new audiences. I started seeing Delbert at Soap Creek. I remember that even before he started filling clubs, he was playing my kind of music. He was absolutely playing the music I loved. I would go out and dance the night away.

"Except for a short time when he and Donna Sue lived here, Delbert was coming and going, and had hits — or we thought he did. His venues got bigger and his crowds got bigger, and I was still a fan in the audience. I still am.

"Delbert and Doug were stars to us. We weren't paying much attention to what the rest of the world was saying about us, but they had a complete unerring sense of what was happening, and what was going to happen right here. All of a sudden, all the hippies were pulling their Levi's and boots and hats out of the closet and coming out to hear our music."[23]

Marcia recognizes the importance of that time in Austin: "When Antone's opened in 1975, that really created a scene for us. It overlapped with the Armadillo and Soap Creek. It was a heyday for live music. There was something great happening every night. Soap Creek would bring in Professor Longhair, the Armadillo brought in everybody, and Antone's became the blues scene of Austin. We were very fortunate to have all that music handed to us, to have the opportunity to play with, and to become lifelong friends with, some of our heroes.

"I made a transition from country to blues between 1975 and 1980. I went solo. I had been moving in the direction of R&B roots. I knew that was where I needed to go. I always felt that country music and rock and roll would age you out. But with blues, the older you got the more revered you are."[24]

Jan Reid talks about the budding Austin music scene: "It was in April of 1973. Willie was playing the Armadillo World Head-quarters with his full band for the first time. No one knew how the concert would go. With clouds of marijuana smoke always pungent in the place, hippies mingled with Willie's redneck fans. But any hostility between the two audiences evaporated as they were swept up in the spell of Willie's jazz-inflected singing and his playing of a battered Martin guitar."[25]

Reid explains that while Willie had discovered his taste for marijuana to take the edge off, and he was perhaps the first coun-try artist to grow a beard and long hair, his real revolt was against the industry, the contracts, arrangements, and session bands that had been forced on him.[26]

Delbert was in the same boat. He had his hopes dashed with two recording companies, but music was his passion and Austin welcomed his art. Reid writes: "[Delbert] sang rhythm and blues like the masters. Fats Domino's 'Blue Monday,' and James Brown's 'Please, Please, Please.' ABC Records went out of business and progressive country started fading; when fashion in Austin music changed from country to blues, he made the transition with ease. Blues was where he started.

"Emmylou Harris recorded his fine ode to failure out West, 'Two More Bottles of Wine.' Delbert was swapping lyrics and interpretations with blues diva Etta James. The title song of his fifth record, *Love Rustler* had cracked Billboard's Top 100—just in time for his record company to go broke.

"Still, people in Austin were standing in lines to get in to see him at the Soap Creek Saloon. With a mop of auburn hair and a broad expressive mouth—'Great lips,' said a woman who used to date him—he moved through the Austin scene like an Irishman out of central casting.

"He could sing and make the harmonica wail, and he knew all the moves. 'How you, pal?' he'd say with a nod to a fan as he sauntered outside on a band break, wearing jeans and loafers and a leather sport coat, lightly carrying a shot glass of [tequila]. Delbert was the consummate, cool, white honky-tonker."[27]

Delbert has always maintained his audience because he is, first and foremost, a live act. Peter Guralnick writes, "In some ways, none of the albums, with the possible exception of *Victim,* has done justice to his talent, simply because they lack the directness, the dangerous incandescence of a live set."[28]

However, the records have always remained close to Delbert's vision. He explained to Guralnick that the music he grew up with was "raw and unpolished, maybe, but that shit was not mediocre. You might talk to a technician and he might tell you how pitiful the mix was, and all that—but goddamn, but goddamn boy. You were hearing somebody's heart beat.

"And when you'd get right down to it, you can burn all the machines and shit, and hand somebody a guitar, and that's what it gets down to. You can either move them or you can't. And it don't have nothing to do with turning knobs. And that, to me, is what I want to keep alive."[29]

In 1974, Delbert was playing on the road, and Donna Sue and Clay were living in Austin. Monty had turned fourteen and was allowed to choose which parent with whom he wanted to live. "He was ready to come live with us. He was looking for better ground, and I was so glad to have him. I had missed so much of his childhood. He was a good kid. He was not that good in school, but Donna Sue tried hard to help him."[30]

By 1976, Donna Sue wanted to move back home to Fort Worth. Things were not going well with this marriage, but Delbert was hell-bent on trying to make her happy, and to make it work. So, he moved their trailer back to Fort Worth, where they parked it behind her good friend, Priscilla Davis's home, commonly referred to as the Davis Mansion. They lived there temporarily, while she set out shopping for a permanent home. Delbert and Donna Sue would soon find themselves brushing all too close to one of the most infamous murder mysteries in American history.

"Clay was a toddler," Delbert says, "and we had moved out of the trailer and into the Davis Mansion. Donna Sue and Priscilla were friends. I was either in Austin or on the road most of the time, so Donna Sue and Clay moved out of the trailer and into the big house with Priscilla. When I was in Fort Worth, I would stay there."[31]

Priscilla was married to one of the wealthiest men in Fort Worth, T. Cullen Davis. Davis had owned Stratoflex, one of the hellish companies Delbert had worked for back in the early 1960s, but it was the friendship between Donna Sue and Priscilla that brought the McClintons to the Davis Mansion. Gary Cartwright wrote about the murders in *Blood Will Tell,* chronicling this "chilling story of sex, drugs, money, murder and mayhem, Texas-style."[32]

As Cartwright summarizes the story: "On the day his oil tycoon father died, T. Cullen Davis wed flashy, twice-married Priscilla Lee Wilborn, dismissed by Fort Worth Society as 'that platinum hussy with the silicone implants, and the RICH BITCH diamond studded necklace.'

"Six violent years later, Priscilla filed for divorce. On August 2, 1976, the eve of the divorce trial, Priscilla and her lover, Stan Farr, returned home to a hailstorm of bullets. Farr and Priscilla's daughter Andrea died. Priscilla, shot in the chest, escaped—and clearly identified T. Cullen Davis as the black-clad assassin."[33]

Delbert recalls the friendship between Donna Sue and Priscilla, and how much they enjoyed the club scene. He describes the Davis Mansion, "It was huge, and filled with all kinds of antiques. Monty was out of school and had moved out on his own. Donna Sue and I would run across the highly polished beautiful wood floors in our socks, and see how far we could slide."[34]

Former Rondels manager and car dealer Jerry Conditt knew Cullen Davis well. He recalls many of the details of that mystery: "Fort Worth was such a small town in those days. I knew Cullen real well," he says, "and, yes, I knew Priscilla. She had been married to Jack Wilborn, another car dealer in Fort Worth. Jack played blackjack with my dad just about every day. He was the nicest guy in the world. It was his daughter, Andrea, who was killed that night.

"Priscilla was—well—promiscuous. And at that time, I think Cullen was making about a million dollars a week. I could tell you a lot of stories about him, but we are already getting off track.

"Anyway, Priscilla took up with Cullen, and it was like water and oil. They were fighting all the time. Fort Worth was a small town, and we were all still friends. Delbert's wife, Donna Sue, was a lot like Priscilla. Donna Sue was a trust-fund baby, and had a little money. She always wanted to be center-stage. She liked to be the center of attention. Sometimes she would run up on stage when Delbert was singing. It was just a little off.

"I think it was a Sunday, the day before the murders happened. I had a fifty-foot cabin cruiser at the time. I called Cullen and told him we were going out the next night on my boat. He wanted to meet us and go out for the night. Then later on the next day, he called me back and said something had come up, he had a change of plans, and wasn't going to be able to make it. And that was the night the murders happened. I am just glad Donna Sue and Delbert were not still living out there."[35]

Delbert adds, "Donna Sue had found a house in Fort Worth, about two weeks before the murders and had moved out. The night of the murders, I was in San Antonio rehearsing with some new guys. Donna Sue was at the new house in Fort Worth. She had gone by the mansion that night and didn't see any lights on so she just went on back home. I was heading back to Fort Worth the next day when I heard that it had all happened. We knew most of those people, and there were some characters of very questionable reputation out there. There was a lot of bad stuff happening out there. I was just glad we were out of there before it happened."[36]

Another chapter of Delbert's life was soon to end. As the 1980s grew near, the progressive movement was waning. In its place, the urban cowboy movement was taking over country music. Denim and diamonds would soon replace bandana headbands and faded jeans.

On September 12, 1978, *Esquire* published Aaron Latham's

"The Ballad of the Urban Cowboy: America's Search for True Grit." It was a story about the new country music scene down in Houston.[37]

Delbert was making some changes as well. In 1978, two years after ABC went out of business, he played some artist showcases in Nashville, and was picked up by Capricorn Records. This business of music was rough, but Delbert McClinton was getting his *Second Wind.*

CHAPTER 12

Second Wind

The Road Warrior

*The urban cowboy thing was going on. In New York, at the
Lone Star Café, the whole Texas deal was blowing up. And
shit, during that time, you were good as gold if you were from
Texas. It was a free pass to almost anywhere.*

—DELBERT McCLINTON[1]

The urban cowboy craze gained national attention, first, with
an *Esquire* magazine article, and then with a 1980 movie by the
same title.

Journalist Aaron Latham follows the true story of the love–hate
relationship of Dew Westbrook and Betty Helmer, as it plays out
in two-step time at Gilley's Club, a mega-dance hall in Pasadena,
Texas. Through their story, he chronicles the celebrated cowboy
culture popular in Houston at the time, and coins the phrase,
"urban cowboy." Dew is not a traditional cowboy. He works in
an oil refinery. But, at quitting time, he trades his hard hat for a
cowboy hat and steel-toed boots for cowboy boots. He and hundreds of other petrochemical cowboys head for Gilley's, billed as
the World's Largest Honkytonk, complete with a mechanical bull
for the inner-cowboy in all of these city folks.[2]

The *Esquire* article was made into a blockbuster movie starring Debra Winger and John Travolta in 1980. *Urban Cowboy* has
been described as a country music version of Travolta's 1977 *Saturday Night Fever* and his 1978 movie *Grease*.

While *Urban Cowboy* was not the financial success of Travolta's
other dance movies, it made Texas popular everywhere. Nowhere
was the urban cowboy craze more prevalent than in New York

City. While the movie focused on country music, the craze enveloped Texas in general: denim and diamonds, boots and hats, and live honkytonk and blues music.

The Lone Star Café opened in New York City in 1976. Longtime club manager Cleve Hattersley says, "Mort Cooperman, one of my best friends, was a former advertising guy with Wells Rich Greene. He was the head of Pepsi, Datsun, and several other big accounts. He was driving home one day, listening to Willie on the radio and everything hit him at once. He said, 'We've gotta have a place for Willie to play up here,' and in no time, he and a couple of his ad friends had put the Lone Star Café together."

Hattersley adds, "It was an old drugstore, and the oddest place to have music. Right in the middle of the largest city in the world, and it had a roadhouse feel to it. The view from the stage was actually obstructed from every seat in the house."[3]

Hattersley went on to explain that while the Lone Star Café began as a country bar, they brought in the rest of Texas music when he joined the team. Hattersley and his wife, Sweet Mary, had led one of the leading progressive country bands in Austin, Greezy Wheels, and had strong connections back home. Mort wanted Stevie Ray Vaughan, Delbert, and the Thunderbirds, and it became a premier place for Texas rhythm and blues. Texans and Texan-wannabes flooded through the doors to be a part of the scene.

Jason Mellard writes about the Texans in New York in *Progressive Country: How the 1970s Transformed the Texan in Popular Culture*, "From the 1970s through the late 1980s, the [Lone Star Café] served as the capital of Texas chic, an embassy of "the Texan" to communicate the shared bluster of two of America's largest and symbolically salient states . . . . Strange assortments of people came through its doors over the years, lending it a voyeuristic, performative air: Mick Jagger and Johnny Paycheck, Abbie Hoffman and Doug Sahm, Grace Jones and Liz Carpenter, John Connally and Jerry Garcia, Julian Schnabel and Tommy Tune. In some ways, the Lone Star Café played a similar symbolic role in transcending oppositions as the hippie-redneck confluence in Austin, only in New York, closing the imaginative gulf between socialite and Sunbelt celebrity."[4]

Cleve Hattersley adds, "And Delbert was the biggest star of the bunch. He is the absolute heart and soul of Texas rhythm and blues. We saw this every time he played. We had James Brown, George Strait, Elvis Costello, Reba McEntire. But, the one that all the other stars came out to see was Delbert. Bob Dylan, Joe Ely, Keith Richards, Jimmy Buffett, the *Saturday Night Live* crew. Everyone wanted to come out when Delbert was playing. He had created his own genre, and nobody could get enough of it."[5]

About the time the urban cowboy craze was hitting the nation, and Delbert and Donna Sue had moved back to Fort Worth, Delbert got a deal with Capricorn Records. Capricorn was the premier label for many southern rock and blues bands in the 1970s, including the Allman Brothers Band, the Marshall Tucker Band, Lynyrd Skynyrd, Bonnie Bramlett, Otis Redding, and Elvin Bishop. Capricorn was a natural fit, and it seemed that Delbert was finally destined for success.

Delbert's first Capricorn album, *Second Wind* (1978), was well produced by Johnny Sandlin, with Delbert's band and the Muscle Shoals Horns. Longtime band members Billy Wade Sanders on guitar, Lewis Stephens on organ and clarinet, Robert Harwell on saxophone, and Dennis Good on trombone made Delbert feel at home in the studio. The Muscle Shoals Horns was a group of successful session musicians who had played and recorded with everyone from Jimi Hendrix to Bob Dylan to B. B. King to Elton John.[6]

Mark Pucci was the publicity director for Capricorn at the time: "Delbert was managed by Don Light in Nashville. I had been a fan since the Delbert and Glen Clean records. When his last ABC record came out and they folded, I was all for picking him up. I don't think I ever saw him perform live until we started working with him in 1978. What a band. Ernie Durawa on drums, Lewis Stephens on keyboards, James Pennebaker on guitar, and whatever else he needed to play. Delbert always had a great band.

"One of my best memories was at the Lone Star Café one night supporting *Second Wind*, I think. Stephanie Turnakowski was there shooting some pictures for a story Martha Hume was writing about Delbert for *Rolling Stone*. It was in the summer, and we had invited a whole bunch of press people out to the show.

Delbert always had a big fan following from the media. And still does. Martha Hume and her husband Chet Flippo were there. Pioneer female rock jock Jessie Scott was doing a live broadcast for WNBC radio that night.

"We had no idea [John] Belushi; [Bette] Midler; Otis Blackwell; Dusty Rhodes, the wrestler; Elvis Costello; Gary Busey, all these people were going to show up to listen to Delbert and the band. Delbert was inviting them up on stage. And I should add that everyone was drinking a lot.

"Someone passed a note up to Delbert to remind him not to say anything bad because the show was being broadcast. Delbert announced, on the air, 'Someone handed me a note that says, 'Don't fuck up because this is on the radio.' And yes, this was before the broadcast industry's six-second delay. But that was one of many amazing nights."[7]

In his autobiography, Elvis Costello writes about one memorable night at the Lone Star Café: "On the way back to England we found our way to the Lone Star Café. The great Texas singer, Delbert McClinton, was on stage . . . I'd been handed a Les Paul, which might as well have been a trombone or a frying pan. It was late in the last set. Otis Blackwell was still up on piano, after he and Delbert had sung 'Don't Be Cruel,' the famous song Otis had written for Elvis Presley. Now Delbert was calling a different kind of Elvis to the stage.

"We played ragged versions of Chuck Berry's 'Don't You Lie to Me,' Hank Williams' 'You Win Again,' and 'Tonight, the Bottle Let Me Down,' the Merle Haggard song that might have been a little too close for comfort."[8]

Dan Aykroyd and John Belushi were big Delbert McClinton fans. The two comedy actors credited Delbert along with the Downchild Blues Band, a Canadian group, as inspirations for their Blues Brothers band. In 1978, they recorded Delbert's "B Movie Boxcar Blues" on the first Blues Brothers album, *Briefcase Full of Blues*, which went to number one on the *Billboard* 200 and went double platinum. It remains one of the highest-selling blues albums of all time.[9]

In February 1979, Delbert and the band landed the musical guest spot on *Saturday Night Live*. The host was *Charlie's Angels* star, Kate Jackson, and Delbert and the band played Chuck Berry's "I'm Talking About You," the single from the second Capricorn record, *Keeper of the Flame*.

Thom Jurek writes in his review of the second Capricorn product, "*Keeper of the Flame* was the follow-up to *Second Wind* and was to prove once again to be the last record Delbert McClinton would record for a label that was going out of business; in this case it would be Capricorn."[10]

Capricorn's Mark Pucci says, "I was one of the last people to leave Capricorn. I was out of town when I got a call from someone at the label who said the phones had been cut off and he didn't know what to do. I got back and we tried to hold things together as well as we could. But, it didn't last long. Delbert had just been in the wrong place at the wrong time. He had been on three labels and they had all gone out of business while he was under contract."[11]

Cocaine had been the drug of choice in the entertainment industry during the '70s and '80s, with many backstage and after-hours parties from coast to coast. Belushi was in the middle of it, backstage at the Lone Star Café, or at his blues club on the other side of town. Delbert remembers that methamphetamine (meth) was also coming on strong. "It was a hard time for me, and for anyone around that scene. You could turn your head two inches to the left or right and someone was there with a snort to put up your nose. Free cocaine, meth, you can't turn that down."[12]

"It was awful. A lot of people didn't survive it," he adds. "I can't believe I did. I never had enough money to buy a bunch of it, but I was certainly a coke whore. It was horrible. I cannot believe I was that way. But, everyone was. It's not like that anymore. You don't see a bunch of people out of control like that. Today, you have to dress up the act with diamonds and big smiles. But back then, it was anything goes."[13]

Even in the heyday of coke and meth, Delbert remembers that the rule for *Saturday Night Live* was "no blow till after the show."[14]

Delbert remembers his first *Saturday Night Live* appearance for another reason—one that would someday change his life forever. "That was the night I met Wendy [Goldstein] for the first time."[15]

Back in Fort Worth, things were not going well with Donna Sue. While Delbert describes his first wife, Sandra Sue, as "mean-crazy," he admits that Donna Sue was "sad-crazy."

"And there was no doubt about it. It was mostly my fault," he admits. "I didn't really offer anything for either Sandra Sue or Donna Sue to build a foundation on. I was a taker. It was a very confusing time. We were both so unhappy and didn't know what to do. I was not bringing in a shitload of money, but I was working all the time. I didn't mind it. I looked forward to it. I knew I could make it. Looking back, I could look like a guy who didn't contribute much, but I wasn't sponging off of these women. Donna Sue had the resources to live how she wanted to live."[16]

Drummer Ernie Durawa grew up playing conjunto music on the west side of San Antonio. He was playing with Doug Sahm in the Eastwood Country Club and the Ebony Club in San Antonio, and, like Delbert's bands in Fort Worth, they would back the Chitlin' Circuit artists when they would come through town.[17] He says, "My first gig with Delbert was Thanksgiving night, 1977, at the old Soap Creek Saloon. About six months earlier, I had been playing with Doug, and Chris Ethridge, the bass player for the Flying Burrito Brothers, said that Delbert was playing across town. We went over and sat in with them, and Delbert said, 'I think we could make each other rich.' I was all for that and gave him my phone number. Didn't hear from him again till he called and said he was coming to Soap Creek, and asked me to join the band. Stevie Ray [Vaughan] used to come listen to us, the Thunderbirds, Paul Ray, and the Cobras. I was playing with Delbert, Doug Sahm, and Gatemouth Brown regularly until I went out on the road with Delbert. I stayed with Delbert from 1977 till about 1982.

"It really was the best of times and the worst of times. We were playing everywhere. We were at the top of the heap in New York City. We had fans up and down the East Coast, and everyone was putting out lines of cocaine for us everywhere we went. We weren't making any real money, but we were living the life. All completely out of control. It was sex, drugs, and rock and roll.

"We were playing in Nashville one night, and when we got back to the motel, some of us went over to the Waffle House. Delbert was on the phone in the room with Donna Sue. She told him she was having an affair. He went nuts. He hung up the phone and tore up the hotel room. When he came over to the Waffle House, he was all cut up and crazy looking. He was grabbing food and cussing and yelling. They thought he was a homeless guy and chased him out of the Waffle House. I've been in a lot of Waffle Houses and I have never seen anyone get kicked out before or since."[18]

Delbert admits, "I had been a liar and a cheater and everything else. But, when she told me she had cheated on me, I completely lost it. I fell apart. There was no making sense of it. I just couldn't believe she would do that to me."[19]

So, Delbert went home to Fort Worth. The second record had barely made it off the press before Capricorn closed its doors. However, he was not slowing down. If anything, he was on the road more than ever, paying his dues as a road warrior, playing across the country. "We had finally upgraded from that old pickup and camper shell—with the mattress I was born on in the back— and a trailer, to two vans, and then to a bus."[20]

Ernie adds, "When I joined the band, we had two vans with CB [citizen band] radios. We would get on the mic and call the guys up front, 'Hey, stop. I gotta pee.' It was pretty low tech."[21]

James Pennebaker had joined the band in 1976, as a fiddle player, and after an off-and-on career with Delbert, forty years later, he is still on stage touring with the band.

After the ABC albums, Delbert had shed the progressive country idea and gone back to rhythm and blues. James went back to Fort Worth, playing in a western swing band with Gary Nicholson, and backing Delbert at occasional gigs at Panther Hall.

A couple of years later, Delbert called James back into the band. "He called out of the blue and said, 'I want to have two guitar players in the band. How do you feel about playing guitar and seeing how it goes?' I didn't think about it for two seconds. I said, 'Sure,' because I had never before—nor have I since—had more fun doing anything more than playing Delbert's music with him."

James adds that Delbert probably needed two guitars because *Keeper of the Flame* was coming out. "Billy Sanders had played on the record. I hadn't. I was brought along to reproduce some of the John Hug guitar parts from the record."[22]

In a 1983 interview in *Guitar Player*, Billy Sanders says, "I look at myself as a good rocket-in-the-pocket kind of player. There's a lot of harmony in the band, at least in the relationship between the band members. You walk into the studio and it's like putting on an old pair of gloves. I'm used to the old shuffle stuff, so we just turn [James] Pennebaker loose."[23]

James talks about their miles on the road: "The greatest thing ever was when we got a bus. Delbert found an old 1953 Flex bus. It was one of those art deco buses. It had no name on the side, but the sign on the front said 'Bobby Whitehead and his Country Playboys.' Bobby Whitehead owned some pawnshops in Fort Worth and I guess he had a little band. We kept that sign up there. It didn't have air conditioning, and had army cots held to the walls with bailing wire. At first we had to drive it ourselves," he recalls.[24]

Ernie adds, "None of us knew how to drive a bus, but we just had to. At the end of the gig, whoever wasn't too drunk or stoned, had to get us on the road."[25]

Delbert says, "I really don't know how we made it through those years. None of us knew how to drive a bus, and we were just driving it like it was a car or a truck. I remember having to pick someone up at the airport in Boulder. It was sleeting and I was driving about fifty-five or sixty. The brakes were not worth a shit but we got there. That old bus was like a tank. One time I was sitting at a red light in Fort Worth, driving it home (where I parked it on the street in front of the house). I felt a bump. I got out to see what happened. A guy had hit me head on and knocked out the whole front of his truck. I could not even see him down there. And it didn't do anything to the bus. It was a good thing when we finally got a real bus driver, Mark Proct."[26]

James says, "Thank goodness Mark Proct became our road manager/sound man/bus driver. He would have to crawl under the back of the bus with a hammer and bang on the solenoid, while someone put their finger on the button on the gearshift to get it into reverse. Mark was a big step up for us. We had to get an extension cord and blow a hair dryer on the starter to thaw out the starter on the bus one morning. Mark knew mechanics, he knew audio, how to set up equipment, and how to get hotel rooms. He managed to get us to where we were going and back home in one piece."[27]

But, once they got home, Delbert knew he needed to do something. He wanted to try to salvage this marriage. At forty, he didn't want to make the same mistakes he had made before.

In Nashville, well-known artist manager Don Light had added Delbert to his roster. When Light died in 2014, Peter Cooper wrote in the *Tennessean*: "Most every day, Gospel Music Hall of Famer Don Light offered this advice: 'If you can find a need and fill it, you've got a job.'"[28]

Cooper added that Light was among Music Row's most quotable figures with lessons like, "Keep your goals and objectives in front of you. That's the reason they put the carrot right out in front of the mule. Otherwise, the mule might forget." Light often reminded artists to "be particularly aware of somebody who tells you, 'Don't worry about a thing,'" and "There's no substitute for experience, and only one way to get it."[29]

Peter Guralnick, who has been called "The Dean of Rock and Roll Storytellers,"[30] recalls his own early impressions of Delbert in that era: "Nick Tosches was living in Nashville, working for Don Light as a publicist, which seemed a most unlikely combination, because it is such a contradiction to his public personality today, but he was such a fanatic about Delbert in a very sincere way. I respected Nick, and listened to Delbert's music and his background.

"I knew I wanted to write about him. Hearing the story of Delbert cutting across a vacant lot somewhere in Fort Worth and hearing Big Joe Turner, and having it strike him like a bolt of lightning. This was what Doc Pomus had told me, and it was so similar to my own experience. That is what struck me. It's not like reading about it in a book. There is no pretense about it. For Delbert it was a visceral experience. And that comes out in his music even today. And in Joe Ely's music as well.

"He and Joe Ely came onto the national stage in the same era and brought this new sound of white rhythm and blues music. Delbert could not be categorized. I hate to keep comparing the two, but even as songwriters, what Delbert wrote and what Joe wrote was so eccentric. They were always to the left of center, even for Texas songwriters.

"Particularly with Delbert, there is this energetic push in his music, almost irrespective of what the lyrics are saying. This uncontainable energy. Delbert and Joe both have it. Delbert's energy has always been a little less jittery. But, both of them just have this push to their music that you are not going to find anywhere else.

"However you describe it, Delbert has created this 'up on the edge of your toes,' forward-moving sound. I would not think of him as a blues singer. A rhythm and blues singer, maybe. Even at that time, he already had that rhythmic element that was so strong, those off-center lyrics and that on-stage energy.

"The first time I saw him perform live was at the Bottom Line in New York. He was on the bill with Alex Taylor. I remember that I took my editor from Seaview Press with me. She was a very sensible, young woman and she swooned over Delbert. And I have seen that happening again and again at Delbert's shows."[31]

Delbert listened to Don Light, and took the experience lesson to heart, playing small clubs and large festivals around the country, while trying to keep his home life from completely falling apart.

With Donna Sue's admission of her own affair, Delbert was determined to salvage that relationship. "I knew I was being a prick. I had no respect for our relationship. But, for her to do the same thing really hit me hard. She was looking for something I couldn't give her. But at the time, I was determined to try."[32]

With twenty-twenty hindsight, Delbert recognizes that his marriage with Donna was good for about three years. Then he fell back into old habits, and she became more and more disillusioned.

In a 1981 interview with Gary Cartwright for *Rolling Stone*, Delbert says the Muscle Shoals/Capitol session for *The Jealous Kind* was sobering, literally and figuratively. "For years, I had been throwing down a pint of tequila during a set," he recalls. "You're up there on the stage and the adrenalin is pumping, Hell, you know you're wonderful. But I'd listen to the tapes later and think, 'Jesus, is that how I sounded? I wouldn't pay to hear that!'"[33]

Cartwright adds, "Uppers, downers, sunshine, multidimensional herbs, it took a heap of madness to get by. There were times when Delbert was moderately sober, times when he looked through the lights and smoke and read what he saw as disappointment on the faces." Delbert tells Cartwright, "They felt cheated 'cause I wasn't drunk and disgusting."[34]

"I decided I wanted to do this album sober. I wanted to remember doing it. I wanted to be responsible for myself. If they were happy times, I wanted them to be happy for real. If it was a bummer, I wanted to handle it like a grownup. You can only fool yourself for so long," Delbert recalls.[35]

He went into the studio with determination. *The Jealous Kind* did not have a single original song on it. "At the time, I didn't think I had anything strong enough," he says.[36] The Bobby Charles title song kicked off a wide spectrum of cover material. Jerry Williams's "Giving It Up for Your Love," Bobby Osborne's "Going Back to Louisiana," Van Morrison's "Bright Side of the Road," and Al Green's "Take Me to the River," were among the songs that set Delbert back on track, showcasing his versatility and powerful voice, capturing the on-stage energy of what continued to be described as one of the best bar bands in the nation.

Going in to the session, Delbert says, "I knew I was taking in a song that was going to be a hit. It was a song by a friend from Dallas, Jerry Lynn Williams. It had been on his record, *Gone*. I knew the first time I heard it that it was a hit song. I handed it to my producer, Barry Beckett, and said, 'This is our hit.' He listened, and said, 'I think you're right.'"[37]

Delbert, Donna Sue, and Clay moved to Malibu to try to rebuild their relationship. They were married but not happy. She wanted out of Fort Worth. Delbert says that they were trying to rekindle the romance in their life. "She was looking for Paris. But as the saying goes, 'you can't find Paris there if you don't bring it with you,' and we didn't bring it with us."[38]

Delbert talked to Gary Cartwright for the *Rolling Stone* story on the day the moving vans were packing his Fort Worth home to move to California. This time would be different, he was saying, as if saying the words aloud would be convincing enough. This time, California would be different. A far cry from the black painted apartment in Venice. This time, a woman wouldn't run out on him a few minutes before midnight, leaving him with a broken heart and two bottles of cheap wine. This time, no spurned wife would pull a pistol on him.

In 1981, Cartwright wrote, "Forty years teaches a man who he is. Success is something you measure in scar tissue. Fame and fortune are products of luck, but success is something personal and uncompromised, something torn from its socket. If Delbert had been successful ten years ago, when he first tried to make it in L.A., he would probably be dead now. Another legendary burnout. They would probably be making a movie about him, about the ultimate one-night stand, where he lurches onstage with nothing but a can of gasoline and a kitchen match."[39]

"Donna Sue found us a great house on top of Saddle Peak. You could see the San Fernando Valley on one side and the Pacific Coast on the other side. It was wonderful. Malibu had a lot of good things. But the things we wanted to fix didn't get fixed," he admits. "And that was mostly my fault."[40]

On the day that Donna Sue and Clay moved into the Malibu house with the beautiful view, they did it without Delbert. That day, Cartwright adds, "He and the band were playing in Baton Rouge, Louisiana. After twenty-five years on the road, he hardly noticed."[41]

Despite the failed attempt to fix the marriage, something was going right. *The Jealous Kind* was tracking well. The first single, "Giving It Up for Your Love" reached *Billboard*'s Top 10, and spent six months on the charts. It seemed that Delbert was finally on his way to stardom.

James Pennebaker recalls, "Delbert and Donna Sue moved to California briefly after 'Giving It Up for Your Love,' to get away and try to get things back on track. He quit playing as much for a little while to concentrate on her. Donna Sue was from money. She liked to live nice. Delbert finally had a hit and she wanted to get away from all the issues weighing them down in Fort Worth. The band kind of disintegrated. It was a period of about a year or so where we didn't play much beyond the big shows.

"During that short time that they lived in Malibu, it was tough for us not playing that much. For Delbert, trying to get his life together and be a husband and father, and for us, going from playing all the time to coasting without regular work.

"Delbert didn't realize how hard it was for us at that time. We had never made a lot of money when we were out on the road all the time, but it had been steady work. We'd come home from the road and Delbert would pay the boys, pay the bills, put fuel in the vehicles, and he would usually not make anything. He would always just hope to make up for it on the next run.

"I remember once, during that time, when we were playing in New York. It was before cell phones, and I called my wife, Debbie, from the pay phone in the bathroom. Delbert walked in and heard me talking. When I hung up, he asked if I was okay. I said, 'Yeah, I'll be alright. Just talked to Debbie and we are about to get our electricity turned off.'

"Delbert said, 'What do you need for electricity?' I told him we would figure it out. He asked me again. I told him. He walked out of the bathroom and came back with an envelope, handing me twice what I needed, plus my pay for the gig."[42]

Cartwright wrote, "Six months after the album's release, *The Jealous Kind* is still on the charts, and the label is still in business."[43]

That should have been a good sign. Muscle Shoals wanted Delbert to tour Europe. The second Muscle Shoals album, *Plain' from the Heart*, was in the works. Delbert didn't have the time to go to Europe. He needed to head back out on the road to support the new record, to make hay while the sun was shining.

The clubs got bigger, and instead of loading equipment into the back doors of beer joints, he was backing up to loading docks of auditoriums and college concert halls. But, Delbert still wasn't making real money—just enough to keep playing.

CHAPTER 13
"I Want to Love You"
Wendy and the Lost Boys

She just picked me up and dusted me off. She helped me
when I wasn't doing so good, told me I could get my act
together and do better. She gave me a confidence that had
lain dormant my whole life.[1]

—DELBERT McCLINTON

Plain' from the Heart, the second record on Muscle Shoals/Capitol, was vintage Delbert McClinton. Surrounded with lifelong friends and mainstays of his band, Billy Sanders, James Pennebaker, Ernie Durawa, Barry (Frosty) Frost, and Robert Harwell, Delbert went all out on a multifaceted project. This was the natural next step after the top-ten hit with "Giving It Up for Your Love" on *The Jealous Kind*.

In late 1981, just as *Plain' from the Heart* was released, Muscle Shoals Sound had a falling out with Capitol, and yes, the label folded. Capitol cut their losses and moved on. It was another verse of a familiar song, but Delbert went back to doing what he did best, digging in, and playing on the road two hundred and twenty-five nights a year.

By now, Delbert and Donna Sue were back in Fort Worth. They had pretty much given up on salvaging anything from their marriage, but neither had the energy to make the move.

During this low period in his life, Delbert was playing in New York regularly. He had met Wendy Goldstein and run into her a few times. She was a news producer for NBC radio and television. Delbert was still coasting on the traction of "Giving It Up for Your Love." He and Bonnie Raitt were opening shows for Willie Nelson.[2]

Delbert and Wendy have somewhat different stories regarding when and where they first met. "I had been introduced to Delbert before the first night he played *Saturday Night Live*. I met him through a mutual friend when he played in New York at the Lone Star Café in 1979, and again at the Bottom Line," she recalls. "The first time he played *Saturday Night Live* [*SNL*], I went with a friend, since I worked two floors below *SNL*. I already loved Delbert's music, and I liked him. I kept up with him. We became friends. They were going to be playing in Philly and then in Washington."

She adds, "My good friend, Joan Scarangello, was also doing radio for NBC in Washington, and I had been wanting to go down and see her. So, I caught a ride with Delbert and the band on the bus."[3]

Delbert's blue eyes twinkle as he remembers, "We decided to take a nap on the bus. We spooned all the way to DC And here we are, today."[4]

Despite any uncertainty about when their relationship started, Delbert credits Wendy for the success he has amassed. "She took a look at everything I had done, and what I should have done, and what I wanted to do. Then she raked it all up into a pile and turned it into something."[5]

Their personal and professional partnership is based on a combination of passion, talent, astute business skills, a strong work ethic, and a deep love for each other. The music that has been central to their lives for more than three decades is second to their mutual respect for one another. Delbert and others close to the couple are quick to credit Wendy for helping transform him from that road-weary musician struggling to break even on the road, to his current level of critical and commercial success.

Delbert often refers to Wendy as "The Fixer," not only for straightening out his business affairs, but also for taking care of his extended family. She has expended a tremendous amount of time and energy resolving problems with the Internal Revenue Service (IRS) and various tax accounting firms on behalf of Delbert, dealing with health insurance and pension programs for his parents, serving as an academic guidance counselor for his then high-school-aged son, Clay, and doing what she could for Delbert's older son, Monty.

Wendy never had thoughts of a career in the music industry. Born in New York City to Martin and Evelyn Goldstein, she grew up in a completely different world from Delbert's Texas childhood.

"My dad was a medical engineer for the United States Government Department of Defense. It was my understanding that he wrote specs for X-ray machines and procured them for use in the field during the Vietnam War. My dad had taken a job with the government when most of his friends went to medical school. He was working on a project with the military hospital in San Antonio in 1968, and I got to fly with him to Texas, and spend the day at HemisFair in San Antonio. That was probably the only time in my childhood that Texas even crossed my mind."[6]

Wendy's mother worked in real estate or other professional jobs throughout Wendy's childhood. "I spent most of my childhood on Long Island and my father worked in Brooklyn. We moved from New York to South Jersey when I was twelve," she recalls. "Secretary of Defense Robert McNamara wanted to move his job to Philadelphia. Education was very important to my parents, so they looked for the best school district in the area that they could find."[7]

Cherry Hill School District in Camden County (New Jersey) was one of the top three districts in the country in 1965, so the Goldsteins moved to Camden County where Wendy and her older sister, Arline, would grow up.

Wendy was an aspiring journalist. "I was an editor of our school newspaper in high school. We would read the *New York Times* in class. Robert B. Semple Jr. was the White House correspondent for the *Times*. When I graduated in 1971, I was accepted at George Washington University in DC. As soon as I moved to Washington, I called Robert B. Semple and asked him to lunch in exchange for some advice. We went to lunch and he said, 'Major in whatever you want, just don't major in journalism. You'll bring so much more to the job.'"[8]

Wendy took his advice and majored in biology, with an emphasis in botany. The summer after her junior year in college, Wendy's friend, Sherry Coben, helped her get a summer job at KYW-TV in Philadelphia, where she had the opportunity to work with up-and-coming national journalists Andrea Mitchell and Jessica

Savitch. This was a good starter job, and she could have stayed at KYW, but Wendy knew she needed to finish college. So, in the fall of 1974, Wendy went back to George Washington and got a job at WRC-TV in DC, one of NBC's flagship stations. She soon moved to WRC Radio, which was starting News and Information Service (NIS), an experiment by NBC to do all news all the time.

"In 1978, Jim Farley came down from NBC, and invited me to go up to New York City and work vacation relief at the NBC radio network. That was what I was doing when I met Delbert the first time. I worked there for four years as a writer, editor, and producer. Another vice president asked me to come work TV with the affiliates, writing and editing these new forty-second news-breaks for Jessica Savitch, Edwin Newman, Chuck Scarborough, Connie Chung, and others. I was working with one of my favorite anchors, Edwin Newman. He was the ultimate writer. I was so humbled writing for him. I learned so much from him. I went on to produce the evening feeds for affiliates, sending them weather, sports, and any breaking news," she said, describing any young journalist's dream trajectory to a long and successful career.

"I really liked Delbert. I loved his music. Whenever he played in New York, I would go out and see him. I would get off work at eleven at night, and my good friend, Doc Pomus, would take me to his shows. Doc was a safe date," she remembers fondly.[9]

Doc was an award-winning blues singer and songwriter, stricken with polio as a child, and in later life, was confined to a wheelchair due to post-polio syndrome. He is best known for writing "Save the Last Dance for Me," "Viva Las Vegas," "This Magic Moment," "A Teenager in Love," "Suspicion," and countless other American classics.[10] He was also a great fan, friend, and supporter of Delbert McClinton.

Delbert recalls, "Malibu didn't do anything to rebuild my marriage, but we weren't really trying, and eventually, Donna Sue wanted to move back to Fort Worth. She bought a little house in Arlington Heights, and completely redid it. She could have been an interior designer. She had some of her mother's gorgeous furniture and we had this beautiful living room with a mirrored wall on one side. Just about the time she finished decorating the house, we completely fell apart."[11]

Delbert says in early 1984, the couple made one fruitless, last-ditch effort—a trip to a romantic Caribbean island where Donna Sue told him she wanted a divorce. There was nothing left. They came home and she moved out with Clay and all of her furniture, leaving him with a big empty house. The couple agreed to share custody of nearly ten-year-old Clay.

"It wasn't even really sad. It was better for both of us and we knew it. So, I went out and bought a cane plant like the kind that grow in the jungle, and a six-foot baby grand piano. That was all I had in the living room. I sat down at that piano and started writing songs. The first song I wrote on that piano was 'I Want to Love You,' for Wendy," he says.[12]

> *I want to love you,*
> *Take you in my arms and love you*
> *It's not just because you're always on my mind,*
> *With me all the time*
> *I just want to love you*
> *I want to kiss you,*
> *Girl, and let you know I miss you*
> *I'm having feelings like I've never had before,*
> *And all I want is more*
> *I just want to love you*
> *Baby, are you ready to stop wasting time?*
> *Would it blind you if I let my love light shine?*
> *I want to trust you,*
> *Turn my feelings over to you*
> *Let you see the frightened child inside of me,*
> *How frail a man can be*
> *I just want to love you*
> *Baby, are you ready to stop wasting time?*
> *Would it blind you if I let my love light shine?*
> *I want to kiss you,*
> *Girl, and let you know I miss you*
> *I'm having feelings like I've never had before,*
> *And all I want is more*
> *I just want to love you.*[13]

Delbert spent all the time he could with Wendy. She was working in New York, and he was playing regularly in the city and up and down the East Coast. Delbert's booking agent of more than three decades, David Hickey, says, "When I started working with Delbert, he was still married to Donna Sue, but his marriage was falling apart. The road was an escape. He wanted to play all he could just to avoid all the drama at home. Then one day he said, 'If you ever need to find me, call this number,' and gave me a 212 [area code] phone number in New York. It was Wendy's. She was working for NBC, and Delbert started wanting to play in New York all the time. During those days, we made a lot of stops at the Lone Star Café and DC and up and down the East Coast."[14]

What was it about Wendy that set her apart from the countless, nameless women he had met on the road? Delbert explains, "She had a lot of class. Wendy is very classy and so smart. And smart women are so fucking sexy. Socrates said, 'Speak so that I may see thee.' That says it all. You can see a beautiful woman, and she opens her mouth and it goes downhill. But the first time Wendy spoke and I 'saw thee,' I fell in love with her immediately."

He adds, "But the most amazing part was that she fell in love with me. She obviously knew better."[15]

Wendy Goldstein was about to change Delbert McClinton's life in ways he couldn't imagine. It was appropriate that she came into his world during the "Giving It Up for Your Love" point of his career because she did just that. "Leaving NBC to live with Delbert was the biggest gamble I ever took," she admits.[16]

Through the next few years, Delbert brought his mother, Vivian, to New York for her first tour of the city, and introduced her to Wendy's world. Wendy recalls, "We took Vivian on a grand tour. I had press [license] plates, so we could park anywhere, and we took her everywhere. We have pictures of her riding the subway and the ferry and seeing the Empire State Building. I took her to NBC, and television star Buddy Ebsen was in the lobby. That was exciting for her. Then we went up to the newsroom, and Roger Mudd was getting ready to do *Newsbreak*. We walked in as they were putting makeup on him. He looked up at Delbert's mom and deadpanned, 'Don't tell anybody they do this!' Delbert's mother had the time of her life and talked about it for years."[17]

On June 30, 1985, this New York native of Jewish descent, Wendy Goldstein, moved to Cowtown. "We could not bear to continue this long-distance relationship. I was moving in with Delbert. Monty and a friend went to New York to drive my car down to Texas, and a moving van had loaded my furniture and most of my belongings. I had a suitcase and most of my clothes with me," she recalls.

Her employers and friends questioned her judgment but gave her the benefit of the doubt. "My dad asked my best friend, Debbie Hessert, if I knew what I was doing. She told him that I was going to be okay," Wendy says. "Debbie said, 'Wendy can always come back. She knows that.'"[18]

In fact, her boss at NBC would not accept her resignation. Instead, she gave her a twelve-month leave of absence, and assured her that she could come back if she changed her mind.

On that hot and humid summer Sunday, Wendy Goldstein sat on the curb at the Dallas-Fort Worth International Airport, waiting for Herman and Vivian McClinton to pick her up. Delbert was in Montana and would not be home for another week.

"I was sitting on the curb with all of my luggage in this miserable heat, watching for Delbert's parents," Wendy recalls. "All around me, I was hearing all of these people say, 'Baa. Baa. Baa.' I am thinking, 'God, these people are talking like sheep!' before I realized that was how they were saying 'Goodbye,' to one another. Herman and Vivian finally found me and took me home to Delbert's house. I spent a week trying to understand Fort Worth before Delbert got home."[19]

She confesses that Fort Worth was like another country. "I wanted to buy a futon. I wanted sushi. I had lived on sushi in New York. No one had heard of futons and they didn't have sushi in Fort Worth. How was I going to live here? But Vivian soon introduced me to chicken fried steak and other Texas cuisine. And I love her chicken fried steak!"[20]

When Delbert finally got home from Montana, Wendy had decorated the living room with a big banner across the mirrored wall that said, "Welcome home, Bear Bait!" And so their life together began.

"Wendy is a fast learner," says David Hickey. "She stepped in and got feedback from Delbert and me, and figured out the touring business and the record business. I had been doing the booking and day-to-day management of finding cheap hotels, sending the newspapers advances, setting up radio interviews. Wendy picked it up pretty fast and learned how the touring business worked by being there and going out on the road with the band and keeping an eye on things."[21]

Longtime band member James Pennebaker elaborates on this period in the singer's career. "Wendy came along at the right time and saved Delbert's life. There is no doubt about it. We were pushing it as far as we could. We played hard and then we played harder. The late '70s into the mid '80s were the cocaine decade in this country. When coke was not enough, someone handed us something else. We did everything we could to keep going. Wendy changed all that. She saved Delbert's life. She moved to Fort Worth to live with him, leaving a great job in New York. She came on the road with the band. She loved him so much. She did it to save his life. She basically said, 'That shit's gonna stop or I'm out of here.' And if she hadn't been there then, we wouldn't be here now. I honestly believe she is responsible for saving his life—and mine, too."[22]

David Hickey adds, "Coke was just part of the culture of the time. The work was so intense. And Delbert ran with some really rough characters back then. Travel was hard. There was no luxury on the road. Delbert had a bus early on, but it wasn't much of a step up from a pickup and a trailer. More often than not, that old bus would break down or the air-conditioning would go out or something. All the gigs were getting played, but it was not easy. If you drank, you had to do blow to get through the night."[23]

He says, "Those Lone Star Café shows were out of control. I went out a few times with them. I sat out on the fire escape of the Lone Star Café and did blow with John Belushi. It was the norm. People were coming out of the woodwork trying to give it to you. And you would come to expect it. Wendy absolutely cleaned all that up when she got involved in Delbert's life. She probably did save his life."[24]

Changes in tax laws and a lack of sound tax advice had caused Delbert and several other Texas musicians serious headaches with the IRS during the early 1980s. Those years are often overlooked because without a major label, Delbert did not receive much national attention, but he was tearing up the highways and trying to pay the bills.

Wendy explains that Delbert had an accountant in Austin: "He had set up these deductions every year, some kind of depreciation, and it wasn't valid. It had something to do with a live video series. Joe Ely was caught up in it too, as well as several other musicians. This guy was taking the deduction every year to the tune of something like thirty-six grand a year, and finally, Delbert was audited. The IRS hit him with this. The accountant knew something was up all along. He said to me early on that he knew they probably weren't going to allow it, but that because they hadn't said no, he kept taking it. The firm had an umbrella insurance policy that ended up paying a portion of the debt the IRS wanted from Delbert.

"I had started taking care of Delbert's bills right after I moved to Fort Worth. Until then, Delbert was sending all the bills to an Austin accountant. I said, 'Somebody's got to pay the bills and you are not going to keep sending them to Austin.' A few months later, that accountant called and said, 'I think Wendy can handle all of this,' and basically dumped all of Delbert's finances into our laps. Shortly after that, we were audited and got the big bill from the IRS.

"This debt was Delbert's and Donna Sue's. Delbert's house was paid for, and we eventually had to sell it, and pay the IRS that money. Oil had tanked, so Donna Sue didn't have any money. I did all this work and got a good lawyer who could help us. The amount kept going up because of interest and penalties. But ultimately, our attorney, Paul Buchanan, got it knocked down to a quarter of a million dollars. We were paying them as much as we could, but it was not fast enough.

"And the IRS would threaten us. They would send these notices, saying that they were coming to the gig and taking the money at the door, and we would say we just wouldn't play. We had to pay the band. We couldn't go and let the IRS take all the money because some of that money belonged to the band. And one IRS agent who was so crazy would call Paul Buchanan. It was before cell phones, so this guy would pull his car over and use a pay phone and say 'I just heard a Delbert McClinton song on the radio. How much is he getting paid for that?' They were attaching anything they could attach. It was really upsetting.

"Delbert was on my bank account so he could cash checks for me, and the IRS took some of my money. That was so wrong. And that's why we couldn't get married. I was paying the tax bill for Delbert and Donna Sue. They were taking some of Donna Sue's oil royalties, which didn't amount to much at that time, and they attached some of Delbert's song royalties, but they couldn't get much of that just because they couldn't find it. But, it was frightening.

"Someone from my bank called one time and said, 'The IRS was in here and they had the name wrong or the Social Security number wrong so they didn't get the funds, but they've been here for your money.' I closed the account. It was probably totally illegal for them to tell me. And that was a business account, the account that paid everybody's paychecks. We were doing everything we could do to pay that debt, but they kept threatening."[25]

To say that the mid-1980s were a struggle would be an understatement. Delbert was not recording. However, he was playing dives, auditoriums, festivals, and concert halls across the nation, building on that road warrior reputation.

"Some people ask me about all the places I have seen while on the road," Delbert says, "But honestly, we go from back door to back door. I have seen a lot of back doors of clubs, and a lot of hotel rooms that all start to look alike, but as far as seeing the sights, I have not really seen much beyond the window of the bus."[26]

And as far as that time being called Delbert's Lost Years, he explains, "I wasn't lost. I know right where I was. I was working for the IRS. They decided that I owed them several hundred thousand dollars. So, a lot of that time, I was back to playing every night, and splitting that between the band members and paying for gas, and a hotel room. I never thought of doing anything else. We always managed to get to the next gig, and after a while, things started to pick up speed."[27]

"Wendy came along and made all the difference in my life. I

needed somebody to believe in me. Until she came along, there wasn't anybody who believed in me but me. I don't think I ever really felt good about myself before Wendy," he says.[28]

Delbert's dad had been diagnosed with Parkinson's disease, and had to take early retirement from the railroad. Vivian had retired from styling hair in her Fort Worth beauty shop, to take care of Herman. Delbert and Wendy were living in Fort Worth when they were home, and spending a lot of time together on the road. Monty and Clay were doing well, and it seemed that Delbert was finally getting a grip on the balancing act between home and the road.

CHAPTER 14
"Take it Easy"
The Worst of Times

I really never understood how to be in love until I met Wendy. We were just meant to be together. There is no doubt that she is the best thing that ever happened to me.

—DELBERT McCLINTON[1]

By 1986, Wendy had taken on the full-time, day-to-day management role, something Delbert had never really had. She was traveling with the band, and handling the day-to-day business. She cashed in her NBC retirement, bought a GMC 4104 school bus for fifteen thousand dollars, and spent another fifteen thousand dollars customizing it. Finally, Delbert had a decent and, for the most part, reliable bus that would stand up to the rigors of the road.

This was the year that Delbert and Wendy faced their own mortality for the first time. Wendy recalls that Delbert was having severe headaches and was seeing a neurologist in Fort Worth. His mother, Vivian, who had been healthy her entire life, lost forty pounds in a matter of weeks. Delbert mentioned it to his neurologist, who asked to see her, and said he would work with her until they figured out what it was. She was diagnosed with ovarian cancer, and Vivian began chemotherapy.

Wendy's older sister, Arline Strongin, was diagnosed with type 2 diabetes. The Goldsteins were in New Jersey helping Arline through a tumultuous divorce. Arline was under a lot of stress. Suddenly, she began slurring her words. She was rushed to the hospital where she was diagnosed with type 2 diabetes, and a blood sugar level of 685, which should have been deadly. Wendy went up to New Jersey to check on her sister. While doctors were trying to get Arline's blood chemistry stabilized, Evelyn Goldstein discovered a lump the size of a pencil eraser in her breast, and was admitted to the same hospital.

Wendy recalls, "My mother didn't want to upset Arline with the news that she, too, was in the hospital, so we tried to keep it a secret. But in my family, we can't keep secrets, so it came out sooner rather than later."[2]

Arline was released from the hospital with a new health regimen, and Evelyn and Martin Goldstein went back home to Florida for her cancer treatment.

Wendy and Delbert were trying to keep things going musically, while dividing time between the two sets of parents. Evelyn had a lumpectomy and radiation, and was deemed cancer free and doing well; but Vivian struggled through surgery and chemotherapy before beginning to feel like her old self again. Wendy says, "She wore wigs and was as lively as ever. We were able to bury our heads in the sand and sort of forgot she was so sick. It was rough, but the chemo did give her two more years."[3]

Life rocked along fairly smoothly, despite the Internal Revenue Service (IRS) and their mothers' health issues into 1987. In 1986, Wendy had sold her co-op in New York, and was required to reinvest the proceeds of the sale within eighteen months to avoid being taxed on the income. She purchased a townhouse in Nashville with plans to use it as a second home. However, family obligations and Delbert's rigorous touring schedule didn't allow that. So, the townhouse sat vacant.

Early in 1987, Arline's divorce was final. She decided to leave New Jersey and move to Florida, to start a new life and to be close to her parents. Evelyn had flown to New Jersey to help Arline drive to Florida. Near Washington, DC, their car was slammed into by a truck. A medical helicopter happened to be flying overhead at the time. The crew saw the accident happen and immediately landed to offer help, extracting Evelyn from the car and flying her to the nearby trauma hospital.

Wendy was traveling with the band. She had the bus drop her at the nearest airport and took the first flight to Washington. Evelyn had a severe head injury, was in a coma, and her pelvis had been broken in three places. One of Wendy's university biology professors, Dr. Kittie Parker, had been like a second mother. Wendy called her mentor as she awaited her flight. She says, "Dr. Parker offered me a place to stay and the use of her car. In the wreck, my sister's dog had gotten out of the car and run away. We searched the area and found her dog at the animal shelter. My father and I stayed at my friend's house for days. And I was at the hospital when my mother came out of her coma."[4]

Evelyn wanted to go home to Florida to get the prescribed inpatient rehabilitation (rehab). During the months that she was in rehab, Martin drove forty-five minutes each way twice a day to see her at the facility. She was an invalid. It was evident that she was not going to get better. She wanted to go home. Wendy adds, "My father was a saint. He took her home and took care of her for nearly eleven years, until she died in 1997."[5]

Early in 1988, Wendy gave Delbert a blank journal, and they decided to take turns writing in it, chronicling their life. Little did they know that they would come to call this the worst year in their lives together. In February, Vivian went into the hospital with pneumonia. While she was in the hospital, they discovered that her ovarian cancer was becoming more aggressive. The IRS was still knocking at the door, and Wendy and Delbert were trying to move to the next step in his career.

Wendy writes in the journal, *Delbert realizes how important it is to be in Nashville. As we try to get our lives in order and try to deal with our roles as caretakers to the world, I am trying to cope with a day of mixed guilt feelings. We need to be in a minimum of four cities. I choose Nashville to work on US. I believe we'll be of more use to others if we are doing better. And time is getting short.*[6]

In a happier journal entry she writes, *We vacationed with the Turlingtons on March 2–5 in Cancun. It was great. They are two of the nicest people ever.*[7]

Gary and Sandra Turlington are longtime Delbert fans and close friends from Lillington, North Carolina. Gary tells the story of the first time he saw Delbert play on *Austin City Limits* in 1976. He was flipping the channels and saw this harmonica player-singer who was fantastic, and his band was hot. Gary waited until they rolled the credits at the end of the show: Delbert McClinton and the list of band members, and Gatemouth Brown and the list of band members. Having no idea who was who, and with no Internet back in the day, Gary decided Gatemouth sounded more like a name for a harmonica player, so he went to the record store and ordered every Gatemouth Brown record he could get. When he got the records, he realized he had the names switched.[8]

Gary and Sandra began going out to all of Delbert's shows when he was in North Carolina, and they soon became friends. That vacation was the first of many they would take together, and today, Gary and Wendy are business partners, and the Turling-tons and McClintons are close friends.[9]

On March 10, 1988, Wendy writes in the journal: *It's official. Dr. Hoffman says I'm in the family way. The due date will be November 16. I want this baby so badly . . . . I wish I could tell the world. But I'm afraid to jinx it. I'm being really good. I think Delbert is feeling good about it. He understands why I need a child of my own. Hope it's a girl, but I really don't care.*[10]

On April 30, Delbert writes, *Wendy and I are going to tell every-one about the baby next week. My mom has been feeling great for the last three weeks.*[11]

When her cancer returned, Vivian opted out of the third round of chemo. She decided to take her chances and enjoy the quality of life that remained. Delbert stayed out on the road while Wendy cut back on her bus traveling. She continued to manage the band from the home office and keep the wheels rolling, while booking agent David Hickey kept the calendar filled.

In late May, Delbert writes in his journal from Tampa, Florida, *Reminds me of the first time I played in Fla. It was Billy, Ronnie Kelly and Jerry Foster and me and Charlie [Stevens]. We drove down to Orlando in Jerry Conditt's borrowed 1962 Cadillac and a U-Haul. But that's all another story.*[12]

The highs and lows of their year fill the pages. Band personnel changes, good nights on the road, full moons, ready to be home with Wendy, doodles, and notes are jotted in the book from the back of the bus.

Life for Delbert was finally settling into a good routine. Every-thing was going smoothly. In June, Delbert writes, *Talked to Monty yesterday. He is so excited about his job and it makes me feel good for him. Clay made fudge on his own this week and he's pretty proud of himself. He even called his grandmother without me asking to ask her if she wanted some fudge.*[13]

Through the end of June, Delbert laments the trouble he was having with one of his guitar players. He was a great musician but not a good fit in the band. The heat of the summer brings with it some heated nights on the road. Over the course of a couple of weeks, Delbert writes, *BC and I locked horns again tonight . . . . Fired BC today. He is history and I've never been so glad to be through having to deal with someone in all my days . . . . We played without BC for the first time last night. I sure am going to miss the way he plays.*[14]

And the summer rolls on. On July 10, Delbert and Wendy went to Maui for a week before they came home to go back out on the road for three weeks. David Hickey continued to book coast-to-coast tours. He says, "I know those long stretches were hard. The band got tired, Delbert got tired. The band would start complaining about their hotel rooms, and why they have to have a night off, and why they have to drive so far. It's more than just playing the shows. There is a lot of wear and tear that goes on behind the scenes even in the best of times."[15]

Delbert writes that he is worried about his mom and dad, but that Wendy's pregnancy is going well; he's feeling good, his weight is down, and the bus is running great. Across the bottom of the page, he scrawls, *These things are good!*[16]

Delbert and the band played an East Coast tour at the end of that July. Wendy went along for this stretch for the chance to stop off and visit her old friend, Douga Miriam, in Fairfax, Virginia. Spending the night at Douga's house, Wendy's water broke. Douga rushed her to the hospital in Fairfax.

Delbert had played the night before in Greensboro, North Carolina. He writes in the journal at 4:00 in the morning on Thursday, July 28, *It looks like we will lose the baby. She is okay but understandably upset. She's waiting for a specialist to come. I talked to a doctor at the hospital and she didn't give much hope. I'm 47 years old and finally got my little girl and then this. I'm so goddamned angry I don't know what to do. You just can't trust being happy.*[17]

On Friday, Delbert writes, *Just got off the plane in DC. Taking a cab to hospital where Wendy is. Doctors will induce labor today and we will lose our little girl. I haven't told my mom and dad yet. But I will later today. Will fly back to Raleigh, NC tomorrow to finish out the week and come back here to take Wendy home. This is a sad day, and I feel very tired and old.*[18]

Wendy says, "The baby was at about twenty-four weeks. One of the nurses explained to me that, *if* she were to survive, there was an eighty-five percent chance that the baby would now have cerebral palsy. Delbert arrived and they induced labor, thinking it would take quite a while. No one was checking on us, and Delbert kept going out in the hall and telling the nurses to come check on me. It was going much faster than they thought. In three hours, she was born."[19]

Wendy writes in the journal, *Casey Cameron Goldstein McClinton came into the world today. It was 3:33 when she arrived. She weighed 1 lb, 8–1/2 oz. She was 12–1/2 inches long. She died at 4:55 pm. She was so pretty with my ears and Delbert's mouth and my nose and somebody's great legs . . . . Delbert got to see her while she was alive. I was not ready yet. Delbert held her and kissed her on her head. I hope she knows how loved she is. We did natural childbirth, which is quite painful, but I'd do it again if I had no other way to have a baby. We will try again and I'll try to stay in bed the whole time.*[20]

Heartbroken, but resilient, Wendy and Delbert pushed forward. They made arrangements to have the baby cremated. And Wendy insisted he go back out on the road and play the show the following night. "It was our biggest money show for that tour. My friend was helping me. He needed to work," she recalls.[21]

Wendy was released from the hospital the next day and flew home alone to Fort Worth. Delbert's parents met her at the airport. Their caregiver drove them home. "I felt like such a loser," Wendy admits. "The doctors had given Vivian a timeframe and she lived three months longer than that. When we had told her about me being pregnant, she seemed to rally. There was something psychological about it. People who are dying will push themselves to live for a significant event. She wanted to live to see the baby. And now, I had lost the baby."[22]

Delbert finished the series of shows on Sunday night in Myrtle Beach, South Carolina, and flew home, leaving the band to come home on the bus. He writes, *This has been a tough one, but Wendy is a tough monkey and so am I. We will try to get pregnant again in February. We both kinda want a November baby.*[23]

A week later, Wendy writes, *8-8-88, a day of magic numbers. Unfortunately, Delbert spent it buying burial plots, signing wills and wrestling with a bad tooth and nicotine jones. I got off easy with postpartum blues.*[24]

Delbert was also struggling with Donna Sue. She didn't want Delbert, but she didn't want Wendy to have him either. She was dating, but she wasn't helping to make life easier for Delbert, or for Wendy.

On August 10, 1988, Wendy writes, *Casey's cremains arrived today. The mailman was so chipper as he delivered his package of death. "Just sign here," he said. We put the ashes in a silk pouch. Vivian has asked that we put the ashes in her arms when she dies. It's such a perfect, yet sad answer. Dr. Hoffman said we're due for things to turn around. I hope so. All we seem to get is more and more bad news. Delbert's aunt Billie Rae called Vivian last night and said the doctor told her she has three months to live. Lung cancer.*[25]

A week later, Delbert took his parents to see their gravesites at the Laurel Land Memorial Park in Fort Worth. He writes, *They wanted to see the spot we picked. I walked with them, one on each arm, my dad stumbling forward, my mom moving slow. She was holding me back, he was pulling me forward.*[26]

Wendy and Delbert were working to get their lives back on track after the loss of the baby, working on his career, and helping with his mother. She writes, *My mom has been doing pretty well. My dad went in the hospital the same week I was recovering. It was hard on us both. Mom has some skin irritations but her spirits are so much better, and she is pretty funny. Delbert's mom is not doing as well. The pain and nausea just get worse and worse. The doctor has nagged us to call Hospice for some help. They are finally going to come tomorrow.*[27]

Delbert's mother continued to decline. In early October, they were notified that Herman's long-term health insurance had run out. It had a one-million-dollar cap per person, and they had reached that with Herman's home health care. Wendy said, "Herman had caregivers, and as Vivian got worse, they were using the caregivers for both she and Herman, but still filing only under Herman. I talked to the insurance people and explained what had happened. They reimbursed the account for several hundred thousand dollars and we were able to continue with the caregivers for both of them for the rest of their lives."[28]

Delbert says, "Wendy has always been the fixer. Like so many other times, I don't know what I would have done without her. She can work magic and make things happen."[29]

As October ended, Wendy, and Delbert, when he was home, was staying at Herman and Vivian's house. Vivian was declining. Delbert writes about the inevitable passing of his mother in detail, and wonders how Herman will take it. They had always assumed that Herman would go first, with his chronic and progressive Parkinson's disease. As things get worse, Delbert depends on Wendy more than ever. Through career chaos, family challenges, heartbreak, and health issues, their relationship continued to grow stronger.[30]

Delbert's life on the road continued to be rigorous but steady. His comments in the journal had become one-line chronicles of day-to-day life, rather than essays and thoughts: *The bus is running good. I think we found the oil leak in a pressure hose. I had to have a new clutch put in last month because that idiot who drove for us for a while in July ruined the last one. I guess we are lucky he didn't kill us all.*[31]

On the last day of October, Delbert writes from Richmond, Virginia, that his mother is very close to death: *I really don't feel like writing, but thought it somehow important to continue to log the progress of this tragedy. I'm okay and the band is sounding good.*[32]

He continues entries in the journal with more bad news of 1988: *My Aunt Billie Rae died yesterday. She was suffering so much that I'm happy it's over for her.*[33]

Billie Rae had been the first person to believe in Delbert's talent. She had been the one who had dragged him out to the talent show in Florida back in 1957. She had introduced him to an eclectic variety of musical styles that he still loves today.

Vivian was soon to join her sister. On Monday, November 28, Delbert writes, *My mother died tonight at 7:30 p.m.*[34]; followed by a brief note on December 1: *We buried my mother at 10 a.m.*[35]

The silk bag of little Casey's cremains was not buried with Vivian. In the last days, as the morphine doses grew stronger, Vivian began having drug-induced nightmares about being buried with the baby's ashes. Wendy and Delbert decided that would not be a good idea. Today, they still have the small bag of ashes.[36]

Delbert and Wendy helped Herman move into a smaller apartment in Fort Worth. And things began to turn around. Delbert writes that someone in Richmond wanted to fly Delbert out to play a private party. He declined the offer, wanting to stay close to his dad through this transition. David Hickey called back and said that money was no object, and Delbert told them ten thousand dollars plus expenses. The man accepted, and Delbert writes in his journal two days later: *I am heading back to Texas with $10,680 in my pocket, that includes airfare. Just as I was about to board the plane, the girl behind the check in desk told me that there was one seat left in First Class, and if I wanted it, she would change my ticket and give it to me. She said she and her husband were fans, and they always came out when I played Richmond. I took her name and number, promised to have them as my guests next time we are in Richmond.*[37]

1988 ended with little fanfare. Their lives had changed dramatically, and Delbert and Wendy were both glad the year was over; 1989 was sure to be better.

CHAPTER 15
"Good Man, Good Woman"
Making It Work

Bonnie [Raitt] and I have been friends for a long time. We played a lot of shows together and always talked about making a record together. She has it all in one package: a tiny woman with great big balls, who can play the hell out of that slide guitar. She had just won five Grammys and was on top of the heap. She called and said she found a song for us to do. She's a good woman.

—DELBERT McCLINTON[1]

The year 1989 proved to be a major turning point in Delbert's career. He had filmed another show for *Austin City Limits* in the fall of 1988. Wendy had written: *Sandra and Gary Turlington went with us and Delbert was spectacular. We were all so proud. He wore a new charcoal silk suit that made him look so sexy. I understand that the superintendent of Austin schools was there, and Lee Atwater, [George H. W.] Bush's campaign manager was there. What a trip!*[2]

1988 was a presidential election year. That November, George H. W. Bush had defeated Michael Dukakis. Plans were made for the inaugural celebration. Atwater was a huge blues fan and was putting an all-star blues revue together. He invited Delbert to be a part of it.

Wendy said that they were torn about accepting the invitation, generally wanting to stay out of politics in public. But B. B. King, one of most apolitical artists of the time, once said, "If the president invites you to the White House, you go, no matter whether you like him or not."[3]

"I called Bonnie [Raitt] to ask her advice," Wendy says. "Bonnie was, to me, someone who was very politically knowledgeable, sensible, and intelligent, and I really wanted her opinion. Bonnie had just had shoulder surgery, so it was a little while before she called me back. By then, I don't think I even bothered her with it. We talked about the surgery, and that she was trying not to take the pain pills because she was glad to be sober, and my question just faded away. I think we had already decided to accept the invitation as a once-in-a-lifetime opportunity, politics aside."[4]

Early in January 1989, Delbert and Wendy sold the house in Fort Worth to give the money to the Internal Revenue Service, with plans to move to Nashville when they returned from the inauguration.

As they were preparing to leave for Washington, DC, they received word that Delbert's first wife, Sandra Sue, had died unexpectedly. She had gone into the hospital for routine sinus surgery, and died of a brain aneurysm during the procedure. Her funeral was to be in Fort Worth on the day of the inaugural event.

Delbert was torn. Should he go to DC, or should he be at the funeral of his former wife and first son's mother? He spoke with Sandra Sue's parents, and they encouraged him to perform at the event. They were proud for him and that he had been asked to play.[5]

The Red, White and Blues Ball was a black-tie, who's who of rhythm and blues artists, and one of the largest events in this genre ever assembled. Along with Delbert, the show featured Etta James, Percy Sledge, Koko Taylor, Stevie Ray Vaughan, Willie Dixon, Bo Diddley, Joe Cocker, Albert Collins, Ron Wood, and more. Delbert's longtime saxophone player, Don Wise, was in the all-star backup band. Don recalls: "I thought I had played just about everywhere, but this was an unusual situation for all of us. I'd never seen so many legendary musicians in one room. And they had short-haired guys in grey suits checking us constantly, with dogs sniffing our cases and equipment. Most of us were familiar with everyone's music. But, there was a trumpet player from another band who had no idea of any of the music beyond his own band's. We didn't really have time to rehearse together beyond a brief sound check. So, while everyone was out partying the night before, I stayed locked up in my hotel room all night writing out trumpet parts, and being mad as hell!

"But when it was time for the show, the music transcended everything and it was such an experience. There were all these great musicians that we normally would not see because we were always crossing paths out on the road, but never in the same place.

"The funniest thing that happened on that gig was when Donald 'Duck' Dunn, the bass player for Booker T and the MGs, got backstage the night of the show and asked, 'Where's the beer?' He told one of those suit guys with the dogs, 'We need some beer back here.' The suit immediately said, 'There will be no beer backstage!' The room got quiet. Then Duck said, 'No beer, no Duck.'

"It would be hard to imagine that rhythm and blues show without a bass player, and within two minutes, we had beer backstage!"[6]

Delbert says the inauguration was kind of a blur. In some ways, it was just another gig, but in other ways, it was a show of a lifetime. Music critic Bob Putignano later reviews the *Celebration of the Blues and Soul: The 1989 Inaugural Concert* DVD:

> Delbert McClinton performs four songs [on the DVD] starting with the jumping and bluesy "Just a Little Bit." Delbert has several members of his own band on board, most notably Don Wise's sax and keyboardist Nick Connolly. But even though Albert Collins and Steve Cropper are in this band, Delbert calls out twice to Wise for not one but two blistering sax solos. The funky "Standing On Shaky Ground" is next where it's obvious Collins is having a ball with tasty guitar fills, but Wise's sax fires twice again. Delbert's vocals are also roaring and he is in total control as a seasoned bandleader.[7]

Delbert and Wendy returned to Fort Worth. This would be the last time they would call Cowtown home. On January 31, 1989, they moved to the townhome in Nashville because, as he explains, "I needed that songwriter's community. I had never done much cowriting before, and Nashville is a really creative place to be. The way I look at it, if you're going to pick cotton, you have to go to the cotton patch."[8]

Wendy says, "The movers unloaded the boxes on January 31,

and we hit the road on February 1, leaving the house filled with unpacked boxes."[9]

Delbert writes: *We were in Nashville long enough to receive our things from the movers, and then we left for a month on the road . . . . Monty will be out with us for a week. I thought it would do him some good to get away for a few days. It's been quite a blow for him since Sue died.*[10]

The tour goes well, but not without the usual bumps in the road. Don Wise remembers: "We were somewhere in the middle of the country, heading to Seattle, during one of the biggest winter storms on record, when the bus broke down. Six of us got off the bus and attempted to push it to get it started, to no avail. We had some shows between wherever we were and the big show in Seattle.

"Wendy did some magic, and we felt like we were in a scene from the movie, *Planes, Trains and Automobiles.* The bus got towed into the next big town. Our driver stayed with the bus, waiting for the part to come in from somewhere. We rented two vans to get to the rest of the gigs. Just as we got to Seattle, we got word that the bus was fixed and was on its way to get us. So, we turned in the vans so we could leave town right after the gig, and got to the hotel to wait for the bus.

"We were staying at a hotel downtown and playing at a big ballroom outside Seattle. The bus got delayed and we had to get to the gig. The best we could do was get on a metro city bus with all of our instruments and ride out to the gig. The drummer is carrying his cases; the bass player is carrying his stuff. And I have my horns. And we were all wearing our Delbert McClinton Band road jackets. We get on the bus and people are looking at us like, 'What the –?' We're struggling to get our cases down the aisle. Wendy is sitting next to someone who looks like he just got out of prison that day. But, we got to the gig. And somewhere, one of us has a picture of all of us trying to push that bus."[11]

Road stories like this are common when talking to Delbert's band members, but they are proud of those scars and memories of the good old days.

Months pass before Delbert writes in his journal again. The entries are heart wrenching. Clay had gotten into some trouble at school. Delbert sided with the principal, and Clay and Donna Sue were not taking his calls. *Called Clay. No answer. Just the answering machine* entries fill page after page of the journal. On a Sunday in April, Delbert visited Fort Worth and took his father to visit Vivian's grave. The Parkinson's had taken its toll, and Herman was now in a wheelchair and could barely speak.

Delbert's father sobbed uncontrollably when he saw the grave. Heartbroken, Herman mumbled about how he wished he had gone when Vivian did. Delbert writes, *I'm writing this down because I don't ever want to forget these things as I see them. These are hard times for all of us, including Clay, and I just don't want to forget these things I feel.*[12]

Musically, things are picking up. Alligator Records is showing some interest. Wendy is learning to be a music manager. And as David Hickey said, she is a fast learner. Another music manager-wife, Judy Hubbard (Ray Wylie Hubbard), speaks of her baptism by fire into the industry. Judy says, "I never planned to be in the music business. My family was in the car business and I grew up in sales, leasing, finance. I was working fulltime at the dealership, and managing and booking Ray.

"I think we all started with the same challenges: Susan Walker [Jerry Jeff Walker], Wendy, and me. We married them at a time when their careers needed reviving. They each had a history of bad management or no management, and none of us is the kind of person who is going to let things fall by the wayside. We didn't have the Internet then, so we learned about publishing and contracts and all aspects of the business by reading books, talking to people, and asking for advice. We are not going to let things not get done. At the same time, as women in this industry then, we have had to work twice as hard to get street credibility.

"I knew the minute I took the reins that my job was to make Ray look good, regardless. And a lot of times, it comes at the wife-manager's expense. But, ultimately, nobody cares as much about the artist as the spouse. I know Wendy has the same feelings. Sometimes I wonder if Ray would be further along with someone who knew more about the business. I didn't come into this with connections and history in the business.

"I think any of us, Wendy, Susan, or me, would have stepped

aside and handed over the business side of things to someone better at the job, for the greater good. But, looking at the big picture, at the end of the day, I honestly believe we are the best man for the job.

"It's not always easy. We have to be the bad guys. We have to say no. Those guys can't say no to anyone. They come off the stage or see someone on the street, and someone asks them to play something or do something, and of course they say that they would love to, and to call the office. Then we're the ones who have to say no.

"One time, Ray was getting on a plane at the Austin airport to go play the Letterman show or something, and ran into Nancy Coplin, our good friend who did all the live music booking for new, up-and-coming artists and bands at the airport. She said, 'Hey Ray, you ought to play here sometime.' Ray, of course, said, 'Sure, I'd love to. Call Judy!' She called me, and I had to say, 'Nancy, Ray's not going to play at the fucking airport.' Nancy and I still laugh about that. But she thought it was worth a try."[13]

Wendy was learning all aspects of the music business, and making headway with Delbert's career. After nearly a decade without a record label, they landed a deal with Alligator Records. They released *Live from Austin*, which earned Delbert his first Grammy nomination for Best Contemporary Blues Album.

Gary Nicholson was a pivotal part of Delbert's success in Nashville. Gary grew up in Dallas, and had cut his teeth in some of the same Fort Worth clubs. He had moved to Los Angeles in about 1970. "We cut a couple of albums as Uncle Jim's Music, for MCA/Kapp. Then my drummer, Don Henley, left my band to start his own little thing," he quips, referring to then powerhouse 1970s band, the Eagles. "They had a lot of success."[14]

Gary had moved back to Texas in 1973, and married his college sweetheart. "The first record I had heard when I moved back was that Delbert and Glen record, and I was crazy about it. I hooked up with him in about 1975, and went out on the road with him a few times and played a lot of local shows," he adds.[15]

"We lost touch for a while. I had my own band. My friend, Jim Ed Norman, got one of my songs on the *Urban Cowboy* soundtrack, and I got my foot in the door as a songwriter.[16] So, we moved to Nashville. I signed with Jim Ed's publishing company. He sold out to Tree Publishing and I worked for them for fifteen years before I went to Sony."[17]

Gary says, "I have always been so crazy about Delbert. He carved his own path. That mixture of country rhythm and blues and rock and roll made a Delbert genre. It is what he has always done naturally, and is the coolest music ever—all mixed together— a brew that is completely organic, with no compromise. He would never change what his vision of his music was to accommodate some commercial construct, which is kind of the standard here [in Nashville]. He would never cut a song he didn't like just so it could be a hit."[18]

Longtime friend Lee Roy Parnell says, "I was stuck in Texas and not getting anywhere. Delbert and I talked a lot about needing to be in Nashville. We both knew we needed something different but we were dragging our feet. We were playing these clubs and dance halls and the same people were on the roster that had been there when we started playing there ten or fifteen years before. We were getting nowhere. My dad encouraged me to go. My cousin, Robert Earl Keen, was living up there writing songs. Delbert and I would challenge each other to go. Finally, he said, 'You know Gary Nicholson, right? He's doing great up there. Go talk to him and I bet he can get you a job at Tree [Publishing].'

"I said, 'If it's so good for me, why don't you go too?' And before long, we both got up to Nashville. And, I know it's true for me, and Delbert would say the same thing, but if it wasn't for Gary Nicholson, I don't know what would have happened to either of us in this town. Gary was like the Texas songwriter ambassador. He took us around and cowrote with us and made us relevant.

"When we got up here, Delbert and I were both on a mission. Time was wasting. When we were not out on the road, we were writing songs and going out at night and sitting in wherever we could. And as we got things going, Delbert and I would sing and play on each other's records. I cut some of his songs, and we did some fun stuff together. Delbert and Wendy were living in that townhouse on Clifton, and I had moved to East Nashville—before it was hip. Back then, it was just dangerous. We were both hanging on to those dreams and trying to make something stick. We are birds of a feather in many ways."[19]

Delbert and Gary teamed up to concentrate on writing songs, and the pair soon became among the most successful songwriters in Nashville. In addition to Lee Roy Parnell, George Strait, Garth Brooks, Martina McBride, Vince Gill, and others recorded their songs.

Gary says that he had been writing for so long in the Nashville mainstream, that to collaborate with Delbert was like being let out of commercial country music jail. One of their first covers of significance was a duet by Garth Brooks and Trisha Yearwood, "Squeeze Me In," and George Strait cut "Same Kind of Crazy" and "Lone Star Blues" early in their writing partnership.[20]

Delbert and his band continued to travel, filling their calendar with one-night stands. Wendy traveled with the band much of the time, and had a toll-free 1-800 line installed at home so Delbert could call home from payphones and hotels along the way.

In mid-July 1989, Delbert writes in his journal, *I had no idea we were so far into the summer until I asked someone what the date was. It seems that I'm one of those soldiers in a 1940s war movie trudging along while the pages of a calendar fly by . . . . But we have a lot of good things going on.*[21]

Clay had failed seventh grade in Fort Worth. For him to get to go into the eighth grade in the fall, he would have to take summer school classes. He moved to Nashville to enroll in summer school and for Wendy to help him with his studies. Clay was getting on track. The arrangement seemed to be working out.

Delbert's *Live from Austin* album didn't win the Grammy. He lost to Stevie Ray Vaughan. However, that was okay because he was excited about his friend Bonnie Raitt's four-award sweep. She, too, had suffered a dry spell and had been touring on her savings just to keep her name out there. But, she had been picked up by Capitol Records, and with Don Was as her producer, she earned three Grammy Awards for *Nick of Time*, and an additional award for a duet with John Lee Hooker on his album, *The Healer*.

Delbert told a reporter, "Her being acknowledged is a thumbs up to go ahead with what I'm doing. Bonnie and I have been on a similar track for years. I'm a fan of hers and she's a fan of mine."[22]

After Bonnie's *Nick of Time* and Grammy sweep, she called Delbert. David Hickey says, "They had been friends for a long time. They had made a pact that if either one of them got a big break, they would pull the other one up. And Bonnie did that for Delbert."[23]

Bonnie had become a big fan of Delbert and Glen back in the early '70s. She says, "Back then, you didn't have to be in a box. You could hear Conway Twitty on the radio next to the Rolling Stones and Hank Williams. Delbert and Glen were a revelation to me. I had never heard white guys be as funky as that."

She adds, "Delbert and I have had mutual admiration for each other and been friends for a long time. He's one of the most soulful, powerful singers I've ever heard, writes great songs, and plays killer harp. He always finds great material and a kickin' band. He's a nexus of honkytonk, R&B, country and blues—and melds all those influences into a funky, smart style all his own. He's admired by so many musicians and beloved by fans from all corners of the world.

"We played a lot of the same places in the 1970s and '80s, including a great run in Texas over New Year's with Willie Nelson. When I got ready to do my follow-up to *Nick of Time* in 1991, I really wanted to do a duet with Delbert on this Womack and Womack song, 'Good Man, Good Woman.' When he said yes, I was thrilled."[24]

Don Was produced Bonnie's *Luck of the Draw* album as well. Delbert flew to Los Angeles for one day to record his vocals for "Good Man, Good Woman." Delbert writes from his hotel room, *When I am here, I always think of the first time I was here in LA. Those feelings and smells are unique to this side of the country. I was 20 years younger and still had more dreams than I could carry.*[25]

On the heels of Delbert and Bonnie's 1989 Grammy nomination, Curb Records signed Delbert to a multi-record deal that kicked off with the 1990 *I'm With You* album. Delbert candidly told a reporter at *The Tennessean:* "[Curb] came calling. I've been on the road for 200-plus dates a year for the last several years. I would like to be able to cut that back some. I would like to be able to work more because I want to, rather than because I have to. I enjoy what I am doing but I would like to reap more of the harvest.

"Hopefully, this record will put us in larger venues. That will let me do what I meant to do in the first place, which is try to write more and just be home more."[26]

Delbert was turning fifty that year. Wendy had been good for him. He admits to having quit a lot of bad habits. "But it was a long time coming," he admits.

He tells a reporter, "I'm having an awful lot of fun doing it the right way. The difference being, when I get through playing I can be through instead of being through sometime the next day. But who wants to hear any more about anybody cleaning up? I don't want to hear anybody tell me about how they cleaned up—we ought to all clean up and quit talking about it."[27]

With the new year came another goodbye. On January 3, 1992, Delbert and Monty were with Herman when he died. He was buried next to Vivian.

However, 1992 was going to prove to be the turning point for Delbert's career.

On February 26, 1992, Bonnie and Delbert's "Good Man, Good Woman" won a Grammy for Best Rock Performance by a Duo or Group. In addition to the duo award, Bonnie won two additional Grammy awards for Best Female Rock Performance for the *Luck of the Draw* album, and Best Female Pop Vocal Performance for "Something to Talk About."[28]

The Grammy was just the boost Delbert's career had needed. It was something on which to hang his future. His 1992 Curb album, *Never Been Rocked Enough*, features the Grammy recording of "Good Man, Good Woman," with Bonnie, as well as guest appearances by Melissa Etheridge and Tom Petty.

Don Was produced several songs on the album in Los Angeles, and the project was wrapped up in New York, with Delbert and Jim Horn sharing production credits. Delbert credits Wendy for bringing it all together.[29]

The Max Barnes–Troy Seals single illustrates Delbert's life at that moment:

> *She's got a roof that don't leak, when the rain's pouring down.*
> *She's got a place I can sleep, where I'm safe and sound.*
> *She's got a lock on her door, but she gave me a key.*

She don't walk the floor, but she worries about me.
Her love has no strings, shackles or chains.
But I'm holding on for dear life.
She's like rolling a seven,
Every time I roll the dice.[30]

"Every Time I Roll the Dice" would become his biggest hit since 1980's "Giving It Up for Your Love." After nearly four decades in the music business, Delbert was finally rolling sevens.

Tanya Tucker found the Pat McLaughlin song, "Tell Me About It," and wanted to do it with Delbert. Her producer, Jerry Crutchfield, called and asked Delbert to do the song with her. Wendy talked to them and explained that they would like to have half the points. Tanya's dad called, and Delbert explained that he was not independently wealthy, and that he could not comfortably help someone above him on the "food chain" for free. He was grateful for the chance but he needed to get something for it. Tanya's dad completely understood.

Delbert and Tanya teamed up for the duet of "Tell Me About It," on her *Can't Run from Yourself* album on Liberty. The song peaked at number 4 on *Billboard*'s country charts and it earned Delbert and Tanya a Grammy nomination for "Best Country Collaboration with Vocals."

Delbert was in preproduction for his second Curb album, when his relationship with the label began to sour. Wendy explains: "Curb talked us into going with them because they said they would always have another major record label with them. Our portion would be smaller, but that would ensure that the records stayed in broad distribution. We were already questioning the sales numbers for the first record when we started working on the second one. Curb said it sold about four hundred thousand, but Nielsen Sound Scans, the national sales and tracking system, said it was more like five hundred thousand.

"We were working on the next record. We knew it needed to be the best we could put out. Curb didn't think we were doing it fast enough because they wanted to capitalize on the duet Delbert did with Tanya. The album was released as a self-titled project with several re-releases, three new songs with only the scratch vocals, and the Tanya-Delbert duet, against the artist's wishes.

"Harriet Sternberg was with us, helping to manage Delbert at the time, and they played us some tracks with scratch vocals and wanted to put that out. We did not want to put out the scratch vocals on any product."[31]

That was the beginning of the end for Delbert and Curb. Curb was not meeting its obligations, not promoting Delbert's records, and had no intentions of releasing Delbert. To illustrate Curb's pattern of signing an artist and then warehousing him in order to better control the chart standings for other artists on their roster, Trigger Coroneos writes a similar story, "How Curb Records Killed Merle Haggard's Commercial Career," in his *Saving Country Music* blog: "In 1990, when Merle Haggard signed with the label, Curb was seen as one of the most trustworthy labels in town. They didn't have to answer to higher ups in New York and Los Angeles, and could pass that freedom on to their artists. There was no reason to think of Curb as anything but a sure bet.

"But when it came time to release Merle's debut album on the label called *Blue Jungle*, it absolutely flopped . . . . It was a commercial disaster, and after putting up the money to buy out his Epic contract, all of a sudden one of country music's most successful stars of all time was in serious financial straits. Two years later, Merle Haggard was declaring bankruptcy.

"Things would get worse. First, Curb refused to release Merle's music in a timely manner. For four years after his first record, and when Merle needed the money the most, Curb released no new music. Haggard would eventually release two more albums on the label, named for the years they were released: *1994* and *1996*, but they were not much help.

"Author David Cantwell quotes journalist Michael McCall in his book about Merle Haggard about why Merle did so poorly while on the Curb Records roster. 'His record company didn't send promotional copies to reviewers until the album had been out for nearly a month,' says McCall. 'And no advertising or promotion had been devoted to the music.'

"Like so many Curb Records artists, Merle didn't have many options aside from riding out his contract, especially since he was already suffering from financial shortcomings. Merle went from a bona fide headliner to an opening act playing honky-tonks and county fairs during the Curb era and the decade saw virtually no promoted radio singles.

"'People wonder where I was for the last ten years. I was on Curb Records,' Haggard said in 2000, after his Curb contact had finally expired. 'He [Curb President Mike Curb] used me as a billboard for younger acts,' Haggard told the *Chicago Sun* in 2000. 'He got people like LeAnn Rimes and Tim McGraw. He didn't do anything to promote my records.'

"Curb Records responded, 'We released three albums on Merle and all three albums hit the charts. When he was going through bankruptcy he asked for a release from his contract and that was granted. Mike still has a great amount of respect for Merle.'"[32]

Delbert recognized that, at best, he was being warehoused as well. Curb was not meeting their obligations, and Wendy had unanswered questions about the financial discrepancies between Curb's reports and the independent Sound Scan report. Most important, Delbert and Wendy saw what Curb was doing to his career, as well as the careers of other artists in the industry. Delbert says, "At that point, I didn't care if I ever got to record again. I was not going to do another record for Curb."[33]

Curb released two more records on Delbert, against the wishes of the artist. They re-released the Muscle Shoals albums, *The Jealous Kind* and *Plain' from the Heart* as *Delbert McClinton Classics — Volume One* and *Delbert McClinton Classics — Volume Two*. Neither of these records would receive promotional effort, and they would do nothing for Delbert's finally flourishing career. While they had been good records in their day, this was ten years later, and recording technology, as well as Delbert's band and his own performance had greatly improved since the decade-old material was recorded. Re-releases rarely get airplay, especially with no promotion.

But Delbert continued to plow through. Lee Roy Parnell says, "Delbert's always been a little crazy. I think you have to be a little crazy to do this. But you can't give up. What else would you do? I cannot imagine doing anything else. I sure can't imagine Delbert doing anything else."[34]

Delbert McClinton at 8 months old, Lubbock, Texas, 1941. McClinton personal archives

Delbert in the fifth grade, Fort Worth, Texas, 1952. McClinton personal archives

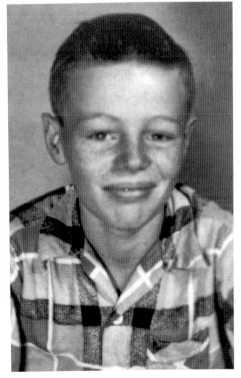

Fifth-grade class South Hi Mount Elementary School in Fort Worth, Texas, 1952. Front row, from right to left: Roger Lapham and Delbert. McClinton personal archives

From left: Jack Bridwell, Vivian Bridwell McClinton, Randall Bridwell, and Delbert, Fort Worth, Texas, 1956. McClinton personal archives

Senior picture, Arlington Heights High School, 1957. McClinton personal archives

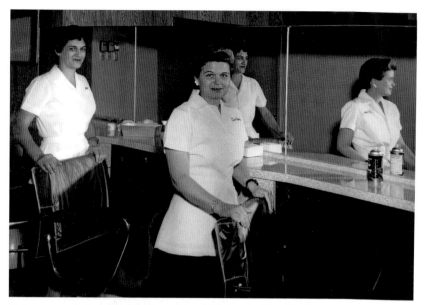

Unknown stylist and Delbert's mother Vivian, Fort Worth, Texas, 1958.
McClinton personal archives

From left, Jack Bridwell and wife, Donna; Herman McClinton; Sandra Sue
McClinton and Delbert, 1960. McClinton personal archives

Delbert McClinton and the Straitjackets, 1960. Courtesy of James Pennebaker archives

The playbill for the Bruce Channel's 1962 "Hey Baby!" British Tour, with a popular young local band, the Beatles, opening for them. McClinton personal archives

Flyer for Big New Year's Eve Blast with Chuck Berry and the Rondels, 1965. McClinton personal archives

The Rondels's first hit single on Smash Records, 1966. McClinton personal archives

Rondels's publicity photo. From left: Jim Rogers, Jerry Forester, Ronnie Kelly, Delbert McClinton, and Billy Wade Sanders, 1965. McClinton personal archives

An early shot of the Rondels with Delbert on piano, 1965. Courtesy of the Jerry Conditt Collection

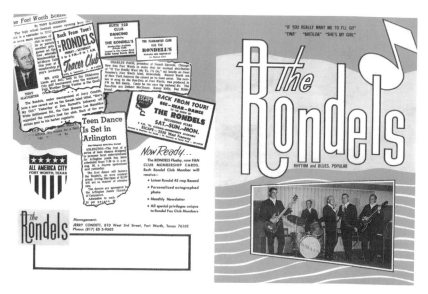

Promotional packet created by Rondels manager Jerry Conditt, 1965.
Courtesy of the Jerry Conditt Collection

Courtesy pass for the Skyliner Ballroom, Fort Worth, Texas, 1962. McClinton
personal archives

Delbert's songwriting pad, 1972. McClinton personal archives

Delbert McClinton headshot, Los Angeles, California, 1972 (Clean Records). McClinton personal archives

The progressive country scene, Austin, Texas, 1973. Lewis Stephens personal archives

Delbert serenades baby Clay, Fort Worth, Texas, 1974. McClinton personal archives

Delbert McClinton Band opening for Willie Nelson, 1977. Courtesy of Lewis Stephens

Road warriors, 1980. Courtesy of James Pennebaker

Delbert with his pride and joy, his 1960 Cadillac, Fort Worth, Texas, 1975.
McClinton personal archives

More cowbell, Club Foot,
Austin, Texas, 1982.
WattCasey.com

Willie Nelson looks on as
Delbert receives Billboard Star
award, backstage, Austin,
Texas, 1978. Courtesy of
James Pennebaker

John Belushi, Jimmy Buffet, Delbert McClinton, and Joe
Ely, Lone Star Café, New York City, 1978. Lewis Stephens
personal archives

Nameless motel on the road, Aspen, Colorado, 1979. Lewis Stephens
personal archives

Delbert sings to Clay at home in Fort Worth, Texas, 1978. McClinton personal archives

Monty McClinton and dad, 1974. McClinton personal archives

The iconic Lone Star Café in New York City, 1979. Lewis Stephens personal archives

Billy Wade Sanders, Delbert, and James Pennebaker, 1980. Courtesy of James Pennebaker

Delbert McClinton Band with Bette Midler, Lone Star Café, 1980. Lewis Stephens personal archives

Broke down and busted in 1982. Courtesy of James Pennebaker

Elvis Costello sits in with the Delbert McClinton Band at the Lone Star Café, 1979. Lewis Stephens personal archives

Band and road crew, 1982. McClinton personal archives

Backstage in Chicago, 1983. Courtesy of James Pennebaker

Victims of life's circumstances, 1985. Lewis Stephens personal archives

Delbert McClinton and Wendy Goldstein, New York City, 1985. McClinton personal archives

Bonnie Bramlett, Delbert, and Terry McBride,1st Farm Aid Concert, Champagne, Illinois, 1985. Courtesy of Terry McBride

Dan Aykroyd, Delbert, and Terry McBride, premiere of the movie *Dragnet,* Los Angeles, California, 1987. Courtesy of Terry McBride

Delbert and Lewis Stephens reading the Gary Cartwright story in Rolling Stone, 1978. Lewis Stephens personal archives

Delbert with John Belushi, Lone Star Café, 1981. Lewis
Stephens personal archives

Lone Star Café, New York City, 1987. Lewis Stephens personal archives

Delbert takes a
break, New York
City, 1987. Lewis
Stephens personal
archives

Delbert and Willie on
stage at Club Foot,
Austin, Texas, 1982.
WattCasey.com

Bonnie and Delbert backstage at the Grammy Awards, Best Rock Duo or Group With Vocals, 1992. © 1992. Photo by Ken Sax/ special thanks to The Recording Academy. Courtesy of Bonnie Raitt

Songwriter Doc Pomus with Delbert at the Lone Star Café in New York City, 1984. Courtesy of James Pennebaker

In the studio with Lyle Lovett recording "Too Much Stuff," for the *One of the Fortunate Few* album, 1997. McClinton personal archives

Vince Gill, Delbert, and Lee Roy Parnell, during a filming of the music video for "Sending Me Angels," 1997. McClinton personal archives

Gary Nicholson, B. B. King, and Delbert McClinton. McClinton personal archives

Kevin McKendree, Delbert, and Bob Britt, Sandy Beaches Cruise, 2016. Courtesy of Joseph Lemieux Jr.

Delbert sings with Etta and Bob Britt and the McCrary Sisters, Sandy Beaches Cruise, 2016. Courtesy of Joseph Lemieux Jr.

Bonnie Raitt, Stephen Bruton, and Delbert McClinton, *Road to Austin,* 2007. Courtesy Gary Fortin, FORMAX Group, LLC

Kevin McKendree, Delbert, and Gary Nicholson with their 2006 Grammy Awards for Best Blues Album: *Cost of Living.* McClinton personal archives

Delbert, Wendy Goldstein, and Delaney McClinton, 2015. Photo by Todd V. Wolfson

Monty, Delbert, and Clay McClinton, 1999. McClinton personal archives

Gary Turlington and Delbert McClinton, 1987. McClinton personal archives

Handwritten lyrics of "One of the Fortunate Few." McClinton personal archives

Willie Nelson, Clifford Antone, Delbert, and Albert Collins backstage at Antones, 1991. Photo by Susan Antone

Family pride: Wendy Goldstein, Delbert McClinton, and Delaney McClinton, 2015. Photo by Todd V. Wolfson

Author Diana Finlay Hendricks and Delbert McClinton, 2016. Photo by Todd V. Wolfson

CHAPTER 16
"Have a Little Faith in Me"

Curb Cuts

Don Was convinced me to record John Hiatt's "Have a Little Faith in Me." At the time, I was probably the only person who had never heard the song. I listened for about thirty minutes and told Don, "I don't think I can do it. There's no way in the world I can phrase this like Hiatt can." And he said, "That's good. He already did it that way." Don convinced me that I could do it my way.

—DELBERT McCLINTON[1]

While the music business was taking most of their time and energy, Wendy and Delbert had not given up on having a baby. They learned about a very good clinic in Florida with the second-highest success rate in the country, and decided to try in vitro fertilization. The first time, it didn't work. They went back in the summer of 1992, and learned that she was already pregnant, the old-fashioned way. The doctor at the Florida clinic knew an obstetrician in Nashville who specialized in high-risk pregnancies, and sent Wendy to see him.[2]

Delbert's first Curb record, *I'm With You,* had earned good reviews in the United States, and hit the top ten in Scandinavia. The Grammy with Bonnie Raitt had validated him. "It also made me listen to what Bonnie was telling me. She recommended her producer, Don Was," he says. "Don is great. I have a lot of admiration for him. He is a genius at making things happen. He's brilliant with arrangements and hearing how to put something together."[3]

The second Curb record, *Never Been Rocked Enough,* released in 1992, did better than Delbert expected. The reviews were good, sales were up, but with virtually no label support, publicity, or radio promotion, it was going nowhere on the charts. Despite the weak promotion, the new record did better than he had expected in Canada, Norway, and Australia, as well as the United States.[4]

Sitting in a hotel room in Kansas City, Missouri, watching torrential sheets of rain through the open window, Delbert writes that the KC Blues and Jazz Fest might be rained out, but later adds that the sun came out and they played in the steam of the late afternoon.

Delbert's appearances grew in stature to include the *Late Show with David Letterman,* multiple *Austin City Limits* tapings, and major music festivals, filling in the gaps in the calendar with the old familiar bars and clubs between here and there. The bus was plugging along despite a new clutch in Missouri, two of the four air conditioners quitting outside of Mobile, and a leaky fuel pump near Raleigh. And Delbert continued to write in the journal.

Later in the summer, headlining a jazz festival, he writes about the glamour of the music business: *It finally stopped raining here in Port Arthur and the show is on. I was standing backstage eating fried chicken from the trunk of a rent car, and this space case walks up and asks if anyone wants some meth. We knew right then that it was gonna be a crazy night. Seven girls from a tit bar all wanted their tits and asses autographed, and Bryan broke two snare drums, but the money was good and it's over.*[5]

He continued to walk that fuzzy line between country and blues and was at home in both worlds. *I think [the duet with Tanya] might be a big record,* he writes. *It's a really good song called, 'Tell Me About It," and we had fun with it. Wynonna's [Judd] agent left word with David Hickey that he wants to talk about some dates together.*[6]

Delbert stepped off a ramp in a New York City studio, and hurt his foot. He had to fly to Memphis for a gig that afternoon, and would wait to get it checked out there. On August 13, he writes, *Went to Baptist Hospital Emergency Room for x-rays of my foot, and found out it's Elvis Week in Memphis. The parking lot is full of people just standing around. This is the same emergency room they took his ass when he died. They say crutches for ten weeks.*[7]

His foot was broken, but too swollen to put in a cast, so they put him in a boot so he could do the Memphis gig.

Delbert admits that he fared better than "the King" on his trip to that emergency room.

The next day, he rode the bus to Little Rock. In another emergency room, he got a cast on his foot. The next stop was Denver. Wendy had called ahead and arranged for the orthopedic surgeon for the Denver Broncos to look at his foot. It needed surgery but he was booked on Letterman and had to postpone it. So, the surgeon put him in another cast.

Delbert flew to New York to perform with Bonnie Raitt on *Late Night With David Letterman*. All Letterman wanted to talk about was the cast on Delbert's foot. Delbert was advised that he shouldn't talk about the accident. However, it is difficult to tell David Letterman that he can't talk about something. Letterman kept bringing it up, "Oh, you fell off a motorcycle? Oh yeah—you can't talk about it."[8]

Delbert flew back to Denver with his son, Monty, to have the orthopedic surgeon put a screw in his foot. It didn't slow him down. Two weeks after the surgery, Delbert was a presenter on stage at the Country Music Awards in Nashville.

The year passes quickly. He writes, *The leaves are starting to turn and I like that. The mornings are cool and my foot is mending. I am able to get around quite a bit better now. I think of the coming months and the changes that are coming with this baby and wonder how I will do. I find myself looking at every little kid I see like it's the first one I've ever seen. I'm going to have to lose some weight and get in better shape. I don't want this kid to see some old fat fart. I can't change my hearing and eyesight, and that worries me.*

I'm already blind, crippled and crazy, so I have been thinking of writing about my life while I still have my memory, so this little guy will know that the ol' man really did exist at one point in time. That might be kind of fun now that some of the worst parts are far enough gone so that I could tell them. What the fuck. Maybe I will, Maybe I won't.[9]

As has happened throughout Delbert's career, he has no concept of his musical acclaim. Playing two hundred nights a year in nameless venues does little to build egos. Although Delbert continues to be described as a "musician's musician," it continues to surprise him. He writes, *At the CMAs, I said hello to Johnny Cash*

*and he knew my name. I was thrilled. A couple of weeks ago, I did
a video with Vince Gill. I was coming out of the makeup trailer and
Carl Perkins was coming in. He looked up and saw me and without
hesitation said, "Hello Delbert." I was thrilled. I had no idea either
of these guys knew who I was.*[10]

Delbert finished the year playing shows with Melissa Etheridge. She would earn her first Grammy for her *Never Enough*
album and she and Delbert would collaborate on some recording projects. Delbert was being asked to make guest appearances
on other people's records, but Curb was not doing anything with
him.

In January 1993, he learned that the duet with Tanya Tucker
had been nominated for a Grammy, but *Never Been Rocked Enough*
was overlooked, and Delbert's frustration peaked. Still, with all
the positive traction in his home life, he could not stay disap-
pointed for long. Wendy was doing great, and the baby was due
in only a few weeks.

In early February, he writes from a Los Angeles hotel: *Yesterday
morning on my way to the airport in Nashville, I saw a guy leaning against a guard rail on Interstate 65. He had on black jeans, a
blue denim jacket, boots and a black cowboy hat. Beside him was a
guitar in a cardboard case. He had his hands on his knees, and he
was throwing up big time. Ahhh. The stuff dreams are made of.*[11]

On February 25, 1993, Delaney Dyer Goldstein McClinton was
born in Nashville. The next day, Delbert writes, *She is absolutely
beautiful and perfect. I find that with each hour I seem to become
more aware that she is finally here. She is so soft and sweet it's hard
to imagine that I'll be able to hold her and talk to her any time I
want. I thought Wendy and I both did well. And I am happy for us
both. This is surely something special.*[12]

If Delaney was a miracle baby, Delbert was surely a new man.
This baby girl put his life into perspective, and offered more reason than ever to do all he could to make things work. And Wendy
was proud of them both.

It's no secret that Delbert has always had a way with the ladies,
and Delaney is no exception. And, of course, a pretty face has
always caught his eye as well. In May, Delbert writes, *I was playing with Delaney and for the first time, got her to smile. She's in*

her swing and every time I stop it on the up-swing, she gives a big smile. She has the most beautiful smile. I had to write it down. Now I'm going back to see her do it some more.[13]

Later that summer, Clay got into some trouble in Fort Worth. He and a friend were going camping. They were speeding and got pulled over. The police found some pot in the car. Everyone decided that it would be in Clay's best interest to move to Nashville to finish school. It was a good move for Clay. He got an after-school job to pay his dad back for his Fort Worth fines. And he started playing guitar in his first band.[14]

In October 1993, Delbert has been at this for nearly four decades, and the road has begun to wear even more heavily on his health and his psyche. If familiarity breeds contempt, it is never more evident than on a tour bus. On October 30, Delbert's entry in the journal reflects the day-to-day madness that comes from living in close quarters with a band: *I guess it's Halloween every day on this bus but today it's really evident. E is the most imbecilic looking person with his Bozo hair and ball cap and that ever-present serial killer look. I am to where I can't stay in the front of the bus when some of these characters are up.*

I'm gonna talk to D later today and tell him he has to clean up. He has on those purple sweats he has had on every day for the last TWO YEARS. And those shoes! God save me from those fuckin' shoes. He now has his winter wear with him which is a long suede coat with a matted fake wool collar that the seams are busted in, so that it looks like he got in to it through the sleeve. And I mentioned to K moments ago that he might want to start wearing a shirt. He has expanded a great deal in the last year so that when he walks back and forth in the front lounge, his huge hairy stomach and that navel that looks like where an eye has been recently plucked, jiggles inches from the faces of those sitting.[15]

The Curb record battles were still an albatross for Delbert. For more than five years, Wendy and Delbert's co-manager, Harriet Sternberg, along with their attorneys, Engel and Engel in Los Angeles, worked tirelessly to get him released from this Curb contract. Beginning in 1994, Delbert and Wendy attempted to speak with the executives at the label, to prevent them from warehousing Delbert, as they developed new artists, but to no avail. Ultimately, Curb attempted to fulfill their obligations by rereleasing the old material, which would guarantee virtually no airplay or national attention.

Reams of paper filled file cabinets with back and forth letters between Curb and the McClinton representatives. Just when it looked as though an agreement might be set, Curb would create another delay.

On July 22, 1994, Delbert prepared for one of America's most prestigious performance venues, a most unlikely place for a Jacksboro Highway rhythm and blues musician. He was headlining at Carnegie Hall, in midtown Manhattan in New York City. Most of the great classical performers have played on this stage, as have legendary jazz and pop musicians. The Beatles had performed at Carnegie Hall in 1964, on their historic first trip to the United States, and the Rolling Stones and Led Zeppelin had followed and rocked the room.

Delbert was among the first authentic American rhythm and blues players to stand on this historic stage. Delbert's show was to benefit Blue World Conservancy, a nonprofit organization dedicated to preserving the world's aquatic resources through education, research, and conservation programs.[16]

Folded in an old Carnegie Hall playbill, in a box of Delbert's memorabilia is a yellow Western Union telegram with special delivery instructions to Carnegie Hall:

HEY DELBERT THE OL WOLFMAN IS SURE PROUD OF YOU FOR TAKING BLUES TO CARNEGIE HALL! AND CONGRATULATIONS TO BLUE WORLD BEVERAGE COMPANY FOR CLEANING UP ALL THE WATER ON THE PLANET. KEEP ON ROCKIN AN ROLLIN. WOLFMAN JACK[17]

Delbert continued to tour, but with no new product, his career was leveling off. In 1995, a new label in town, Rising Tide, showed a strong interest. Wendy says, "Ken Levitan was running Rising Tide, a subsidiary of Universal. He wanted Delbert. We really wanted out of the Curb contract. But it would be two more years before we were finally free and clear from Curb."[18]

Wendy adds that they have her friend and mentor, Harriett

Sternberg, to thank for the most important part of the negotiations in the move from Curb to Rising Tide/Universal. Harriet insisted that no matter what happened in future mergers,
sales, or buyouts, Delbert's contract could never be transferred
to Curb Records; it was exclusively with Rising Tide/Universal.
Most important, Curb would have nothing to do with any part of
any future Delbert McClinton recordings.[19]

CHAPTER 17

Acquired Taste
The Millennial Groove

*I've learned more about what I do in the last fifteen years
than I have in the previous fifty as far as performing. I have
had a great flash of insight in the last five years. I have
become a more active participant in life. With this band, I am
not afraid to do anything, anywhere, any time. And do it top
notch. I feel invincible in my efforts.*

—DELBERT McCLINTON[1]

In 1997, Delbert was finally released from the Curb contract, and
opened a new door with the Universal subsidiary, Rising Tide. His
first record with Rising Tide is still considered among his best.
It had been a long time coming, and Delbert released an album
full of pent-up energy. He says that he felt like Curb had held
him prisoner, and time was of the essence.

Produced by Delbert, Gary Nicholson, and Emory Gordy Jr.,
it is evident that Ken Levitan at Rising Tide was putting a lot of
stock in Delbert. In addition to Delbert's own powerhouse band,
he assembled an all-star cast for these sessions, including B. B.
King, Lee Roy Parnell, John Prine, Mavis Staples, Vince Gill, Patty
Loveless, Bekka Bramlett, Pam Tillis, and Lyle Lovett. Delbert says,
"It's the difference between going in and recording with friends,
and just doing it with personalities. All the people who joined
me on this were friends, and in doing it that way, it felt right and
was just a lot of fun."[2]

One of the Fortunate Few debuted higher on the charts than
any previous album. Delbert had written or cowritten seven of
the ten songs. Like his previous albums, the genre lines blur

between rhythm and blues and country. The signature combination of strong lyrics and a powerhouse band prove that Delbert is hitting his stride as he nears his sixtieth birthday.

When asked how to describe this sound, Delbert says, "I don't know. I think I would say it's American music."[3]

Three months after the release of *Fortunate Few*, though, he was doomed again. Universal shut down Rising Tide, pulling all promotion for the record. Delbert says, "At that point, we decided we could do it better ourselves."[4]

Delbert and Wendy decided to record a new album themselves, and lease it to a record company. He and Gary Nicholson produced *Nothing Personal*, and leased it to New West Records, the independent label launched by Cameron Strang in 1998. It was released in 2001.

In an article in *Music Business Worldwide*, Cameron shares his 7 Lessons Learned from My Career. Number 2 is: "Be persistent . . . and remember: *you* never know who knows who." Cameron says, "My brother had seen Delbert McClinton in New Orleans in the 1980s, and had his records. I finally saw Delbert live at the Vancouver Jazz Festival in 1991. I was totally blown away and bought all of his records. When I started New West, I knew he had been on Rising Tide, and Universal had closed down the label, and I knew that that he hadn't made a record in a long time, so I cold-called his house in Nashville to try and sign him.

"God bless Delbert and his wife Wendy, who answered the phone at the time. They probably thought I was crazy.

"I met a fellow named Stephen Bruton at the Iron Works Barbecue at Austin, Texas. We were both drinking grape soda and I think that caught his attention. We started talking and it turned out he produced some records I really loved, including an album by Alejandro Escovedo, the great Austin artist. I didn't know much about [Stephen] but we became friends and I put out his own record. One day, I ran into Stephen, and we talked about what we were doing. He asked me what I wanted to do next. I told him I really wanted to put out a record by Delbert McClinton.

"He looked at me and said, 'I've known Delbert since we were kids!'

"Stephen called Delbert on the phone and said, 'I met this kid at the Iron Works Barbecue. I've been making some music with him.' And Delbert was like: 'That kid's been calling my house!'

"Wendy and Delbert invited me to Nashville. I flew up and Delbert picked me up at the airport. We drove around Nashville listening to his new record in his car. He asked me what I thought. He said, 'Do you think you could sell it?'

"It was *Nothing Personal,* and it won a Grammy and sold hundreds of thousands of copies."[5]

Wendy recalls, "Stephen [Bruton] introduced us to Cameron Strang, who ran New West. He told us that Cameron was the best guy in the world, and that he does what he says he is going to do. Cameron was selling his albums out of the trunk of his car, but he was so great. We believed in him. He has always been passionate about what he was doing and he loved music. He is such a good person. I still worship him. He was fair. We were getting paid. He worked hard for us and we worked hard for him."[6]

Cameron adds, "New West, as a company, was pretty straightforward. We tried to do a good job, and provide a service to the artists. The goal was to let them make the records they wanted to make and play the music they wanted to play."[7]

Nothing Personal was to be the biggest hit of his career to date. It earned Delbert a Grammy for Best Contemporary Blues Album, and was the number one blues album for 2001, according to *Album Network* magazine. *Nothing Personal* also charted in the top twenty in *Billboard* country albums.

Cameron goes on to say, "We were nominated for Grammys on three of Delbert's studio albums. We won two, and sold hundreds of thousands of records. Delbert got New West on the map and earned us a lot of respect. We went on and did all kinds of great things with the label, the Flatlanders, John Dee Graham, [Kris] Kristofferson, Steve Earle, the Drive-By Truckers. Delbert put us on the map. Delbert put *me* on the map."[8]

Cameron Strang was a thirty-year-old Vancouver law school graduate when he started New West Records. "I was the only employee for several years. When Delbert came on board, we built a great company. Delbert and Wendy worked with me, and helped me work with so many great artists. We wanted everyone to be able to make a living doing what we do."[9]

As New West grew, Cameron created a publishing company based on that same philosophy. One day, Edgar Bronfman Jr., then-CEO of Warner Bros. Records, called Cameron and asked for a private meeting. Cameron told an interviewer, "I was like, 'Starbucks probably isn't private enough . . . maybe my house?'

"So Edgar came over and we talked for three or four hours in the backyard. We didn't talk specifically about publishing, my company or those kind of things—just business in general, life, how we saw artists and the music industry. At the end of it, he turned to me and said, 'I'd like to buy your business, and I'd like you to run Warner/Chappell.'"[10]

From that initial backyard conversation, today, Cameron Strang is the only person in the music industry to simultaneously run both a frontline major record label *and* a leading music publisher—Warner Bros. Records and Warner/Chappell.[11]

Cameron adds, "I owe a lot of credit to Stephen [Bruton] for vouching for me, and to Delbert and Wendy for their willingness to include me in some fashion in Delbert's career. They made a huge impact on my career. You never know who you will talk to who knows someone who knows someone who knows someone."[12]

Nothing Personal, a career-best album, and the first solo Grammy gave Delbert a lift. He was back on the "A" lists, playing on the *Late Show with David Letterman*, *Late Night with Conan O'Brien*, and *Mountain Stage*, among others.

In early fall of 2001, Delbert was invited back to Lubbock to be inducted in the Buddy Holly Walk of Fame. The *Nothing Personal* album was receiving rave reviews from critics from the *New York Times* to *Rolling Stone*, and the *Lubbock Avalanche-Journal* ran a full-page story about the hometown boy.

His oldest brother, Jack Bridwell, introduced Delbert to the crowd at the Lubbock Memorial Civic Center. In his remarks, Jack told the sold-out audience that, "though the family was proud of his self-taught talent and accomplishments, our support frequently narrowed to 'Delbert, why don't you get a real job.' Despite this admonition, and with both feet planted firmly in midair, Delbert thankfully pursued his dream.

"He won't remember this, but when we were in school, I argued that I'd rather be smart than have talent. He won though. He has all that talent and he married smart . . . and we have finally given up on trying to get Delbert a 'real job.'"[13]

In December 2001, Delbert and the band celebrated another homecoming. They went home to Fort Worth for the first time after winning the Grammy for *Nothing Personal*. The Jacksboro Highway joints had long since been abandoned and bulldozed to make room for big box stores and nameless warehouses, but this time, Delbert would not be loading in to the back door of the Skyliner Club from a gravel parking lot.

Delbert was coming home to play the most prestigious venue in Tarrant County, the Bass Performance Hall. Another of Fort Worth's native sons, international pianist Van Cliburn, had suggested to patriarchal philanthropists Nancy and Perry Bass that they build a first-rate concert hall in the city. In 1997, the multimillion-dollar concert hall, modeled after classical European opera houses, opened its doors.

That night, Delbert and the band did not have to worry about the distraction of gunshots in the parking lot or bomb scares in the bar. In fact, as noted in the playbill, all patrons attending the Delbert McClinton concert would be provided with complimentary cough suppressant tablets, "in an effort to help reduce distracting noises and enhance the theatre-going experience."[14]

Whether the Bass Performance Hall or a honkytonk on the edge of town, Delbert says, "My past always shows up whenever I play Fort Worth, even though most of my old friends are dead now. It seems like every time I come home, I chase ghosts and old memories."[15]

The success of *Nothing Personal* led to a second album, released in 2002, and appropriately titled, *Room to Breathe*. "I did that record for me and my fans," Delbert says. "I wasn't beholden to anyone else. The only reason I have stuck around as long as I have is because of the fans. My fans are all that matter to me when I think about a record . . . I owe everything to all those people who came out to see me when I was playing all over the country, I feel so lucky to have that fan base. They've stuck by me, you know? That's a good feeling."[16]

As the twenty-first century dawned, Delbert was finally getting the breaks that had been just out of reach for so long. The new millennium would bring with it room to breathe, literally.

Venues were getting bigger as were the revenues. And Delbert was learning that you *can* go home again.

The new millennium with New West Records was bigger and better than Delbert and Wendy could have imagined. Critics continued to praise the live performances, agreeing that even the best of the studio records could not hold a candle to the soulful energy of a live Delbert McClinton show. In 2003, New West released a two-disc live album, recorded in Europe on his world tour. Delbert did not plan to release a live album from the concert at the Bergen Blues Festival when the show was recorded for Norwegian radio. Geoffrey Himes writes in the *Washington Post*, "The lack of preplanning prevented the problems that afflict so many live albums—the under-rehearsed guest stars, the self-conscious banter and the showoff solos. Instead, it's just another night on the road for the seven member Delbert McClinton band . . . . On *Live*, his gravelly baritone sounds powerful and persuasive . . . . [The album] is dominated by ten recent songs written by McClinton and/or his producer Gary Nicholson, and these numbers make it clear that McClinton's best work is being done right now."[17]

In 2006, Delbert's *Cost of Living* earned him another Grammy for Best Contemporary Blues Album. He had brought his "A" team together for the project. Kevin McKendree, James Pennebaker, Bill Campbell, Al Anderson, Tom Hambridge, Gary Nicholson, Don Wise, Glen Clark, Bob DiPiero, and a host of other familiar names fill the liner notes. Delbert wrote or cowrote almost all the songs on this project, making it one of the best examples of his songwriting skills.

Kevin McKendree has played piano with Delbert since 1997. He had moved to Nashville to work with Lee Roy Parnell, and as Lee Roy's work slowed down, Delbert's was picking up speed. "I had been playing with both of them, and just made the shift to Delbert full time. There have not been that many changes in the twenty years I've played with him. Well, I have to say we are making more money, we have a better bus. Better hotel rooms. But the shows are consistently good.

"Playing with Delbert is the best feeling on stage that I have ever had with anyone. I feel at home working with him. He is the extension of my playing, and I am the extension of his singing. As a band, we improvise; we play short or stretch it long. We never play two shows the same. We have fun. If I could sing, I would want to sing like Delbert. In any band—like any job—there is something that rubs you the wrong way about the boss. But, not with Delbert. There is no one I have ever had more joy playing with than him."[18]

Delbert credits these musicians with his continued success. "I've had a lot of fools in my band. And I've been a fool in my band. But, there comes a point where you gotta say, 'Well, do you want to be a fool or do you want to keep doing this—making music and having a good time?' So, I surrounded myself with non-fools. It's a very stable atmosphere. I pay my guys good, as they should be. I'm not trying to be greedy. I just want everybody to be happy."[19]

Guitarist Bob Britt has played with Delbert for several years. "It's a blast. Delbert's material is custom-made for me. It's always fun and never tiresome. We all love what we do, and that is why we are here. Kevin [McKendree] has been with him for nearly twenty years, and he feels the same way. It's really a part of our souls. And on stage, it's like we can read each other's minds.

"I was playing Delbert's stuff for a long time before I met him, when I was with Wynonna [Judd] and John Fogerty, but it wasn't until I started playing with Delbert that I knew how it feels to be a part of something bigger than ourselves. And there is something about the organization. Wendy and Delbert know that is the most important thing. They are so generous, and they just try to be good to people. It makes it easy to love what we do."[20]

When *Cost of Living* was nominated for the Grammy in 2006, Delbert's song, "Midnight Communion," was nominated for Best Male Country Vocal Performance. Keith Urban won that category for "You'll Think of Me," but Delbert was lined up with country legends George Jones and Willie Nelson, and newcomers Brad Paisley and Toby Keith in the nominations, proving again that his music cannot be defined in one genre.

Delaney was three weeks away from her thirteenth birthday. Delbert took her as his date, to the awards show. Delaney recalls, "Our part was in the pre-televised segment. It was filmed, but not on live TV. Dad was a presenter, so we were sitting in a little dressing room backstage. Dad went out and presented, and then came back and went to the restroom. We were back there watching and they announce, 'Best Contemporary Blues Album: Delbert McClinton's *Cost of Living.*' And Dad is nowhere. We are all saying, 'Oh my God! We won! Where is he? He's in the bathroom!' So, Gary [Nicholson] and Kevin [McKendree] have to go out and accept the award. Dad comes out of the bathroom, and I run up and scream, 'You won! You won! You won!' and he said, 'What? Slow down,' before he realizes what happened. It was exciting."[21]

Delbert tells his own memorable story of that awards show. "We had two tickets to floor seats during the televised portion of the show, and Delaney and I went to that part. When there was a commercial break, people could mill around a little. Delaney would pop up and go down the row and talk to Nelly, Bonnie Raitt, Sheryl Crow, Faith Hill, or Gwen Stefani or other people she recognized. She would say, 'Hi. I'm Delaney and I love your music!,' and then bounce back to her seat before the cameras came on again. I was so proud of her. Nothing fazed her. She was in her element, working the crowd like a natural."[22]

Back in Nashville, Delbert was not going to rest on his laurels. Just as he had done when "Giving It Up for Your Love" had provided a bump in his career, he got back out on the road. In 2009, he would go back to producer Don Was for his thirteenth studio album, *Acquired Taste.*

Don says, "I had really enjoyed working with him on Bonnie's [Raitt] record, and then on 'Every Time I Roll the Dice,' back in the '90s. Coming out of Detroit, I grew up on R&B. Delbert has always had that perfect way of phrasing. He could take that Texas blues, rock and roll, and really understand the roots of rhythm and blues. I have always admired him for that.

"Bonnie revered him as an authentic artist, which is really high praise. She doesn't give her seal of endorsement often. She knows the real guys from the riffraff. A few years later, Keith Richards contacted me about producing a Rolling Stones album and wanted to hear some work I had done. I sent him Delbert's 'Every Time I Roll the Dice' as one of the tracks.

"Delbert has this raw, rough, organic thing going for him. It's deceptively raw. He's like spice and chocolate, smooth and rough at the same time. After 'Dice,' it seems that time flew by. I was working with Kristofferson and the Stones and Dylan, and Cameron Strang at New West was around for some of that. So, when this new Delbert project came up, we all thought it was a good fit.

"We went in to work on *Acquired Taste* with Delbert, and it was completely different than what he had done before. His voice was richer and stronger than it had been twenty years before. I thought he was better than the stuff he had done at seventeen and thirty. He was in his element. Maybe his voice had lost a little of the sheen, but he was going from the gut. There is something that happens to some of the really good ones. It becomes a real art form when they rely on honesty rather than chops. You can't create that in the studio. That comes from somewhere deep inside."[23]

Margaret Moser reviewed *Acquired Taste* for the *Austin Chronicle*: "Delbert McClinton is Texas' roadhouse Renaissance man with the King Midas voice, turning golden anything he sings. The three-time Grammy winner has been riding high on his third wind since 2001's *Nothing Personal* reminded everyone what a badass he is (as did 2005's *Cost of Living*)."[24]

For the first time since the Rondels, Delbert had a band with a name. *Acquired Taste* credits Delbert McClinton and Dick50. Why? Delbert says, "We had high hopes. If an artist wins a Grammy and the record is only in his name, he is the only one credited with the award. But if the band is named on the album, everyone gets a little part of the hoop-tee-doo."[25]

By now, Delbert had surrounded himself with a band that was more than a group of players. Each was bringing an integral piece to the project. The name? "We play a lot of dice on the bus. The only way to score is with a five or a one. When you'd roll nothing, someone started saying, 'I rolled Dick.' Then Dick50 just became sort of a joke—a code word for having nothing—and we went with it."[26]

Produced by Don Was (with the exception of a couple of tracks coproduced by Delbert and Gary Nicholson), this album brought another round of critical acclaim and Delbert had settled comfortably into the twenty-first century.

New West would release one more album. Delbert and Glen's *Blind, Crippled and Crazy* brought Delbert and his old friend, Glen Clark, back together after forty years for a reunion project that proves their chemistry stands the test of time. The youthful energy of the Clean records gives way to the wisdom of two road scholars who have played hard and learned some lessons the hard way. Delbert and Glen admit they did this record because they had always promised each other they would. As Delbert says, "We did it for us."[27]

The track titles fit the tone, "Whoever Said It Was Easy," "Oughta Know," "Been Around a Long Time," and "Just When I Needed You Most" paint a picture of a couple of guys who have paid a lifetime of dues and are still reaping the benefits.

Nick Tosches writes, "It was Charles Olson, a poet bigger than Texas, who said, 'He who controls rhythm, controls.' These words were first published in 1954, the year of Big Joe Turner's 'Shake Rattle and Roll,' of Elvis Presley's first record, the year most commonly associated with the dawn, the first full blast, of rock and roll. And though they are words that perfectly define and express the essence of the power of the greatest poets from Sappho to Dante, indeed to Olson himself, they also define and express the essence of the power of the greatest rock 'n' rollers as well, from Big Joe Turner to Jerry Lee Lewis to the Rolling Stones to the guy whose latest record here lies at hand."[28]

Tosches adds that Delbert McClinton is the son of the afterglow of that dawn, that first full blast. "Born in Lubbock, raised in Fort Worth, he wrote his first song/poem on a scrap of Kotex paper in a high school classroom, made his first record in 1959, and in the years since has lived a roadhouse odyssey . . . whose telling yet awaits its honkytonk Homer."[29]

CHAPTER 18
"Sandy Beaches"
The Delbert Cruises

The Sandy Beaches Cruise is the best and cheapest therapy anybody can ever get to fall back in love with life. Guaranteed to energize your life force . . . it's taken on a life of its own.
—DELBERT McCLINTON[1]

Delbert played his first music cruise in 1992. What began as just another gig would become one of the most lucrative business ventures in the Delbert McClinton story, but like everything else in his career, it would not happen overnight. And even with Wendy's skills, he would need additional help.

Gary Turlington had become a fan when he saw Delbert perform on *Austin City Limits* in 1976. A couple of years later, he saw that Delbert was going to be playing in Raleigh, North Carolina, only about thirty miles up the road from his hometown of Lillington. As he and his wife, Sandra, were leaving the show, Gary stopped to speak to a girl who was selling T-shirts. "I asked her for an address to write a letter to Delbert. I sent him a letter. A few weeks later, I got a letter back, inviting us out to a show. It was the most unlikely friendship in the world. We were from entirely different backgrounds but we have been good friends ever since," he says. "Today, Delbert and Wendy are the closest friends we have."[2]

Gary was a third-generation builder and architect, and the kind of friend who means it when he says, "Let me know if you need anything." So, when Delbert bought his first Silver Eagle bus in the late 1980s, he called on Gary to customize it.

Gary remembers, "They needed a stateroom in the back and

a kitchen, and asked if I could build it. I had never customized a bus, but I'd built plenty of houses. I figured I could, and I did. From then on, I have made myself handy, and enjoyed being a fly on the wall through Delbert's career. I never dreamed I would be building buses, much less, running a music cruise."[3]

Delbert says Gary is one of his alter egos. "He can do everything I can't. He can fix things, he can build things, and he can make things work. He can get through life without looking like an idiot. He just handles everything. He's like Stephen Bruton. With him, I think I can do anything."[4] Delbert recognized that Gary had a multitude of talents. He could customize buses (and quickly figured out how to drive them), fix just about anything that broke, and make a good director of security when needed, running buddy, and best friend.

While today they are common in the cruise industry, music-themed cruises were still a novel idea in the early 1990s. Ships featured lounge musicians and house bands, but few had headliners on stage. In December 1992, a group from Kansas decided to feature Delbert McClinton, Marcia Ball, Koko Taylor, Buckwheat Zydeco, and several other musicians.

At the time, a cruise was like another gig to Delbert. Wendy was pregnant with Delaney and opted out of the first trip, so Delbert took Ronnie Kelly (the Rondels), and Gary and Sandra Turlington went along. The rhythm and blues tour group numbered about three hundred guests, only a portion of the ship's passengers, so, as Gary explains, "The rhythm and blues music could not start until after hours—when the regular cruise shows were over."[5]

Multiple Grammy nominee and Blues Music Award winner Marcia Ball adds, "Roger Naber, the guy who was behind the Ultimate Rhythm and Blues Cruise was kind of like the Clifford Antone of Kansas City, and owned the Blues Emporium for almost thirty years. When they came up with the idea, this was just a special interest group on the ship full of traditional vacationers."[6]

On that cruise, Delbert and Gary Turlington sat on a beach in St. Thomas, talking about the concept of a music cruise. Delbert saw a potential in this, but wanted to take it a step further. He didn't want to focus on a single genre. He wanted to bring together seven or eight kinds of music and handpick the musicians who would perform. It would be a chance for these musicians to play with one another, listen to each other, and completely immerse themselves in the music. Everyone would be isolated from the day-to-day business of music, and would get to do what they loved best. Gary recalls that Delbert envisioned a cross-pollination of musical styles, with talented artists he had worked with forever— talented session musicians, headliners, all good people.[7]

By January 1995, a month before Delaney's second birthday, Wendy Goldstein and Gary Turlington had created a partnership and chartered a small cruise ship. It was to be the first Delbert McClinton Sandy Beaches Cruise, and would feature Delbert, Marcia Ball, Lou Ann Barton, Stephen Bruton, Nick Connolly, Anson Funderburgh with Sam Myers, Henry Johnson and the Rhythm Kings, Hal Ketchum, Lee Roy Parnell, and Wayne Toups.

Wendy and Gary quickly determined that if they were able to charter an entire ship, they could run the shows the way they wanted to, and not wait until after hours for the artists to play on the stages. They learned that bargains could be had by buying a block of rooms on a regular cruise, but to charter the entire ship, they would be charged full price for every cabin. Gary says, "That first year, we chartered a small Dolphin ship that would hold about nine hundred guests, but only had about four hundred people show up. We even gave away some cabins at a blues festival, and those people didn't even show up. We hocked everything we had, and muscled through it. We figured it was fun but that was it. Wendy twisted and turned and finally said, 'Let's do it again.' Without much persuasion, I agreed. We were in it for this much, and everyone who went had a great time and wanted to go again. Why not give it another whirl. How could we miss?"[8]

The owner of Dolphin Cruise Line saw the onboard revenue, the casino income, the bar income, and the ultimate opportunity in this new venture. He was willing to work with Wendy and Gary on this unique project.

It took three or four years to break even, and they continued to have more fun each year. Gary says, "It has always been an adventure, sometimes more than others. The second year, we had the 'Storm of the Century.' We lost power on the ship and could not get into port. We drifted for two days, but people still talk about it today. They say that was their favorite ship. That was the *Sea Breeze*, and it ended up sinking a few years later—but not when we were on it!"[9]

The year 2018 will mark the twenty-fourth Delbert McClinton Sandy Beaches Cruise. Now the roster includes more than forty acts and more than one hundred and twenty musicians. Sandy Beaches calls the Holland America Cruise Line home and 60 to 70 percent of the cruisers have been on prior Delbert McClinton cruises.[10]

Many veterans count the years they have been going on cruises with Delbert by pausing and asking, "Let's see. How old is Delaney now?" She was a year old, the year of the first cruise, and some veteran cruisers have not missed the boat once.

Gary admits that they have not kept formal statistics about the repeat cruisers, but they have all created lifelong friends. "It's like a family reunion," he says. "And it has become very personal."[11]

Molly Reed started with the Delbert McClinton organization in 1998, as the merchandise manager, the person who travels with the band and sells shirts, caps, and records at the shows. "Wendy needed a merch person, and I talked to her on the phone. I could hear Delbert in the background, saying, 'We don't need anyone else on the bus taking up space. I don't want a girl on the bus.' But, I met them, and we clicked. I got the job and began handling sales at shows, along with inventory and bookwork."[12]

Soon Molly's on-the-road merchandise duties grew to include a Band Merchandise Room on the cruise, where guests could purchase all of the featured artists' souvenir items and records. Today, the ship staffs a cashier who can bill items to the guests' cabins, but in the early days, Molly says, "We only took cash and had a knuckle-buster credit card machine. But, today, our merch store is like a really nice record store, with volunteers helping to staff the store through the week."[13]

Wendy had hired her friend, Ragena Warden, to help with the office management. She ended up having to take on the reservations and other cruise administrative details. Gary explains that from the beginning, the cruise has had very little advertising beyond word of mouth, posters, and fan club newsletters, along with a few ads in music magazines. Wendy and Ragena worked tirelessly year round, building personal relationships with the guests through multiple phone calls, letters, and emails, long before the ship left port.

Today, Wendy handles band management, passenger relations, and sales, and Gary runs the ship management, charter negotiations, stage management, and graphic design. Details important to the cruisers include healthy meal options, gluten-free and vegan selections, and after-hours bars. Delbert sets the dress code: all casual, all the time and no dress-up requirements, even in the top-shelf restaurants. Today, Molly has taken over office management, and handles the details like room assignments, individual accounts, and day-to-day operations.

Molly adds, "For a long time, the cruise phone number should have been 1-800-RAGENA. She was so instrumental in making everything work. We learned everything from her."[14]

The cruise grew from those early Dolphin ships to the S-Class ships chartered for the cruise today. The number of guests has quadrupled, from four hundred to nearly eighteen hundred, but it hasn't always been smooth sailing, Gary admits. "We did not go into this knowing anything about running a travel agency or a cruise. If we didn't have other sources of income, I think we would all have been flat-busted long ago, but I am glad we struggled through. It is not about the money.

"We decided to go out of San Diego one year. When we left port, it was raining sideways, and was terribly cold. It never warmed up and the cruisers didn't like it. We had cut a two-year deal with that ship to get a better price, but the second year out of San Diego, a lot of people just didn't come."[15]

Gary has earned his keep more times than Delbert can count. "The year of the 'Storm of the Century,' the *Sea Breeze* broke down. Captain Kapatelis was our ship captain. He looked the part, very Greek, stately, straight out of the movies. He and I had become friends as we worked through the logistics for the cruise. During that storm, one of the ship's steam lines broke, and he and I stayed up several nights working on it before we finally got it fixed."

He adds that he believes they would still be with Dolphin today if the cruise line had not changed hands. They sold out to Premier, who didn't really want to work with charter cruises. Two years into that relationship, Premier went bankrupt two months before the Sandy Beaches Cruise was to set sail. Gary said, "We had already paid them for the cruise, and we lost everything."

Gary and Wendy got on the phones, and found another ship. They funded that cruise out of their own pockets. They chartered with the Regal Empress, a cruise line with a one-ship fleet, for several years. He says, "The Empress saved our bacon that first year, but they could not sail the week that was originally planned. So, in addition to having to pay the new cruise line out of our pockets, we had to pay back a lot of people who were not able to change their vacation dates. We lost everything on that trip, but everyone who went had a great time. And most of those who couldn't make those dates came back with us the next year. Today, they are some of our most loyal cruisers."[16]

More than a weeklong vacation for musicians and fans, the cruise has been a catalyst for the phenomenal fan-friends-family base that some call a cult following for Delbert. It has also been a place for Delbert to pass it forward. He brings multiple genres of music together on the lineup and by the end of the week, the musicians are sitting in on each other's sets and playing together after hours. This unique opportunity for musicians grows into national tours, cowriting, and even album projects. A Caribbean luxury cruise may seem a far cry from a roadhouse on the Jacksboro Highway, but the soul carries through every note.

Music cruises run the gamut today, from outlaw country to legendary pop stars. There is a cruise for every interest. Newcomers ask what makes the Delbert McClinton Sandy Beaches Cruise so special.

Marcia Ball has been a headliner since the first of Delbert's cruises. She says, "It's a family reunion for everyone, musicians, and fans. Your ticket is a backstage pass to get to be a part of something magical. Some artists would not dig that, but those of us who do this cruise live for this week. We love it. I have been on other music cruises, but they don't have this vibe. On Delbert's cruise, we know everyone—and if we don't, we want to know them. We get a chance to play with each other and listen to other bands, play dominoes, dance, and have a lot of fun."[17]

Lee Roy Parnell adds, "I have to give it to the cruisers. They are not really fans. They really are like family. They are a part of the show. And when we go home and go out on the road, those Sandy Beaches Cruisers show up at our gigs all over the country. And we feel like we are part of something bigger than ourselves. I have met people on the cruise who are old friends when I see them out on the road. What Delbert and Wendy and Gary and Sandra have put together is brilliant. But the fans are what make it incredible."[18]

Shelley King was named the Texas State Musician in 2008 and has become a favorite on the cruise. "I have only done it for three years, but have friends who have done it for more than two decades. I would hear about it and be so jealous! The lineup is always so amazing, and to get invited to play is like being invited into an exclusive club of people who are all living the dream, from the musicians to the guests, and even the crew. Everyone has such a good time. There is no stress, no drama. For one week, we focus on what brought us into this business in the first place. It's all about the music."[19]

Delaney McClinton has grown up on the Sandy Beaches Cruises. Today, she has an extended family of thousands and has taken on a significant role of bringing new talent to the attention of Wendy and Delbert, not just on the cruise but in Nashville and around the country. "My dad and I are a lot alike. We are both consumed by music. We bond over music. He has introduced me to legends, and I have showed him some of the newer acts out there. He respects my tastes," she says, proudly adding that she has brought the Band of Heathens, Alyssa Bonagura, Kree Harrison, and other young artists to the cruise, and they have been as well received as the legends.[20]

Singer-songwriter HalleyAnna was a first-time artist on Delbert's cruise in 2016. "When I heard Delbert open with 'Take Me to the River,' the first night, I knew I was in the right place. Getting to be a part of something this special is a life-changer. There are so many things that will stay with me forever: the showcases, the after-hours jams, finding a room to write a song with a new friend, or getting to sing harmonies with one of your heroes. Seeing nothing but ocean all the way around the ship. No phones, no worries. Sitting on the floor and swapping songs into the wee hours, or having lunch with a songwriter you've listened to forever. Out in the middle of the ocean, you get the feeling that you are in the center of the universe. One of my favorite memories was having dinner with a couple of longtime cruisers and just listening to their stories of previous years. And these things don't just happen. Delbert, Wendy, and Delaney work hard to make everyone feel at home the whole week. It's like family—if you are used to a family of musicians. I don't have enough words to describe it. You have to be there to understand."[21]

Hall of Fame songwriter Bob DiPiero has had more than a thousand songs recorded in his career, many of which have topped the charts. He says, "Delbert has done a lot for songwriters with the cruise. Sometimes people don't think about where a song comes from. Delbert puts songwriters on center stage, and it is a unique part of the entertainment for the audience. We have songwriter shows, and people love to hear the songs done by the writers, and the stories behind the songs: what inspired them and how they came about. And while we are out on the boat, we all spend a lot of time writing together or making plans to write together. It just happened to come together. One year I was on the boat with Al Anderson and he got sick and couldn't play his slot. So, I got to jump in and do a songwriter thing. That was the first of the songwriter shows. There really is something for everyone— different genres from rhythm and blues to gospel to country to comedy. We are down in one of the lounges doing an acoustic songwriter show, and someone is up on the back deck doing a full-blown rocking show."[22]

When asked about his favorite cruise, Gary Turlington is quick to answer, "The last one—they keep getting better." Delbert disagrees. "The next one. It's going to be the best one yet."[23]

CHAPTER 19
"Sending Me Angels"
Family Ties and Old Friends

A lot happened while I was out chasing my dreams.
—DELBERT McCLINTON[1]

Delbert likes to talk about his family and friends, and they like to talk about him. There is little doubt that his singular blend of life experiences have molded him into the musician, bandleader, songwriter, father, husband, and respected individual he is today.

Delbert admits that he has been three distinctly different fathers to his three children, Monty, Clay, and Delaney. Along the way, he is the first to say he hasn't always made the best choices, but he has always been true to his music.

Today, family and friends are a priority for Delbert. His youngest daughter, Delaney, lives in Nashville. Clay, his middle son, lives with his wife, Brandy, in the Texas hill-country, west of Austin. Monty, his eldest son, lives in Fort Worth. Delbert's grandchildren, Emellia Grace and Calvin Ross, live in Aledo, just south of Fort Worth, with their mom, Patty McClinton, and in Fort Worth, with their dad, Monty.

Delaney is very active in the local music scene, volunteering with benefits and pitching in backstage at major events around town in her spare time. In recent years, she has taken a greater role in the Sandy Beaches Cruise, consulting with her parents on new acts for the lineup, and is mature beyond her years. She reflects on her greatest lesson from her father: "Always be gracious. He truly loves the people who allow him to do this. He has always told me to, 'speak so that I may see thee,' which means to be true to my words and actions, and act in a way that makes people want to be around me.

"He was playing two hundred nights a year when I was a child, but when he was home, he was completely engaged in our life. Even on the road, we have always argued about who got to say 'I love you,' last. And we always have tried to one-up each other with, 'I love you more than all the stars in the sky, or all the grains of sand.' And he used to make up stories on the spot. I grew up with his imaginary characters like Margaret, the mouse, and Dot, the ladybug, and their continuous adventures.

"My worst memory? Learning to drive. I thought it would be easier to learn to drive with him, because he is generally more laid back than Mom. But, he has a habit of making very dramatic sounds and reacting to things, flailing his arms and saying, 'Oh God!' He is still the worst backseat driver!

"My mom and I are very close. We have always done everything together. We have the same sense of humor. She is the funniest person I know. I am so grateful for her. We are so similar. I love that she has such grace and strength, and is a really good friend to her friends.

"And my dad loves me better than anyone else. I consciously look for someone who is like my dad. Displaying affection is so important. He is always very present. He is focused. He will mute the TV and pay attention to me and listen to what I say. I think that is the greatest gift any parent could ever give a child.

"Both of my parents are extremely generous. If I could inherit any of their traits, I hope it is that. They will always give more than they have to someone in need. They are both truly kind and honest. Even if I don't fully have their means, I hope to always be able to share what I do have with others."[2]

Delaney adds that the extended McClinton family is very dynamic. "My niece and nephew, Emellia Grace and Calvin Ross [McClinton], are the most well-behaved, sweetest kids on the planet. Last year, my mom and dad took them to Disney World for the first time, and they made my dad ride Space Mountain. Mom will ride anything, but my dad is a little more cautious.

"I've always been close to Clay, my 'little big brother'—he is an inch shorter than me! I never thought about the fact that he was only my half-brother. We have loved Brandy from the get-go. Clay has always been so supportive of me. And Brandy is so good for Clay."[3]

Delbert's second child, Clay, agrees, "Dad was really busy when I was young, but I understood. I grasped that concept: when you are an artist, and you are passionate about your art, you have to do it. That made sense to me. It was what he did. It was where he worked.

"We always had music around the house: Hank Williams, old country and blues, Jimmy Reed, Merle Haggard. My earliest memories are of him playing guitar for me. I got a guitar and harmonica when I was about twelve. He would let me sit in with him on stage, and sing on the choruses and build my confidence. And he has always wanted me to be better than him—at music and at life—in the choices I make. He didn't want me to make his mistakes.

"My mom [Donna Sue] was great, too. She was fun, pretty, loving, and even when she came up with the idea that she wanted to leave, she was sad about it. Not that she was leaving, but that it didn't work out like they thought. But, she loved life.

"My older brother, Monty, is a good musician, too. As a brother, he is great. He thinks about things differently. He is very charismatic and can talk to anyone. He has two beautiful kids. And I have had the best extended family, from Stephen Bruton and Lewis Stephens, and Kevin McKendree and James Pennebaker. The band has always been a part of our family. I've grown up with them."[4]

While the band has changed personnel through the years, some of the members have been constants in Delbert's life. In the sometimes-solitary business of music, Delbert has avoided one of the major pitfalls of loneliness.

Counting his closest friends, he is quick to include longtime guitarists Billy Sanders and Stephen Bruton. "Billy Sanders was the best friend of all time. He could light up a room before the door was fully opened. I still miss him." Delbert says, recalling familiar stories of Billy in the Straitjackets, the Rondels, and off-and-on roles in the band until his death nearly fifty years after their first show together.

Stephen Bruton was another of Delbert's lifelong friends. Another Fort Worth native, Stephen was part of the Texas migration to Los Angeles in the early 1970s and played with Delbert and Glen. Stephen became Glen Clark's roommate when Delbert moved back to Fort Worth. "Stephen was my alter ego. He had the personality and wit and talent. He had it all. And we had a lot of fun together."

Glen Clark is one of the funniest people Delbert has ever known. Like the closest of brothers, Delbert shares stories, some off-color, and all off-the-record, about Glen's old rust-colored Volkswagen Microbus and the House of Pies, and wonders how they survived. He remembers when the band toured to support the *Blind, Crippled and Crazy* album. "The band gave him the nickname of 'Highly'—'Highly Inappropriate,'" Delbert says. "He was the band entertainment for the entire tour. And it takes a lot to entertain a bunch of musicians on a bus."[5]

Songwriting partner Gary Nicholson is a regular lunch partner, and they talk practically every day. "As songwriters, Delbert and I complement each other. As friends, we think alike."[6] It was a natural for them to write "Same Kind of Crazy (As Me)," which was recorded by Delbert and Gary, as well as George Strait.

Gary Turlington tells of sitting on the bus one day with long-time guitar player Dave Millsap counting members of Delbert's band. "We got up to about two hundred, and I know we didn't name them all," he says. One of Delbert's former keyboard players, Lewis Stephens, said as he boarded one of the first large Sandy Beaches cruise ships, 'Delbert's finally got a boat big enough to hold all of his former drummers.'"[7]

Personnel changes aside, band members are high on the list of Delbert's close friends. His longtime road manager, Keith DeArmond, paved the way for too many miles to count. Road manager Molly Reed is sincere when she says, "We are family. There is not one asshole on the bus. We're in the trenches together. The bus is not a party on wheels. Everyone gets along, through the thick and the thin. We have had health crises, bus breakdowns, hotel issues, and a few money issues at the end of the show, but we are there for one another. We appreciate getting to work with amazing people, and it carries through on stage. It's fun, but it's a job. John McElroy is the production manager, and he is a major player. And the fans are so great. We cannot say enough about the fans."[8]

David Hickey has been Delbert's booking agent for three hundred years, according to Delbert. And as David recalls, they have never had a contract between them. "We shook hands in a grocery store in Fort Worth sometime way back in the twentieth century, and we are still at it."[9]

Delbert talks about his current band, "It's the best band I have ever had. James Pennebaker [guitar] is family. He's been playing with me off and on, since he was nineteen, back in the 1970s, and he will be with me forever, as long as he wants to. Mike Joyce [bass guitar], Kevin McKendree [piano], and Bob Britt [guitar] and I write together a lot, as well as play. Dana Robbins [saxophone] and Quentin 'Q' Ware on trumpet. And Jack Bruno [drums]. I finally have a drummer I can live with," he exclaims. Delbert, Kevin, and Bob also coproduced the most recent album, *Prick of the Litter*, in Kevin's Franklin, Tennessee, studio.[10]

At first glance, Gary Turlington and Delbert are unlikely best friends. The third-generation builder from North Carolina and the blue-eyed soul singer from Fort Worth, Texas, are the kind of friends who can finish sentences for one another, or sit quietly for hours on end, and watch old movies. *The Treasure of the Sierra Madre*, Gary says, "is a movie we can watch over and over and it never gets old." Delbert and Gary are both voracious readers, World War II buffs, and history fans, from ancient history to twentieth century studies. Their conversations range from the latest techno-gadget to the transformation of one of Delbert's ever present chile peppers.[11]

Delbert leaves chile peppers in various stages of ripeness everywhere he goes: on his desk at home in Nashville, on a balcony rail in San Miguel, on the window ledge of the bus, or above the sink in the Austin condo. He sets them out and checks them daily, fascinated by the way they change and transform from blossoms to buds to green to yellow to red peppers, and works of art as they dry. These chiles are like those friendships — changing, growing, and transforming, but as timeless as favorite lyrics.

I told you I was doin' just fine
Didn't need nothin' in this life of mine
Was havin' a good time just bein' free
But you smiled that smile and just wouldn't listen
Now you're makin' it hard for me to keep resistin'
Oh baby, you're 'bout to get the best of me.[12]

CHAPTER 20
"Best of Me"
Staying Power

When I hear "Honey Hush," or anything Joe Turner does, it transports me back into that world. If that don't make you want to get up and move, then you're probably dead. I hear horn parts for the hum of the city sometimes. Honest to God. I hear horn parts for music everywhere. Since I discovered it in myself, that enthusiasm for music has never waned. I've dragged it into and out of and over and around and through a lot of shit.

—DELBERT McCLINTON[1]

Truly "One of the Fortunate Few," Delbert has managed to live his dreams, sometimes in spite of himself, expanding his roots to encompass the world, while continuing to color just outside the lines of any single genre. The stars have aligned for him. Those stars may have leaned toward the blues, but Delbert has managed to keep them on the bright side for the better part of seventy-seven years.

A career spanning more than six decades is unusual in any profession, but in the music business, it is virtually impossible. What is the secret to Delbert's staying power? How has he stayed relevant for generations of music fans?

Music writer Robert Oermann says, "Music is more than those ten records you hear on a radio station all day long. Radio stations want to be wallpaper. So, every record sounds like the one before it. But, music is much more alive than that. Music will always outsmart the radio industry.

"Fans keep the music alive. Delbert's fans are the most loyal people in the world. Delbert is of a generation that he can remember when rock and roll was born. He is so enthusiastic about music. His life spans the history of rhythm and blues and rock and roll, and beyond. He has never lost the joy of discovering good music, hearing good music, and playing good music. And he sings his ass off at every show."[2]

Musicologist Kathleen Hudson asked him about his staying power in a 1997 interview. "You've been around so long. Why?" she asked. "Too broke to quit is the main thing that has kept me going," he replied.[3]

Twenty years later, Hudson says, "Delbert is just Delbert. Whatever air he's breathing and whatever song he is singing, he is being authentic. He has never tried to be anything else. It happens to cross color lines and genre lines and gives us a reason to shake our hips. That is heart and soul."[4]

Country music singer Tanya Tucker says, "The aches and pains are just a part of it now. Working the road for as long as Delbert and I have, we just roll with the hurting. I think it's harder on a girl. Delbert can throw on a pair of jeans and a T-shirt and get out there and do it. He is still one of the sexiest men I know. He has a great look. He reeks with magnetism. He's eat up with it. When he opens his mouth to sing, he hits you right in the gut. He touches you where nobody else can.

"My dad always said, 'They don't come out to hear you. They come out to see you. Give them a show.' Delbert does that every time he climbs on that stage. He gives them what they came for and more. You want to see him play. Hearing him is just the gravy on top. Delbert has the whole package—and he's sexy as hell. And he's still doing it better than a lot of people a quarter of his age."[5]

Music executive T Bone Burnett says, "First of all, Delbert is undeniably good. He is soulful, deeply honest, and has an extraordinary history filled with integrity that encompasses every part of his music. And he has the advantage of never having 'made it,' so to speak. Roy Orbison said to me once that he felt like he was dragging this legend around. Elton John says it's difficult to play a new song. That's when the audience goes to the men's room. It's hard to keep generating your repertoire when people only want to hear the songs they know. Dylan is another one who never 'made it,' in that way. He didn't have a period where he defined himself so fully that he has to stick to that self forever. Delbert has been consistently good for sixty years. But, Delbert and Dylan have both created an underground audience that is incredibly loyal. Their audience doesn't believe that you're only as good as your last hit. They keep coming out and keep discovering him, because Delbert is good."[6]

Songwriter Ray Wylie Hubbard recognizes, "Delbert's a songwriter first and always will be. Pop culture is celebrity conscious. But, those celebrities burn bright and fast and then they are gone. Guys like Delbert and Billy Joe [Shaver] and Willie [Nelson] are writing great songs and putting it all out there, mile after mile, year after year. Delbert's a powerful songwriter who can entertain like hell. He's honest. Whether there is a market for it or not, he's always going to do it. It's all he's got, but he's got it all."[7]

Music writer Peter Guralnick adds, "For Delbert, there has never been a flagging of commitment or enthusiasm. He has a sense of never wanting to let himself down, pushing forward and never coasting. In coasting, you give up the things that drew you to the music in the first place. You can find the same commitment in writing or carpentry. People with passion maintain that passion by never taking anything for granted and seeing that each moment calls on you to live up to your own standards. Delbert has an easy-going manner, but he has a truthfulness in his performance, the intensity and total commitment to every detail. Delbert is the length and breadth of American music, and will always represent the best of what we are."[8]

Asleep at the Wheel's Ray Benson has shared stages with Delbert since the 1970s. He talks about staying relevant in the music business, "Every five years, a new audience discovers us, and every ten years, a new generation comes along. Delbert has a fiercely loyal crowd. He started gathering people back in the 1960s, and those people still come out to the shows. His audience grows, and gets younger as new generations discover him. And he is eternally young. It's not easy. Michael Murphey left the fold years ago. Jerry Jeff doesn't do anything anymore, but still could. Rusty [Wier] died. We lost Townes [Van Zandt] and Doug [Sahm]. We thought Ray [Wiley Hubbard] would be dead by now, but he's out there, better than ever. Delbert. Willie. Us. None of us ever thought we would still get to be doing this. And today, we are doing things beyond our wildest dreams. Maybe it's human resilience, good work, and persistence. The secret? A rolling ball gathers lint."[9]

National radio host Don Imus adds, "Delbert still sings his ass off. Lyle Lovett told me one time, 'If we could all sing like we want to sing, we'd sing like Delbert McClinton.'

"His phrasing is as good as Sinatra, or anybody I've ever heard. He is one of the best artists I have ever heard. He is a wonderful songwriter. His lyrics are clever. And yeah. He has God's gift for a voice. And he's a good person. He treats people right."[10]

Warner Bros. Records CEO Cameron Strang says, "Delbert is such a great talent, such a great singer. He has an incredible relationship with his fans. He's seen a lot and knows a lot, but is so humble and talented. It's not ever going to stop for him. This is what he does. He doesn't ever rest on his laurels. He will always reach for his best, and his best keeps getting better.

"Delbert has a different type of calling than a lot of musicians. All that work and all those shows, all that playing with greats. He was learning when nobody was watching, and today he is real. He is authentic. That's what makes him different from most of the artists you meet."[11]

Bonnie Raitt says, "None of us can believe we'd still be making a living doing this, getting our first record deals in our twenties and still playing today. I don't want to gush, but you would be hard-pressed to find anyone who would listen to Delbert's music and not love it. He spans generations and musical styles. He may not be a pop star, but he's a true classic who's carved out a steady fan base over six decades on the road, hosted many years of his Sandy Beaches Cruises, and still keeps coming up with great new music. His legacy is assured. With great luck, we'll both still be singing together for many more years to come!"[12]

James Pennebaker began playing guitar with Delbert in 1976. He says, "God knows, Delbert has never been a superstar, but he has been able to blaze his own trail and do it his way. He has a fan base—more of a cult following—and he has done very well. No one has ever had more loyal fans. And now he can work as much or as little as he wants. I believe he'll be doing this till they throw dirt in on him. He's outlived a lot of his bandmates. And the mileage on that boy—hard miles. But, look at his friends, fans, and family. They have made as much of a difference in his life as he has made in theirs. They've always been there for him and always will. That is the true sign of success."[13]

Delbert has been featured on seven *Austin City Limits* (*ACL*) programs, dating back to 1976. Terry Lickona, executive producer of *ACL*, says, "Delbert is one of a handful of artists who have been tied so closely to the history of our show, as a thread that runs through from our beginnings. As *ACL* has evolved and grown and expanded, Delbert's music has done the same. We have always been loyal to those artists who were there in the beginning: Delbert, Lyle [Lovett], and of course, Willie [Nelson] who did our first pilot show.

"Some artists come out of nowhere and rocket to the top and become worldwide superstars overnight, and maintain staying power: Elton John, Paul McCartney, and Prince, when he was with us, to name a few. Some shoot to the top and fade away or burn out just as quickly. Very few have staying power.

"Delbert may not be a household word everywhere, or the biggest star, or make the most money, but he is consistent. He is always good. He is always on. I have never seen a bad performance. I have never heard a bad record. He has charisma and command, and has the audience in the palm of his hand. And that makes great television. You can see the excitement in the audience. You can see the reaction from the fans. It's a visceral thing. You can't put your finger on it, but you know it when you feel it.

"There are three defining qualities that make a great artist. Having a voice that holds peoples' attention (and you recognize Delbert's voice within two seconds of the first note); writing and selecting good songs; and the ability to let the audience be a part of the experience, to respond, and participate. The best music is a shared experience between the artist and the audience. Delbert does all of that and more."[14]

Terry adds that a glance at Delbert's *ACL* appearances illustrates one more quality. "Diversity. The fact that we have featured him with such a variety of artists down through the years. Every time he appears on the show, he appeals to the hard-core blues fans, the western swing fans, the singer-songwriters. Delbert relates to people on all levels. He has a great groove and sets the house on fire. And that makes great television in Texas and around the world. And that is why we love to continue to have him on *ACL* on a regular basis."[15]

Music writer Joe Nick Patoski says, "The easy way out would be to declare Delbert McClinton as the greatest voice to ever come out of Texas and be done with it." He adds that, "Others work the milieu very well, but none so deftly obscures the color line that separates rhythm 'n' blues from country and western as well as Delbert.

"Along came Delbert, quoting from the same old roadhouse catalog he's always carried with him proving you didn't need to wear a hat or dress funny to get a crowd worked up. Folks who didn't know diddley-squat about Texas honky-tonks or the steps to the Push or the Skyliner began to catch on in a big way and the roadhouse fever spread like wildfire.

"Each and every syllable speaks volumes of a life well spent in joints alongside the two lane blacktop with low ceilings, a pool table, a juke box, and bandstand—necessities for any character trafficking in the wild side of life. The main difference is with Delbert, it ain't no shuck. He's the real thing. And knowing that makes his particular groove cut even deeper still. Like a bone-handled knife."[16]

Epilogue

National Public Radio's Scott Simon has just written a new biography with Tony Bennett. Much has happened in Tony's life since the release of his first memoir—nearly twenty years ago—when he was seventy-two.

In twenty years, I plan to write the sequel to this book. Stay tuned.

The year 2017 marks his sixtieth year on stage and Delbert is at the top of his game. He is playing in major venues from New York to California, and is planning his 24th Annual Sandy Beaches Cruise in January 2018. Meanwhile, his most recent album, *Prick of the Litter* (released in January 2017 on his own new label, Hot Shot, with distribution through Thirty Tigers), proves that he's still as hard to pigeonhole into any one style of music as ever. As Richard Skanse observed in his review for LoneStarMusic-Magazine.com, "McClinton has always mixed equal measures progressive honky-tonk, rock 'n' roll, and meaty blue-eyed soul into his own brand of rhythm 'n' blues, but his first solo album since 2009's *Acquired Taste* finds him stepping out of the road-house and sliding confidently into the Jekyll and Hyde dual role of rakishly debonair big band crooner and smoky cocktail lounge jazz cat. And it all fits him like a custom-tailored velvet jacket."[1]

Just as he did on *Acquired Taste*, Delbert made it a point to share credit for *Prick of the Litter* with his road band—though this time around, instead of "Delbert McClinton & Dick50" on the cover, it's "Delbert McClinton & Self-Made Men." It's a testament to how much he values the contributions of everyone in his extended musical family, even though there's never been a question about who's driving the boat and calling the shots, be it in the studio or onstage.

His longtime saxophonist, Don Wise, says, "Delbert is a true band *leader*. He is in charge. Some bands don't go anywhere because they vote on everything like a committee, from the tempo of the songs to how early to leave for North Carolina.

"We had to add a fill-in drummer for a short tour, and got one of the most well-respected drummers in Nashville. Rehearsals went fine, but on the stage, he would slow down the tempo of the songs. I could see Delbert was not having a good time, so I spoke to the guy after the first show, and said, 'Stay with the tempo Delbert counts off!'

"He responded with, 'Well, the recording isn't that fast,' and I said, 'That recording was done twenty-five years ago, and Delbert puts it where HE wants it every night. Just follow him. Next time, it might be even slower than the recording.'"[2]

Don adds, "Delbert continues to make his music brand new. He has never gone through the motions. Many artists stick around in show business doing their handful of hits with a few dancing girls behind them and they have become nostalgia acts. Not Delbert. He is relevant. He is fresh. And he is a band*leader*, writing meaningful lyrics, recording quality, new material, and putting on a show every time he steps on stage. He tells stories with a musical backdrop. Music too good for most radio stations. His songs are the roots and branches of different genres of American music."[3]

When discussing his songwriting style, Delbert explains what others have struggled to describe. "Call it blues or country rock or American roots or whatever, but one of the most important things about my songs continues to be that there is always a way out. Nothing I write spirals into the abyss. It's all 'I'll be all right.' The music is mostly so positive, in that 'I'll be okay' . . . 'and maybe if' . . . 'I'm hoping that' . . . frame of mind. . . . I always want to have an uplifting draft in the breeze of the song."[4]

In a 1966 *Playboy* magazine interview with journalist Ron Rosenbaum, Bob Dylan said, "Popular songs are the only art form that describes the temper of the times. It's more than live—it's *Alive*. It's not in museums or shelves in a library."[5]

Today, more than fifty years after that Dylan interview, does Delbert believe that statement still rings true? "Songwriters are a voice of the people," McClinton reflects. "My own stories and the experiences of others are, or could be, true. I write and sing about the problems, the dreams, the hopes of the everyday person. Bad grammar used properly is poetry. It is art, and it is what we sound like today. I write songs the way I am going to sing them. Phonetically. 'Del-bonics,'" he adds.[6]

One might wonder whether Delbert has ever doubted his career and life choices. He says, "I have never been jaded about music. I have never ever wondered if I was doing the right thing. I have never doubted what I was doing, though I have not always been able to back that up. I am still a work in progress. I still have that hunger in there—that thing that has always been there. It keeps me calm. I am not doing this for anybody else. I am playing and writing and singing for me. If I make me happy, I am doing what I need to be doing. And if I make other people feel good along the way, that's the bonus."[7]

Decades after Delbert McClinton first took the stage at the Big V Jamboree in the burned-out Liberator Theatre and sang "Crazy Arms," Delbert, Glen Clark, and Gary Nicholson wrote the opening song for the *Blind, Crippled and Crazy* album that answers the questions of Delbert's relevance, longevity, lessons learned, and staying power:

> *I ain't old but I been around a long time*
> *Long enough to know age is just a state of mind*
> *Some things just get better like fine wine*
> *I ain't old, but I been around a long time*
>
> *I've seen 'em come and go and come back around again*
> *Some of life's hard lessons finally started sinkin' in*
> *If you don't do nothing you're gonna live to regret*
> *You won't have to live with what you can't forget*
> *I ain't old but I been around a long time*
>
> *Some people say you burn out if you go too fast*
> *But I just want to live it up as long as it lasts*
> *If there's a secret to life I've ever found*
> *It's all about staying in the here and now*
> *I ain't old, but I been around a long time.*

Keep your expectations under control
You just might surprise yourself
To see how far you go
Don't hold too tight, let it all unwind
Keep a positive state of mind
I ain't old, but I been around a long time.[8]

Afterword

Delbert McClinton and I had no formal agreement about this project. I wanted to chronicle Delbert's story; I did not want this to be an "authorized" biography; and I wanted Delbert and Wendy to trust me to tell his story without limits or censure.

Beyond a typical biography, this is the story of the times as they were changing: a history of significant American musical moments and movements. The life and times of Delbert McClinton provide a soundtrack for many of America's greatest musical scenes and snapshots in American history. Chance meetings and casual recollections take on first-person, American history lessons, as Delbert wanders through defining moments drawn from the pages of history books. From watching an early space missile test off Cape Canaveral in Florida to the JFK assassination, presidential inaugurations and Farm Aid concerts, tour bus breakdowns and high-profile crime scenes, McClinton's unique story of American history brings with it a strong rhythm section, an authentic lyrical narrative, heartfelt vocals, and a hot harmonica lead.

In compiling more than three hundred hours of interviews, I have learned much more than will fit between the covers of this book. This experience has opened doors to newfound friendships and broad horizons. Many stories, some off-the-record and some that were better spoken than written, were left out of the book. Jay Curlee's award-winning *Rocking the Boat* DVD shares many great stories that I didn't want to duplicate. There were a few people with whom I did not get the chance to talk. Among them, Delbert's oldest child, Monty, politely declined to be interviewed, and I respected his privacy.

Examining the life story of a musician as significant as Delbert McClinton is a daunting task. There are pendulum swings in all lives, and Delbert's is certainly no exception. He has walked the muddy banks of America's cultural currents; written his own chapters of music history; participated in the music industry's rejection of racial divisiveness; and, in the process, brought us music that can make us smile, cry, dance, or just tap our feet.

While Delbert has certainly borne witness to life's circumstances, he has never given up on his dream. So, his story becomes one of perseverance, perhaps even redemption.

Early in the project, I chose to title this book after a song of his, "One of the Fortunate Few." Exactly why I had chosen that song was not completely clear to me until this book project was near completion.

My husband, Mark, and I met with Delbert and his wife, Wendy, for a celebratory margarita and Mexican dinner at a South Austin restaurant. We smiled a lot as we swapped stories. Delbert was relaxed. The old saying "comfortable in his own skin" came to mind. Delbert's story had become a success story.

However, there was more than that. It was easy to observe how deeply Delbert and Wendy cared for each other. How much they complemented each other. How much their now shared success story meant to both of them.

When we got home that night, Mark said, "Their success story has ultimately become a love story. That's the story."

Shouldn't we all be that fortunate?

Appendix

Live Performance Song List

Delbert McClinton never plays the same show twice, but the band keeps a list of songs most likely to be played during a set. Guitarist Bob Britt shares this current song list, circa 2017.

Up tempo

C	Back to Louisiana
D	Best of Me
C	Do It
G	Everytime I Roll Dice
C	Giving It Up
D	I'm With You
Bb	Leap of Faith
A	Lie No Better
C	Linda Lou
D	Livin' It Down
E	Monkey Around
G	Never Been Rocked
A	New York City
G	Old Weakness
G	Oughta No
C	Plain Old Making Love
A	Same Kind of Crazy
E	Shaky Ground
G	Shotgun Rider
B/D	Skip Chaser
C	Squeeze Me In
D	Take Me to the River

A   Two More Bottles of Wine
Bb   Why Me

Mid-tempo

E   B Movie
A(F#-) Doin' What You Do
Bb   Fine and Healthy Thing
Ab   Holy Cow
E   Neva
F   One of the Fortunate Few
G   People Just Love to Talk
E   Right to Be Wrong
F   Rosy
A   Sandy Beaches
G   Starting a Rumor

Down tempo

F   Bad Haircut
E   Blues as Blues Can Get
G   Down Into Mexico
Bb   Dreams to Remember
F   Fever
F/C Have a Little Faith
A   I Want to Love You
A   Jealous Kind
A-   More & More Less & Less
C   Pullin' the Strings
Bb   Read Me My Rights
Bb   Rebecca Rebecca
G   San Miguel
Bb   Sending Me Angels
E   When Rita Leaves
F#   You Were Never Mine

Notes

Prologue

1. Delbert McClinton, interview by the author, April 24, 2015, Austin TX.

2. Brandy McClinton, interview by the author, May 1, 2016, San Marcos, TX.

3. Ibid.

4. Delbert McClinton, interview by the author, April 24, 2015, Austin, TX.

5. Ibid.

6. Ibid.

7. Clay McClinton, interview by the author, May 1, 2016, San Marcos, TX.

8. Delbert McClinton, interview by the author, April 24, 2015, Austin, TX.

9. Ibid.

10. Don Imus, interview by the author, August 5, 2015, Brenham, TX.

11. Delbert McClinton, interview by the author, September 2015, Austin, TX.

Chapter 1

1. Delbert McClinton, personal journal entry, 1987.

2. Troy Kimmel, email message to the author, June 11, 2016.

3. McClinton, personal journal entry, 1987.

4. Ray Westbrook, "AJ Remembers: Ransom Canyon." *Lubbock Avalanche-Journal*, August 14, 2011, http://lubbockonline.com/life-columnists/2011–08–14/ransom-canyon-was-cattle-ranch-it-was-town#.V2AJq-YrL4M.

5. Art Leatherwood, "Llano Estacado," in *Handbook of Texas Online*, accessed June 11, 2016, http://www.tshaonline.org/handbook/online/articles/ry102.

6. Lawrence L. Graves, "Lubbock, TX," in *Handbook of Texas Online*, accessed June 11, 2016, http://www.tshaonline.org/handbook/online/articles/hd104.

7. Delbert McClinton, interview by the author, July 8, 2015, San Miguel de Allende, MX.

8. Michael Hall, "Gotta Lubbock," *Texas Monthly* (May 2002).

9. Delbert McClinton, telephone interview by Michael Hall, July 17, 2001. Wittliff Collections at Texas State University, SWWC Accession No. 2001–143 Folder 1.

10. Terry Allen, interview by the author, June 8, 2016, Santa Fe, NM.

11. Angela Strehli, interview by the author, May 24, 2016, San Francisco, CA.

12. Joe Nick Patoski, interview by the author, April 11, 2015, Wimberley, TX.

13. Delbert McClinton, personal journal entry, 1987.

14. Delbert McClinton, interview by the author, July 8, 2015, San Miguel de Allende, MX.

15. Delbert McClinton, interview by the author, April 24, 2015, Austin, TX.

16. Delbert McClinton, interview by the author, July 8, 2015, San Miguel de Allende, MX.

17. McClinton, personal journal entry, 1987.

18. Delbert McClinton, interview by the author, June 2, 2016, Nashville, TN.

19. Delbert McClinton, interview by the author, May 31, 2016, Nashville, TN.

20. Delbert McClinton, interview by the author, July 8, 2015, San Miguel de Allende, MX.

21. Delbert McClinton, interview by the author, July 10, 2015, San Miguel de Allende, MX.

22. Delbert McClinton, interview by the author, July 9, 2015, San Miguel de Allende, MX.

23. McClinton, personal journal entry, n.d.

24. Ibid.

25. Delbert McClinton, interview by the author, May 31, 2016, Nashville, TN.

26. Ibid.

27. McClinton, personal journal entry, n.d.

28. Ibid.

29. Delbert McClinton, interview by the author, July 9, 2015, San Miguel de Allende, MX.

Note: The Harley Sadler Tent Shows were secular traveling shows that were part medicine show, part theatre, part music, and a little vaudeville. Long after they fell from popularity in large cities, they continued to travel through rural Texas until Sadler folded the tents and began a second career as a Texas legislator. (Ashby, Clifford, and Suzanne Depauw May. *Trouping Through Texas: Harley Sadler and His Tent Show*. Bowling Green, Ohio: Bowling Green State University Popular Press, 1982.)

30. Terry Allen, interview by the author, June 8, 2016, Santa Fe, NM.

31. Delbert McClinton, interview by the author, June 9, 2016, Nashville, TN.

32. Meredith McClain, "Caprock Chronicles: Strange Phenomena Seen over Lubbock Skies in 1951." *Lubbock Avalanche-Journal*, February

14, 2016, http://lubbockonline.com/life/2016-02-13/caprock-chronicles-strange-phenomena-seen-over-lubbock-skies-1951.

33. Ibid.

34. Delbert McClinton, interview by the author, May 31, 2016, Nashville, TN.

Chapter 2

1. Delbert McClinton, interview by the author, May 31, 2016, Nashville, TN.

2. Ibid.

3. Richard F. Selcer, *Fort Worth: A Texas Original!* (Austin: Texas State Historical Association, 2004).

4. Ibid.

5. Ibid.

6. Ann Arnold, *Gamblers and Gangsters, Fort Worth's Jacksboro Highway* (Austin: Eakin Press, 1998).

7. Ibid.

8. Joe Nick Patoski, interview by the author, April 11, 2015, Wimberley, TX.

9. Delbert McClinton, interview by the author, June 20, 2016, Austin, TX.

10. Delbert McClinton, interview by the author, July 8, 2015, San Miguel de Allende, MX.

11. Delbert McClinton, interview by the author, July 9, 2015, San Miguel de Allende, MX.

12. Ibid.

13. Delbert McClinton, interview by the author, July 8, 2015, San Miguel de Allende, MX.

14. Delbert McClinton, interview by the author, June 2, 2016, Nashville, TN.

15. Paul Hemphill, *Lovesick Blues: The Life of Hank Williams* (New York: Viking, 2005).

16. Ibid.

17. Delbert McClinton, interview by the author, April 24, 2015, Austin, TX.

18. Delbert McClinton, personal journal entry, 1991.

19. Delbert McClinton, interview by the author, July 8, 2015, San Miguel de Allende, MX.

20. Ibid.

21. Delbert McClinton, interview by the author, April 24, 2015, Austin, TX.

Chapter 3

1. Delbert McClinton, interview by the author, April 24, 2015, Austin, Texas.

2. Ibid.

3. Big Joe Turner (rights assigned to his wife, Lou Willie Turner), Progressive Music Publishing Company, Unichappel Music, Inc., 1954.

4. Gary Cartwright, "Twenty-Five Years of One Night Stands," *Rolling Stone* (May 28, 1981): 76.

5. Delbert McClinton, interview by the author, April 24, 2015, Austin, Texas.

6. "Big Joe Turner Was the Brawny-Voiced "Boss of the Blues." Rock and Roll Hall of Fame, accessed June 21, 2016, https://www.rockhall .com/inductees/big-joe-turner/bio/.

7. Ibid.

8. Delbert McClinton, interview by the author, June 2, 2016, Nashville, TN.

9. Peter Guralnick, *Last Train to Memphis* (New York: Little, Brown and Co., 1994), 105.

10. Ibid., 146.

11. James J. Mulay, "Rock and Film," *Encyclopedia Britannica*, accessed June 24, 2016, http://www.britannica.com/contributor/James-J-Mulay/4362.

12. Jeremy Marks, "Oh Daddio! How Blackboard Jungle Changed Rock & Roll," *Boogie Chillin'*, accessed March 20, 2017, https://boo giechillen.wordpress.com/"oh-daddio"-how-blackboard-jungle-changed-rock-roll/.

13. Ibid.

14. Delbert McClinton, interview by the author, June 2, 2016, Nashville, TN.

15. Max C. Freedman and James E. Myers, performed by Bill Haley and the Comets, Decca Records, 1954.

16. "500 Greatest Songs of All Time," Rolling Stone, accessed March 12, 2016, http://www.rollingstone.com/music/lists/the-500-greatest-songs-of-all-time-20110407.

17. Delbert McClinton, interview by the author, May 31, 2016, Nashville, TN.

18. Delbert McClinton, interview by the author, September 14, 2016, Austin, TX.

19. Delbert McClinton, interview by the author, July 7, 2015, San Miguel de Allende, MX.

20. Delbert McClinton, interview by the author, July 8, 2015, San Miguel de Allende, MX.

21. Delbert McClinton, interview by the author, July 7, 2015, San Miguel de Allende, MX.

22. Delbert McClinton, interview by the author, July 9, 2015, San Miguel de Allende, MX.

23. Delbert McClinton, personal journal entry, circa 1987.

24. Ibid.

25. Ibid.

26. Kathleen Hudson, *Telling Stories Writing Songs: An Album of Texas Songwriters* (Austin: University of Texas Press, 2001), 104–108.

27. Delbert McClinton, interview by the author, April 24, 2015, Austin, TX.

28. Delbert McClinton, personal journal entry, circa 1987.

29. Delbert McClinton, interview by the author, July 7, 2015, San Miguel de Allende, MX.

30. Delbert McClinton, interview by the author, June 1, 2016, Nashville, TN.

31. "Arlington Heights High School," Wikipedia, accessed May 11, 2016, https://en.wikipedia.org/wiki/Arlington_Heights_High_School.

Chapter 4

1. Delbert McClinton, interview by the author, July 11, 2015, San Miguel de Allende, MX.

2. For the sake of consistency, we will spell the band's name as *Straitjackets* throughout this book.

3. Delbert McClinton, scrapbook #1, private collection, accessed June 2, 2016.

4. Ibid.

5. Eddie Miller, interview by the author, November 30, 2016, Fort Worth, TX.

6. Delbert McClinton, scrapbook #1, private collection, accessed June 2, 2016.

7. Ibid.

8. Delbert McClinton, interview by the author, July 11, 2015, San Miguel de Allende, MX.

9. Ibid.

10. Delbert McClinton, interview by the author, July 9, 2015, San Miguel de Allende, MX.

11. Delbert McClinton, personal journal entry, circa 1987.

12. Delbert McClinton, interview by the author, August 4, 2015, Nashville, TN.

13. Delbert McClinton, scrapbook #1, private collection, accessed July 1, 2016.

14. Joe Nick Patoski, interview by the author, April 11, 2016, Wimberley, TX.

15. Ibid.

16. Don Was, interview by the author, May 14, 2016, Los Angeles, CA.

17. Gary Cartwright, "Twenty-Five Years of One Night Stands," *Rolling Stone*, May 28, 1981, 34.

18. Gary Cartwright, email message to the author, August 15, 2015.

19. Delbert McClinton, "Victim of Life's Circumstances," Universal Music Publishing Group, 1974.

20. Joe Nick Patoski, interview by the author, July 19, 2013, Wimberley, TX.

21. Karl Hagstrom Miller, *Segregating Sound* (Durham: Duke University Press, 2010).

22. Mark Kurlansky, *Ready for a Brand New Beat: How "Dancing in the Streets" became the Anthem for a Changing America* (New York: Penguin, 2013), 1–4.

23. Gregg Andrews, interview by the author, July 31, 2015, San Marcos, TX.

24. Delbert McClinton, interview by the author, July 9, 2015, San Miguel de Allende, MX.

25. Delbert McClinton, interview by the author, April 24, 2015, Austin, TX.

26. McClinton, personal journal entry, circa 1987.

27. Ibid.

28. Ibid.

29. Ibid.

30. Ibid.

31. Delbert McClinton, interview by the author, July 10, 2015, San Miguel de Allende, MX.

32. Delbert McClinton, interview by the author, April 18, 2016, Austin, Texas.

33. Ibid.

34. Delbert McClinton, interview by the author, July 8, 2015, San Miguel de Allende, MX.

35. Delbert McClinton, interview by the author, July 9, 2015, San Miguel de Allende, MX.

36. Mike Nichols, *Lost Fort Worth* (Charleston, SC: The History Press, 2014).

37. Ann Arnold, *Gamblers and Gangsters: Fort Worth's Jacksboro Highway in the 1940s and 1950s* (Austin, TX: Eakin Press, 1998).

38. Delbert McClinton, scrapbook #1, private collection, accessed July 2, 2016.

39. Delbert McClinton, interview by the author, July 10, 2015, San Miguel de Allende, MX.

40. Ibid.

41. Ibid.

42. Delbert McClinton, interview by the author, July 9, 2015, San Miguel de Allende, MX.

43. Delbert McClinton, interview by the author, July 10, 2015, San

Miguel de Allende, MX.

44. Mike Nichols, *Lost Fort Worth* (Charleston, SC: The History Press, 2014).

45. Delbert McClinton, interview by the author, April 18, 2016, Austin, TX

46. Delbert McClinton, interview by the author, September 14, 2016, Austin, TX.

47. Ibid.

48. Delbert McClinton, personal journal entry, n.d.

49. Michael McCall, "The Good Life: Veteran Singer finds happiness at home," *The Tennessean*, accessed July 6, 2015, http://weeklywire.com/ww/10-13-97/nash_music-lede.html

50. Cartwright, "Twenty-Five Years of One Night Stands," 33.

51. Philip A. Lieberman, *Radio's Morning Show Personalities: Early Hour Broadcasters and Deejays from the 1920s to the 1990s* (Jefferson, NC: McFarland & Company, 1996), 58.

52. Delbert McClinton, interview by the author, April 18, 2016, Austin, TX.

Chapter 5

1. Delbert McClinton, interview by the author, July 9, 2015, San Miguel de Allende, MX.

2. Laurie Jasinski, ed., *The Handbook of Texas Music*, 2nd ed. (Denton: Texas State Historical Association, 2012), 561–62.

3. KFJZ background and history, accessed July 28, 2015, https://en.wikipedia.org/wiki/KFJZ.

4. Jasinski, *The Handbook of Texas Music*, 561–62.

5. Delbert McClinton, interview by the author, July 10, 2015, San Miguel de Allende, MX.

6. Bruce Channel, interview by the author, August 13, 2015, Nashville, TN.

7. *Handbook of Texas Online*, Gary S. Hickinbotham, "Montgomery, Marvin [Smokey]," accessed July 9, 2016, https://tshaonline.org/handbook/online/articles/fmoce.

8. Bruce Channel, interview by the author, August 13, 2015, Nashville, TN.

9. Delbert McClinton, interview by the author, July 10, 2015, San Miguel de Allende, MX.

10. Bruce Channel, interview by the author, August 13, 2015, Nashville, TN.

11. Delbert McClinton, personal journal entry, circa 1987.

12. Delbert McClinton, interview by the author, July 10, 2015, San Miguel de Allende, MX.

13. Bruce Channel, interview by the author, August 13, 2015, Nashville, TN.

14. Ibid.

15. Delbert McClinton, interview by the author, July 9, 2015, San Miguel de Allende, MX.

16. Ibid.

17. Delbert McClinton, interview by the author, September 14, 2016, Austin, TX.

18. Delbert McClinton, interview by the author, July 9, 2015, San Miguel de Allende, MX.

19. Delbert McClinton, interview by the author, April 24, 2015, Austin, TX.

20. Delbert McClinton, interview by the author, July 7, 2015, San Miguel de Allende, MX.

21. "Howdy Mr. President: A Fort Worth Perspective of JFK," University of Texas, Arlington Library Special Exhibit, accessed August 13, 2016, http://library.uta.edu/jfk/motorcadeFW.html#2.

22. Delbert McClinton, interview by the author, September 14, 2016, Austin, TX.

23. Delbert McClinton, interview by the author, September 15, 2016, Austin, TX.

24. Delbert McClinton, interview by the author, April 24, 2015, Austin, TX.

25. Ibid.

26. Ibid.

27. Don Imus, interview by the author, August 5, 2015, Brenham, TX.

Chapter 6

1. Delbert McClinton, interview by the author, June 2, 2016, Nashville, TN.

2. "Found Dead in Car: Asphyxiation Case Probed by Police," *Lubbock Avalanche-Journal*, June 9, 1965.

3. Bruce Nixon, "Billy Sanders: The Subtle Side of Texas R&B," *Guitar Player*, December 1983, 61.

4. Howard DeWitt and Lee Cotten, "Delbert McClinton: The Musical Journey of a Rock Pioneer," *DISCoveries*, July 1992, 26–31.

5. Nixon, "Billy Sanders," 63.

6. Peter Guralnick, *Lost Highway,* enhanced edition (New York: Little, Brown, 2012), Kindle edition.

7. Ibid.

8. Delbert McClinton, interview by the author, July 8, 2015, San Miguel de Allende, MX.

9. Jerry Conditt, interview by the author, May 2, 2016, Harlingen, TX.

10. Peter Guralnick, *Lost Highway.*

11. References to North Texas State University will be edited to reflect the current name, the University of North Texas, for this book.

12. Jerry Conditt, interview by the author, May 2, 2016, Harlingen, TX.

13. Ibid.

14. Ibid.

15. Ibid.

16. DeWitt and Cotten, "Delbert McClinton."

17. Ibid.

18. Jerry Conditt, personal archives, accessed July 2, 2015.

19. Jerry Conditt, interview by the author, May 2, 2016, Harlingen, TX.

20. Ibid.

21. Delbert McClinton, interview by the author, May 31, 2016, Nashville, TN.

22. Jerry Conditt, interview by the author, May 2, 2016, Harlingen, TX.

23. Ibid.

24. Delbert McClinton, interview by the author, June 2, 2016, Nashville, TN.

25. Ibid.

26. Delbert McClinton, KCUL Live 35 flyer, personal archives, June 19, 1965.

Chapter 7

1. Delbert McClinton, interview by the author, July 9, 2015, San Miguel de Allende, MX.

2. Howard DeWitt and Lee Cotten, "Delbert McClinton: The Musical Journey of a Rock Pioneer," *DISCoveries*, July 1992, 26–31.

3. Delbert McClinton, interview by the author, July 9, 2015, San Miguel de Allende, MX.

4. Ibid.

5. DeWitt and Cotten, "Delbert McClinton."

6. "About Bill Mack," Bill Mack Country, accessed July 24, 2016, http://www.billmackcountry.com/aboutbillmack.htm.

7. Bill Mack, interview by the author, July 23, 2016, Fort Worth, TX.

8. Ibid.

9. Jerry Conditt to Congressman Jim Wright, 1965 November 6, Conditt personal archives.

10. Reid Orvedahl, *Marrying to Avoid the Draft*, ABC News, February 1, 2016, accessed July 18, 2016, http://abcnews.go.com/Primetime/story?id=132298&page=1.

11. Ibid.

12. Ibid.

13. Jerry Conditt, Rondels Blue Book, personal archives, n.d.

14. Delbert McClinton, interview by the author, April 24, 2015, Austin, TX.

15. Delbert McClinton, "Outlaws," personal journal entry, n.d., accessed July 24, 2016.

16. Jerry Conditt, news clippings and advertisements, personal archives, n.d.

17. Ibid.

18. Ibid.

19. Jerry Conditt, interview by the author, May 2, 2016, Harlingen, TX.

20. Mike Callahan and David Edwards, "The Dot Records Story, Part 2," last updated November 10, 1999, accessed July 24, 2016, http://www.bsnpubs.com/dot/dotstoryb.html.

21. Bill Mack, interview by the author, July 23, 2016, Fort Worth, TX.

22. Doug Sahm, interview by the author, October 14, 1997, San Marcos, TX.

23. Bill Mack, interview by the author, July 23, 2016, Fort Worth, TX.

24. Peter Guralnick, "Delbert McClinton: The Hard Road from Fort Worth to the Top Ten," *Westward: Dallas Times Herald*, March 8, 1981.

25. DeWitt and Cotten, "Delbert McClinton."

26. Ibid.

27. Delbert McClinton, interview by the author, June 3, 2016, Nashville, TN.

28. Ibid.

29. Delbert McClinton interview by the author, June 2, 2016, Nashville, TN.

30. Delbert McClinton interview by the author, June 1, 2016, Nashville, TN.

Chapter 8

1. Delbert McClinton, interview by the author, April 18, 2016, Austin, TX.

2. Glen Clark, interview by the author, August 10, 2015, Fort Worth, TX. (In 1946, George Bragg founded the Texas Boys Choir, now known as the Texas Center for Arts and Academics. By 1958, when Glen Clark was a member, the group had traveled more than fifty thousand miles throughout the United States and Mexico, performing choral music.)

3. Ibid.

4. Ibid.

5. Ibid.

6. Ibid.

7. Ibid.

8. Ibid.

9. Jim Macnie, "Neil Young Bio," *Rolling Stone*, accessed July 30, 2016, http://www.rollingstone.com/music/artists/neil-young/biography.

10. Vincent Bugliosi and Curt Gentry, *Helter Skelter—The True Story*

of the Manson Murders 25th Anniversary Edition (New York: W.W. Norton & Company, 1994).

11. Bill Mack, interview by the author, June 23, 2016, Fort Worth, TX.

12. Jan Reid with Shawn Sahm, *Texas Tornado: The Times and Music of Doug Sahm* (Austin: University of Texas Press, 2010), 39–42.

13. Glen Clark, interview by the author, May 9, 2016, Fort Worth, TX.

14. Delbert McClinton, interview by the author, July 10, 2015, San Miguel de Allende, MX.

15. Delbert McClinton, interview by the author, April 24, 2015, Austin, TX.

16. Glen Clark, interview by the author, May 9, 2016, Fort Worth, TX.

17. Delbert McClinton, interview by the author, April 24, 2015, Austin, TX.

18. Delbert McClinton, "Two More Bottles of Wine," Universal Music Publishing, 1973.

19. Delbert McClinton, interview by the author, April 24, 2015, Austin, TX.

20. Gary Cartwright, "Twenty-Five Years of One Night Stands," *Rolling Stone*, May 28, 1981, 34.

Chapter 9

1. Delbert McClinton, interview by the author, July 2, 2016, Nashville, TN.

2. Glen Clark, interview by the author, August 10, 2015, Fort Worth, TX.

3. Ibid.

4. Ibid.

5. Ibid.

6. T Bone Burnett, interview by the author, June 10, 2016, Los Angeles, CA.

7. Ibid.

8. Ibid.

9. "Discography and Store," T Bone Burnett, accessed March 25, 2017, http://www.tboneburnett.com/.

10. Glen Clark, interview by the author, August 10, 2015, Fort Worth, Texas.

11. Bob Colacello, "Remembering Earl McGrath: Music Producer, Art Gallerist and Indefinable Cultural Force," *Vanity Fair*, accessed January 21, 2016, http://www.vanityfair.com/culture/2016/01/earl-mcgrath-music-producer-art-gallerist.

12. Delbert McClinton, interview by the author, July 2, 2016, Nashville, TN.

13. Glen Clark, interview by the author, May 9, 2016, Fort Worth, TX.

14. Delbert McClinton, interview by the author, July 2, 2016, Nashville, TN.

15. Ibid.

16. Glen Clark, interview by the author, May 9, 2016, Fort Worth, TX.

17. Richie Unterberger, *AllMusic Review*, accessed August 9, 2015, http://www.allmusic.com/album/McClinton-glen-mw0000138886.

18. Joe Nick Patoski, interview by the author, April 11, 2016, Wimberley, TX.

19. "Delbert and Glen," *Rising Storm* (blog), September 1, 2011, http://therisingstorm.net/delbert-and-glen-delbert-and-glen/.

20. Glen Clark, interview by the author, May 9, 2016, Fort Worth, TX.

21. Howard DeWitt and Lee Cotten, "Delbert McClinton: The Musical Journey of a Rock Pioneer," *DISCoveries*, July 1992, 26–31.

22. Glen Clark, interview by the author, May 9, 2016, Fort Worth, TX.

23. Ibid.

Chapter 10

1. Delbert McClinton, interview by the author, April 24, 2015, Austin, TX.

2. Delbert McClinton, interview by the author, August 11, 2016, Nashville, TN.

3. Delbert McClinton, interview by the author, May 31, 2016, Nashville, TN.

4. Delbert McClinton, interview by the author, June 1, 2016, Nashville, TN.

5. Ibid.

6. Delbert McClinton, interview by the author, June 2, 2016, Nashville, TN.

7. Howard DeWitt and Lee Cotten, "Delbert McClinton: The Musical Journey of a Rock Pioneer," *DISCoveries*, July 1992, 26–31.

8. Delbert McClinton, interview by the author, June 1, 2016, Nashville, TN.

9. Glen Clark, interview by the author, August 10, 2015, Fort Worth, TX.

10. Peter Guralnick, "Delbert McClinton: The Hard Road from Fort Worth to the Top Ten," *Westward: Dallas Times Herald*, March 8, 1981.

11. Delbert McClinton, interview by the author, June 2, 2016, Nashville, TN.

12. Delbert McClinton, interview by the author, April 24, 2015, Austin, TX.

13. Ibid.

14. Ibid.

15. DeWitt and Cotten, "Delbert McClinton."

16. Delbert McClinton, "Victim of Life's Circumstances," Universal Music Publishing, 1992.

17. Joe Ely, interview by the author, May 19, 2016, Austin, TX.

18. Jan Reid, *The Improbable Rise of Redneck Rock* (Austin: University of Texas Press, 2010) 300.

19. Bob Kirsh, *Love Rustler* by Delbert McClinton (Nashville: ABC Records, 1977), liner notes.

20. Delbert McClinton, interview by the author, March 24, 2015, Austin, TX.

21. DeWitt and Cotten, "Delbert McClinton."

22. Delbert McClinton, interview by the author, June 1, 2016, Nashville, TN.

Chapter 11

1. Delbert McClinton, interview by the author, June 9, 2015, San Miguel de Allende, MX.

2. Jan Reid and Don Roth, "The Coming of Redneck Hip," *Texas Monthly*, November 1973, http://www.texasmonthly.com/the-culture/the-coming-of-redneck-hip/.

3. Jan Reid, *The Improbable Rise of Redneck Rock* (Austin: University of Texas Press, 2004), 6.

4. Jan Reid, *Texas Tornado: The Times and Music of Doug Sahm* (Austin: University of Texas Press, 2010), 76.

5. Bill Mack, interview by the author, July 31, 2016, Fort Worth, TX.

6. Delbert McClinton, interview by the author, April 24, 2015, Austin, TX.

7. Joe Nick Patoski, interview by the author, April 11, 2016, Wimberley, TX.

8. Joe Nick Patoski, *An Epic Life: Willie Nelson* (New York: Little, Brown and Company, 2008), 219–20.

9 Ibid.

10. Colin Escott, "Road Scholar: Delbert McClinton," in *Tattooed on Their Tongues: A Journey Through the Backrooms of American Music* (New York: Schirmer Books, 1996), 203.

11. Joe Ely, interview by the author, May 19, 2016, Austin, TX.

12. Ibid.

13. Ibid.

14. Delbert McClinton, interview by the author, August 11, 2016, Nashville, TN.

15. Ibid.

16. Travis D. Stimeling, *Cosmic Cowboys and New Hicks: The Countercultural Sounds of Austin's Progressive Country Music Scene* (New York: Oxford University Press, 2011).

17. Joe Ely, interview by the author, May 19, 2016, Austin, TX.

18. Delbert McClinton, interview by the author, August 11, 2016, Nashville, TN

19. Joe Nick Patoski, interview by the author, April 11, 2016, Wimberley, TX.

20. Angela Strehli, interview by the author, May 24, 2016, Los Angeles, CA.

21. Ibid.

22. Ibid.

23. Marcia Ball, interview by the author, April 16, 2016, Austin, TX.

24. Ibid.

25. Reid, *Texas Tornado*, 79.

26. Ibid.

27. Ibid.

28. Peter Guralnick, "The Hard Road from Fort Worth to the Top Ten,"*Westward: Dallas Times Herald*, March 8, 1981.

29. Ibid.

30. Delbert McClinton, interview by the author, July 9, 2015, San Miguel De Allende, MX.

31. Ibid.

32. Gary Cartwright, *Blood Will Tell* (New York: Simon and Schuster, 1979).

33. Ibid.

34. Delbert McClinton, interview by the author, July 9, 2015, San Miguel De Allende, MX.

35. Jerry Conditt, interview by the author, May 2, 2016, Harlingen, TX.

36. Delbert McClinton, interview by the author, July 9, 2015, San Miguel De Allende, MX.

37. Aaron Latham, "The Ballad of the Urban Cowboy: America's Search for True Grit," *Esquire*, September 12, 1978.

Chapter 12

1. Delbert McClinton, interview by the author, September 13, 2016, Austin, TX.

2. Aaron Latham, "The Ballad of the Urban Cowboy: America's Search for True Grit," *Esquire*, September 12, 1978.

3. Cleve Hattersley, interview by the author, June 6, 2016, Austin, TX.

4. Jason Mellard, *Progressive Country: How the 1970s Transformed the Texan in Popular Culture* (Austin: University of Texas Press, 2013).

5. Cleve Hattersley, interview by the author, June 6, 2016, Austin, TX.

6. "Muscle Shoals Horns," *AllMusic Online*, accessed August 19, 2016, http://www.allmusic.com/artist/muscle-shoals-horns-mn0000399945/.

7. Mark Pucci, interview by the author, May 23, 2016, Atlanta, GA.

8. Elvis Costello, *Unfaithful Music and Disappearing Ink* (New York: Blue Rider Press, 2015).

9. Roger Gatchet, "Still on a Mission from God: Interview with Dan Aykroyd," *All These Blues*, first broadcast 18 May 2007 by KENW.

10. Thom Jurek, AllMusic Review, accessed August 19, 2016, http://www.allmusic.com/album/keeper-of-the-flame-mw0000100838.

11. Mark Pucci, interview by the author, May 23, 2016, Atlanta, GA.

12. Delbert McClinton, interview by the author, August 17, 2016, Nashville TN.

13. Ibid.

14. Ibid.

15. Delbert McClinton, interview by the author, July 9, 2015, San Miguel de Allende, MX.

16. Delbert McClinton, interview by the author, August 17, 2016, Nashville, TN.

17. The Chitlin' Circuit was a name given to a group of theatres and nightclubs throughout the Midwest and southern United States that were safe for African American artists, comedians, and other entertainers to perform in during the era of racial segregation.

18. Ernie Durawa, interview by the author, May 25, 2016, Austin, TX.

19. Delbert McClinton, interview by the author, July 9, 2015, San Miguel de Allende, MX.

20. Ibid.

21. Ernie Durawa, interview by the author, May 25, 2016, Austin, TX.

22. James Pennebaker, interview by the author, January 13, 2016, Delbert McClinton Cruise.

23. Bruce Nixon, "Billy Sanders: The Subtle Side of Texas R&B," *Guitar Player*, December 1983, 63.

24. James Pennebaker, interview by the author, January 13, 2016, Delbert McClinton Cruise.

25. Ernie Durawa, interview by the author, May 25, 2016, Austin, TX.

26. Delbert McClinton, interview by the author, August 17, 2016, Nashville, TN.

27. James Pennebaker, interview by the author, January 13, 2016, Delbert McClinton Cruise.

28. Peter Cooper, "Master Music Talent Scout Don Light dies," *USA Today*, June 19, 2014, accessed August 21, 2016, http://www.usatoday.com/story/life/music/2014/06/19/gospel-music-hall-of-famer-don-light-dies/10960229/.

29. Ibid.

30. Mike Greenblatt, "Rant 'n' Roll: One Great Read," *The Aquarian Weekly*, January 27, 2016.

31. Peter Guralnick, interview by the author, May 24, 2016, Boston, MA.

32. Delbert McClinton, interview by the author, August 17, 2016, Nashville, TN.

33. Gary Cartwright, "Twenty-Five Years of One Night Stands," *Rolling Stone*, May 28, 1981, 78.

34. Ibid.

35. Ibid.

36. Ibid.

37. Delbert McClinton, interview by the author, September 14, 2016, Austin, TX.

38. Delbert McClinton, interview by the author, June 2, 2016, Nashville, TN.

39. Cartwright, "Twenty-Five Years," 34.

40. Delbert McClinton, interview by the author, August 17, 2016, Nashville, TN.

41. Cartwright, "Twenty-Five Years," 78.

42. James Pennebaker, interview by the author, January 15, 2016, Delbert McClinton Cruise.

43. Gary Cartwright, "Twenty-Five Years," 79.

Chapter 13

1. Silas House, "Delbert McClinton – Let the Good Times Roll," *No Depression Online*, October 31, 2002, accessed August 4, 2015, http://nodepression.com/article/McClinton-mcclinton-let-good-times-roll.

2. Delbert McClinton, interview by the author, July 9, 2015, San Miguel de Allende, MX.

3. Wendy Goldstein, interview by the author, July 10, 2015, San Miguel de Allende, MX.

4. Delbert McClinton, interview by the author, July 9, 2015, San Miguel de Allende, MX.

5. Ibid.

6. Wendy Goldstein, interview by the author, July 10, 2015, San Miguel de Allende, MX.

7. Ibid.

8. Ibid.

9. Ibid.

10. "Biography of Doc Pomus," Felder Pomus Entertainment, accessed August 21, 2016, http://www.felderpomus.com/docpomus1.html#ShortBio.

11. Delbert McClinton interview by the author, August 17, 2016, Nashville, TN.

12. Ibid.

13. Delbert McClinton, "I Want to Love You," Delbert McClinton Music, 1984.

14. David Hickey, interview by the author, August 27, 2016, Fort Worth, TX.

15. Delbert McClinton, interview by the author, August 26, 2016, Nashville, TN.

16. Wendy Goldstein, Interview by the author, May 15, 2016, Austin, TX.

17. Wendy Goldstein, interview by the author, July 11, 2015, San Miguel de Allende, MX.

18. Wendy Goldstein, Interview by the author, May 15, 2016, Austin, TX.

19. Ibid.

20. Ibid.

21. David Hickey, interview by the author, August 26, 2016, Fort Worth, TX.

22. James Pennebaker, interview by the author, August 14, 2015, Nashville, TN.

23. David Hickey, interview by the author, August 26, 2016, Fort Worth, TX.

24. Ibid.

25. Wendy Goldstein, interview by the author, July 9, 2015, San Miguel de Allende, MX.

26. Delbert McClinton interview by the author, July 10, 2015, San Miguel de Allende, MX.

27. Delbert McClinton interview by the author, July 11, 2015, San Miguel de Allende, MX.

28. Delbert McClinton, interview by the author, August 23, 2016, Nashville, TN.

Chapter 14

1. Delbert McClinton, interview by the author, July 9, 2015, San Miguel de Allende, MX.

2. Wendy Goldstein, interview by the author, August 27, 2016, Nashville, TN.

3. Ibid.

4. Ibid.

5. Ibid.

6. Wendy Goldstein, paisley journal entry, McClinton family archives, March 1988.

7. Ibid.

8. Gary Turlington, interview by the author, July 12, 2015, San Miguel De Allende, MX.

9. Ibid.

10. Goldstein, paisley journal entry, March 1988.

11. Delbert McClinton, paisley journal entry, McClinton Family archives, April 1988.

12. McClinton, paisley journal entry, May 1988.

13. McClinton, paisley journal entry, June 1988.

14. McClinton, paisley journal entry, July 1988.

15. David Hickey, interview by the author, August 26, 2016, Fort Worth, TX.

16. McClinton, paisley journal entry, July 1988.

17. Ibid.

18. Ibid.

19. Wendy Goldstein, interview by the author, August 27, 2016, Nashville, TN.

20. Goldstein, paisley journal entry, July 29, 1988.

21. Wendy Goldstein, interview by the author, August 27, 2016, Nashville, TN.

22. Ibid.

23. McClinton, paisley journal entry, August 1, 1988.

24. Goldstein, paisley journal entry, August 8, 1988.

25. Goldstein, paisley journal entry, August 10, 1988.

26. McClinton, paisley journal entry, September 6, 1988.

27. Goldstein, paisley journal entry, September 12, 1988.

28. Wendy Goldstein, interview by the author, May 15, 2016, Austin, TX.

29. Delbert McClinton, interview by the author, April 24, 2015, Austin, TX.

30. Wendy Goldstein, interview by the author, August 27, 2016, Nashville, TN.

31. McClinton, paisley journal entry, October 13, 1988.

32. McClinton, paisley journal entry, October 31, 1988.

33. McClinton, paisley journal entry, November 12, 1988.

34. McClinton, paisley journal entry, November 28, 1988.

35. McClinton, paisley journal entry, December 1, 1988.

36. Wendy Goldstein, interview by the author, August 27, 2016, Nashville, TN.

37. McClinton, paisley journal entry, December 4, 1988.

Chapter 15

1. Delbert McClinton, interview by the author, May 31, 2016, Nashville, TN.

2. Wendy Goldstein, paisley journal entry, McClinton family archives, September 1988.

3. Asawin Suebsaeng, "B.B. King and GOP Strategist Lee Atwater Used To Jam and Party Together," *The Daily Beast*, May 15, 2015, accessed August 28, 2016, http://www.thedailybeast.com/articles/2015/05/15/b-b-king-and-gop-strategist-lee-atwater-used-to-jam-and-party-together.html.

4. Wendy Goldstein, interview by the author, May 15, 2016, Austin, TX.

5. Ibid.

6. Don Wise, interview by the author, May 18, 2016, Knoxville, TN.

7. Bob Putignano, "Sounds of Blue: A Celebration of Blues and Soul," *Yonkers Tribune*, May 4, 2014, accessed August 28, 2016, http://www.yonkertribune.com/2014/05/sounds-of-blue-a-celebration-of-

blues-and-soul-the-1989-presidential-inaugural-concert-by-bob-putignano.

8. Delbert McClinton, interview by the author, July 9, 2015, San Miguel de Allende, MX.

9. Wendy Goldstein, interview by the author, August 27, 2016, Nashville, TN.

10. Delbert McClinton, paisley journal entry, McClinton family archives, February 8, 1989.

11. Don Wise, interview by the author, May 18, 2016, Knoxville, TN.

12. McClinton, paisley journal entry, April 1989.

13. Judy Hubbard, interview by the author, May 17, 2016, Wimberley, TX.

14. Gary Nicholson, interview by the author, May 12, 2016, Nashville, TN.

15. Ibid.

16. The song was "Jukebox Argument," performed by Mickey Gilley.

17. Gary Nicholson, interview by the author, May 12, 2016, Nashville, TN.

18. Ibid.

19. Lee Roy Parnell, interview by the author, August 30, 2016, Nashville, TN.

20. Ibid.

21. Delbert McClinton, brown leather journal entry, McClinton family archives, June 21, 1989.

22. Salvatore Caputo, "Rhythm and Blues Veteran Is Back Stronger than Ever," *The Arizona Republic*, March 3, 1990.

23. David Hickey, interview by the author, August 26, 2016, Fort Worth, TX.

24. Bonnie Raitt, interview by the author, June 30, 2016, Los Angeles, CA.

25. McClinton, brown leather journal entry, March 7, 1991.

26. Thomas Goldsmith, "Roots-rocker Delbert McClinton Roars Back with 'I'm With You'," *The Tennessean*, May 13, 1990.

27. Ibid.

28. "34th Annual Grammy Awards," last modified February 19, 2017, accessed March 26, 2017, https://en.wikipedia.org/wiki/34th_Annual_Grammy_Awards.

29. Delbert McClinton, interview by the author, July 12, 2015, San Miguel de Allende, MX.

30. Troy Seals and Max Barnes, "Every Time I Roll the Dice," Warner/Chappell Music, Inc., Universal Music Publishing Group, 1993.

31. Wendy Goldstein, interview by the author, July 11, 2015, San Miguel de Allende, MX.

32. Trigger Coroneos, "How Curb Records Killed Merle Haggard's Commercial Career," *Saving Country Music* (blog), April 18, 2016, http://

www.savingcountrymusic.com/how-curb-records-killed-merle-hag
gards-career/.

33. Delbert McClinton, interview by the author, August 23, 2016, Nashville, TN.

34. Lee Roy Parnell, interview by the author, August 30, 2016, Nashville, TN.

Chapter 16

1. Delbert McClinton, interview by the author, August 23, 2016, Nashville, TN.

2. Wendy Goldstein, interview by the author, August 26, 2016, Nashville, TN.

3. Dave Richards, "They Had A Little Faith In Him," *Pittsburgh Post Gazette*, November 6, 1992. 5B.

4. Delbert McClinton, black and white journal, July 22, 1992, McClinton Family Archives.

5. Delbert McClinton, black and white journal, August 1, 1992, McClinton Family Archives.

6. Delbert McClinton, black and white journal, n.d., McClinton Family Archives.

7. Delbert McClinton, black and white journal, August 13, 1992, McClinton Family Archives.

8. Wendy McClinton, interview by the author, September 15, 2016, Nashville, TN.

9. Delbert McClinton, black and white journal, September 28, 1992, McClinton Family Archives.

10. Delbert McClinton, black and white journal, October 2, 1992, McClinton Family Archives.

11. Delbert McClinton, black and white journal, February 5, 1993, McClinton Family Archives.

12. Delbert McClinton, black and white journal, February 26, 1993, McClinton Family Archives.

13. Delbert McClinton, black and white journal, May 14, 1993, McClinton Family Archives.

14. Delbert McClinton, interview by the author, June 2, 2016, Nashville, TN.

15. Delbert McClinton, black and white journal, May 14, 1993, McClinton Family Archives.

16. Wendy McClinton, interview by the author, September 15, 2016, Nashville, TN.

17. Wolfman Jack, Western Union Telegram, July 21, 1994. McClinton Family Archives.

18. Wendy Goldstein, interview by the author, San Miguel de Allende, Mexico, July 11, 2015.

19. Ibid.

Chapter 17

1. Delbert McClinton, interview by the author, September 15, 2016, Austin, TX.

2. Sunny Stephens, "Delbert McClinton Proves He's One of the Fortunate Few," *Music City Bluesletter* (January 1998).

3. Ibid.

4. Silas House, "Let The Good Times Roll," *No Depression* (November-December 2002): 76.

5. Tim Ingham, "Warner Bros. Records Boss Cameron Strang: 7 Lessons From My Career," *Music Business Worldwide*, accessed September 24, 2016, http://www.musicbusinessworldwide.com/cameron-strang-7-lessons-career/.

6. Wendy Goldstein, interview by the author, July 11, 2015, San Miguel de Allende, MX.

7. Cameron Strang, interview by the author, September 24, 2016, Los Angeles, CA.

8. Ibid.

9. Ibid.

10. Ibid.

11. Ibid.

12. Ibid.

13. Jack Bridwell, introductory remarks at the Buddy Holly Walk of Fame induction, Lubbock, Texas, August 26, 2001. McClinton family archives.

14. *Performing Arts of Fort Worth Hall Series 2001–2002 Playbill*, McClinton Family Archives.

15. Ibid.

16. House, "Let The Good Times Roll," 77.

17. Geoffrey Himes, "Delbert McClinton: Live" *Washington Post*, December 26, 2003.

18. Kevin McKendree, interview by the author, May 14, 2016, Nashville, TN.

19. Robert Baird, "Victim of Life's Circumstances," *Stereophile*, December 2003, 83.

20. Bob Britt, interview by the author, May 14, 2016, Nashville, TN.

21. Delaney McClinton, interview by the author, January 15, 2016, Sandy Beaches Cruise.

22. Delbert McClinton, interview by the author, July 11, 2015, San Miguel De Allende, MX.

23. Don Was, interview by the author, May 16, 2016, Los Angeles, CA.

24. Margaret Moser, "Delbert McClinton & Dick50: Acquired Taste (New West)" *Austin Chronicle*, September 18, 2009, accessed September 10, 2016, http://www.austinchronicle.com/music/2009–09–18/860260/.

25. Delbert McClinton, interview by the author, June 2, 2016, Nashville, TN.

26. Delbert McClinton, interview by the author, June 1, 2016, Nashville, TN.

27. Ibid.

28. Nick Tosches, *One of the Fortunate Few* by Delbert McClinton (Nashville: Rising Tide, 1997), liner notes.

29. Ibid.

Chapter 18

1. Delbert McClinton, interview by the author, September 16, 2015, Austin, TX.

2. Gary Turlington, interview by the author, July 15, 2015, San Miguel De Allende, MX.

3. Gary Turlington, interview by the author, September 7, 2016, Lillington, NC.

4. Delbert McClinton, interview by the author, June 2, 2016, Nashville, TN.

5. Gary Turlington, interview by the author, July 15, 2015, San Miguel De Allende, MX.

6. Marcia Ball, interview by the author, April 16, 2016, Austin, TX.

7. Gary Turlington, interview by the author, September 7, 2016, Lillington, NC.

8. Ibid.

9. Gary Turlington, interview by the author, July 15, 2015, San Miguel De Allende, MX.

10. Gary Turlington, interview by the author, September 7, 2016, Lillington, NC.

11. Ibid.

12. Molly Reed, interview by the author, June 3, 2016, Nashville, TN.

13. Ibid.

14. Ibid.

15. Gary Turlington, interview by the author, September 7, 2016, Lillington, NC.

16. Ibid.

17. Marcia Ball, interview by the author, April 16, 2016, Austin, TX.

18. Lee Roy Parnell, interview by the author, August 30, 2016, Nashville, TN.

19. Shelley King, interview by the author, April 16, 2016, Austin, TX.

20. Delaney McClinton, interview by the author, January 15, 2016, Delbert McClinton Cruise.

21. HalleyAnna, interview by the author, September 8, 2016, Martindale, TX.

22. Bob DiPiero, interview by the author, August 22, 2016, Nashville, TN.

23. Gary Turlington and Delbert McClinton, conversation with author, July 12, 2015, San Miguel De Allende, MX.

Chapter 19

1. Delbert McClinton, records journal entry, McClinton family archives, circa 2002.
2. Delaney McClinton, interview by the author, January 13, 2016, Sandy Beaches Cruise.
3. Ibid.
4. Clay McClinton, interview by the author, May 1, 2016, San Marcos, TX.
5. Delbert McClinton, interview by the author, September 15, 2016, Austin, TX.
6. Gary Nicholson, interview by the author, May 12, 2016, Nashville, TN.
7. Gary Turlington, interview by the author, September 7, 2016, Lillington, NC.
8. Molly Reed, interview by the author, June 3, 2016, Nashville, TN.
9. David Hickey, interview by the author, August 26, 2016, Fort Worth, TX.
10. Delbert McClinton, interview by the author, April 24, 2015, Austin, TX.
11. Delbert McClinton and Gary Turlington, interview by the author, July 9, 2015, San Miguel de Allende, MX.
12. Delbert McClinton and Gary Nicholson, "Best of Me," Sony/ATV Music Publishing, Carol Vincent & Associates, 1997.

Chapter 20

1. Delbert McClinton, interview by the author, September 15, 2016, Austin, TX.
2. Robert Oermann, interview by the author, May 18, 2016, Nashville, TN.
3. Kathleen Hudson, interview by the author, August 12, 2015, Kerrville, TX.
4. Ibid.
5. Tanya Tucker, interview by the author, September 9, 2016, Nashville, TN.
6. T Bone Burnett, interview by the author, June 10, 2016, Los Angeles, CA.
7. Ray Wylie Hubbard, interview by the author, May 25, 2016, Wimberley, TX.
8. Peter Guralnick, interview by the author, May 24, 2016, Boston, MA.

9. Ray Benson, interview by the author, April 20, 2016, Austin, TX.

10. Don Imus, interview by the author, August 5, 2015, Brenham, TX.

11. Cameron Strang, interview by the author, September 24, 2016, Los Angeles, CA.

12. Bonnie Raitt, interview by the author, June 20, 2016, Los Angeles, CA.

13. James Pennebaker, interview by the author, August 14, 2015, Nashville, TN.

14. Terry Lickona, interview by the author, September 28, 2016, Austin, TX.

15. Ibid.

16. Joe Nick Patoski, *Honky Tonk 'n Blues* by Delbert McClinton (Nashville: MCA, 1994), liner notes.

Epilogue

1. Richard Skanse, LoneStarMusicMagazine.com Review, accessed April 6, 2017, http://lonestarmusicmagazine.com/delbert-mcclinton-self-made-men-prick-litter/.

2. Don Wise, email message to the author, July 11, 2016.

3. Ibid.

4. Delbert McClinton, interview by the author, April 24, 2015, Austin, TX.

5. Bob Dylan and *Playboy* Magazine Editors, *Bob Dylan: The* Playboy *Interviews (50 Years of the* Playboy *Interview)* (Beverley Hills, CA: Playboy Enterprises, 2012), Kindle edition, 7.

6. Delbert McClinton, interview by the author, July 10, 2015, San Miguel de Allende, MX.

7. Ibid.

8. Delbert McClinton, Glen Clark, and Gary Nicholson, "Been Around a Long Time" (Nasty Cat Music, WRLT Music, Gary Nicholson Music), 2013.

Selected Discography

Albums

Delbert and Glen—Delbert and Glen (Clean Records, 1972)
Subject to Change—Delbert and Glen (Clean Records, 1973)
Victim of Life's Circumstances—Delbert McClinton (ABC Records, 1975)
Genuine Cowhide—Delbert McClinton (ABC Records, 1976)
Love Rustler—Delbert McClinton (ABC Records, 1977)
Second Wind—Delbert McClinton (Capricorn Records, 1978)
Keeper of the Flame—Delbert McClinton (Capricorn Records, 1979)
The Jealous Kind—Delbert McClinton (Muscle Shoals Sound, Capitol, 1980)
Plain' from the Heart—Delbert McClinton (Muscle Shoals Sound, Capitol, 1981)
Live from Austin—Delbert McClinton (Alligator Records, 1989)
I'm With You—Delbert McClinton (Curb Records, 1988)
Never Been Rocked Enough—Delbert McClinton (Curb Records, 1992)
One of the Fortunate Few—Delbert McClinton (Rising Tide Records, 1997)
Nothing Personal—Delbert McClinton (New West Records, 2001)
Room to Breathe—Delbert McClinton (New West Records, 2002)
Live—Delbert McClinton (New West Records, 2003)
Cost of Living—Delbert McClinton (New West Records, 2005)
Live from Austin, Texas—Delbert McClinton (New West Records, 2006)
Acquired Taste—Delbert McClinton and Dick50 (New West Records, 2009)
Blind, Crippled and Crazy—Delbert and Glen (New West Records, 2013)
Prick of the Litter—Delbert McClinton and the Self-Made Men (Hot Shot Records/Thirty Tigers, 2017)

Videos

Live from Austin, Texas—Delbert McClinton (New West Records, 2006)
Rocking the Boat: A Musical Conversation and Journey Starring Delbert McClinton—Jay Curlee, Director (JC Communications, 2007)
The Road to Austin—Gary Fortin, Director (FORMAX Group, 2015)

Austin City Limits Performances

1977—Delbert McClinton/Gatemouth Brown (205)
1979—Delbert McClinton/Cate Brothers (408)
1983—Delbert McClinton/Rank and File (810)
1989—Delbert McClinton/The Crickets (1406)
1993—Delbert McClinton/Lee Roy Parnell (1806)
1995—Asleep at the Wheel's 25th Anniversary Show (2103)
1997—Delbert McClinton/Miss Lavelle White (2213)

Selected Songs

"Ain't Lost Nothin'"—Delbert McClinton
"All Night Long"—Delbert McClinton and Gary Nicholson
"All Them Other Good Things"—Delbert McClinton
"All There Is of Me"—Delbert McClinton and Kevin McKendree
"Alright by Me"—Delbert McClinton and Kevin McKendree
"B-Movie Boxcar Blues"—Delbert McClinton
"Bad Haircut"—Delbert McClinton and Kevin McKendree
"Baggage Claim"—Delbert McClinton
"Been Around a Long Time"—Delbert McClinton, Gary Nicholson, and
    Glen Clark
"Best of Me"—Delbert McClinton and Gary Nicholson
"Better Off With the Blues"—Delbert McClinton, Gary Nicholson, and
    Donnie Fritts
"Birmingham Tonight"—Delbert McClinton
"Blues About You Baby"—Delbert McClinton and Al Anderson
"California Livin'"—Delbert McClinton
"Can't Nobody Say I Didn't Try"—Delbert McClinton
"Cease and Desist"—Delbert McClinton
"Cherry Street"—Delbert McClinton, Kevin McKendree, and Gary
    Nicholson,
"C.O.D."—Delbert McClinton
"Cold November"—Delbert McClinton
"Cost of Living"—Delbert McClinton
"Couldn't Have Been a Millionaire"—Delbert McClinton
"Crazy 'Bout You"—Delbert McClinton
"Dead Wrong"—Delbert McClinton
"Desperation"—Delbert McClinton
"Doin' What You Do"—Delbert McClinton, Bob Britt, and Mike Joyce
"Do It"—Delbert McClinton
"Don't Do It"—Delbert McClinton and Gary Nicholson
"Don't Leave Home Without It"—Delbert McClinton, Gary Nicholson,
    and Sharon Vaughn
"Don't Want to Love You"—Delbert McClinton and Billy Lawson

"Down into Mexico"—Delbert McClinton, Gary Nicholson, and Bob
DiPiero

"Everything I Know About the Blues"—Delbert McClinton, Gary Nicholson, and Benmont Tench

"Good as I Feel Today"—Delbert McClinton, Gary Nicholson, and Glen
Clark

"Good Man, Good Woman"—Delbert McClinton

"Gotta Get it Worked On"—Delbert McClinton and Max D. Barnes

"Hammerhead Stew"—Delbert McClinton and John Barlow Jarvis

"Have a Little Faith in Me"—Delbert McClinton

"Here Comes the Blues Again"—Delbert McClinton

"Honky Tonkin' (I Guess I Done Me Some)"—Delbert McClinton

"I Had a Real Good Time"—Delbert McClinton, Gary Nicholson, and
Tom Hambridge

"I Like Lovin'"—Delbert McClinton, Bob Britt, and Mike Joyce

"I Need to Know"—Delbert McClinton, Gary Nicholson, Anson Funderburgh, and Renee Funderburgh

"In the Middle of the Night"—Delbert McClinton, Bob Britt, Glen Clark,
and Kevin McKendree

"I Received a Letter"—Delbert McClinton

"I Want to Love You"—Delbert McClinton

"I Want to Thank You Baby"—Delbert McClinton

"If I Could Be Your Lover"—Delbert McClinton and Glen Clark

"If You Don't Leave Me Alone (I'm Gonna Find Somebody Who Will)"—
Delbert McClinton

"If You Really Want Me To, I'll Go"—Delbert McClinton

"It Ain't Whatcha Eat but the Way How You Chew It"—Delbert McClinton

"I'm Dying as Fast as I Can"—Delbert McClinton

"I've Got Dreams to Remember"—Delbert McClinton

"Jungle Room"—Delbert McClinton and Fred Knobloch

"Just You and Me"—Delbert McClinton and Donnie Fritts

"Kiss Her Once for Me"—Delbert McClinton, Gary Nicholson, and Tom
Hambridge

"Lesson in the Pain of Love"—Delbert McClinton

"Let Me Be Your Lover"—Delbert McClinton

"Lie No Better"—Delbert McClinton and Gary Nicholson

"Livin' It Down"—Delbert McClinton, Gary Nicholson, and Benmont
Tench

"Lone Star Blues"—Delbert McClinton and Gary Nicholson

"Lovinest Man"—Delbert McClinton

"Mama's Little Baby"—Delbert McClinton, Kevin McKendree, and Gary
Nicholson

"Maybe Someday Baby"—Delbert McClinton

"Midnight Communion"—Delbert McClinton, Gary Nicholson, and Rus-
sell Smith

"Money Honey"—Delbert McClinton and Gary Nicholson

"Monkey Around"—Delbert McClinton, Gary Nicholson, and Benmont Tench

"More and More, Less and Less"—Delbert McClinton and Gary Nicholson

"My Love Is Burnin'"—Delbert McClinton

"Neva"—Delbert McClinton

"Never Been Rocked Enough"—Delbert McClinton and Troy Seals

"Never Saw it Comin'"—Delbert McClinton, Kevin McKendree, and Gary Nicholson

"New York City"—Delbert McClinton and Tom Faulkner

"Nothin' Lasts Forever"—Delbert McClinton

"Object of My Affection"—Delbert McClinton

"Oh My"—Delbert McClinton

"One of the Fortunate Few"—Delbert McClinton, Gary Nicholson, and Tom Hambridge

"Out of My Mind"—Delbert McClinton, Kevin McKendree, and Gary Nicholson

"The Part I Like Best"— Delbert McClinton and Glen Clark

"Peace in the Valley"—Delbert McClinton, Gary Nicholson, and Tom Hambridge

"People Just Love to Talk"—Delbert McClinton, Kevin McKendree, and Rob McNelley

"Pullin' the Strings"—Delbert McClinton, Bob Britt, and Mike Joyce

"Read Me My Rights"—Delbert McClinton and Johnny Neel

"Real Good Itch"—Delbert McClinton

"Right to Be Wrong"—Delbert McClinton, Gary Nicholson, and Tom Hambridge

"Rosy"—Delbert McClinton, Bob Britt, and Mike Joyce

"The Rub"—Delbert McClinton

"Ruby Louise"—Delbert McClinton

"Same Kind of Crazy"—Delbert McClinton and Gary Nicholson

"Sandy Beaches"—Delbert McClinton and John Jarvis

"San Miguel"—Delbert McClinton, Bob Britt, Glen Clark, and Kevin McKendree

"Sending Me Angels"—Delbert McClinton

"She's Not There Anymore"—Delbert McClinton, Kevin McKendree, and Tom Hambridge

"Skip Chaser"—Delbert McClinton, Bob Britt, Glen Clark, and Kevin McKendree

"Smooth Talk"—Delbert McClinton and Gary Nicholson

"Solid Gold Plated Fool"—Delbert McClinton

"Some People"—Delbert McClinton

"Somebody to Love You" –Delbert McClinton and Gary Nicholson

"South by Southwest"—Delbert McClinton, Gary Nicholson, and Lee

Roy Parnell

"Squeeze Me In"—Delbert McClinton and Gary Nicholson

"Starting a Rumor"—Delbert McClinton, Guy Clark, and Gary Nicholson

"Sure Feels Good"—Delbert McClinton, Gary Nicholson, and Glen Clark

"Take it Easy"—Delbert McClinton

"To Be With You"—Delbert McClinton and Glen Clark

"Too Much"—Delbert McClinton

"Too Much Stuff"—Delbert McClinton and Gary Nicholson

"Troubled Women"—Delbert McClinton

"Two More Bottles of Wine"—Delbert McClinton

"Two Step Too"—Delbert McClinton

"Until Then"—Delbert McClinton, Kevin McKendree, and Tom Hambridge

"Victim of Life's Circumstances"—Delbert McClinton

"Watchin' the Rain"—Delbert McClinton

"When Rita Leaves"—Delbert McClinton and Gary Nicholson

"When She Cries at Night"—Delbert McClinton, Al Anderson, and Bob DiPiero

"Whoever Said It Was Easy"—Delbert McClinton and Al Anderson

"Who's Foolin' Who"—Delbert McClinton and Steve Bogard

"Why Me?"—Delbert McClinton and J. Fred Knobloch

"Willie"—Delbert McClinton and Gary Nicholson

"Won't Be Me"—Delbert McClinton and Gary Nicholson

"Wouldn't You Think"—Delbert McClinton, Gary Nicholson, and Benmont Tench

"You Never Were Mine"—Delbert McClinton, Gary Nicholson, and Benmont Tench

"Your Memory, Me, and the Blues"—Delbert McClinto

Bibliography

Every effort has been made to properly locate, identify, and credit photographers, songwriters, and song publishers. In cases where the photographer is not known, or a publicity shot has been used, the source or collection that has supplied the photograph is listed. Song lyrics are used in accordance with the American Musicological Society's "Best Practices in the Fair Use of Copyrighted Materials in Music Scholarship" (http://www.ams-net.org/AMS_Fair_Use_Statement.pdf).

Interviews

Terry Allen, Gregg Andrews, Susan Antone, Cary Baker, Marcia Ball, Ray Benson, Bob Britt, Etta Britt, T Bone Burnett, Gary Cartwright, Watt Casey Jr., Bruce Channel, Glen Clark, Jerry Conditt, Nancy Copin, Jay Curlee, Bob DiPiero, Ernie Durawa, Miranda Eggleston, Joe Ely, Sharon Ely, Wendy Goldstein, Alan Govenar, Peter Guralnick, HalleyAnna, Gary Hartman, Cleve Hattersley, Annie Heller-Gutwillig, David Hickey, Judy Hubbard, Ray Wylie Hubbard, Kathleen Hudson, Don Imus, Laurie Jasinski, Kathy Kane, Shelley King, Terry Lickona, Bill Mack, Brandy McClinton, Clay McClinton, Delaney McClinton, Delbert McClinton, Patty McClinton, Kevin McKendree, Jason Mellard, Gary Nicholson, Robert Oermann, Lee Roy Parnell, Joe Nick Patoski, James Pennebaker, Mark Pucci, Bonnie Raitt, Molly Reed, Jan Reid, Richard Skanse, Lewis Stephens, Cameron Strang, Angela Strehli, Nick Tosches, Tanya Tucker, Gary Turlington, Janice Williams, Don Was, Don Wise, Todd Wolfson, Red Young.

Print

Antone, Susan. *Antone's: The First 10 Years*. Austin, TX: Blues Press, 1985.

Arnold, Ann. *Gamblers and Gangsters: Fort Worth's Jacksboro Highway in the 1940s and 1950s*. Austin, TX: Eakin Press, 1998.

Carr, Joe, and Alan Munde. *Prairie Nights to Neon Lights: The Story of Country Music in West Texas*. Lubbock: Texas Tech University Press, 1995.

Clayton, Lawrence, and Joe Specht, eds. *The Roots of Texas Music*. College Station: Texas A&M University Press, 2003.

Clifford, Craig, and Craig Hillis, eds. *Pickers and Poets: The Ruthlessly Poetic Singer-Songwriters of Texas*. College Station: Texas A&M University Press, 2016.

Corcoran, Michael. *All Over the Map: True Heroes of Texas Music*. Austin: University of Texas Press, 2005.

Davis, Steven L. *Texas Literary Outlaws*. Fort Worth: Texas Christian University Press, 2004.

Endres, Clifford. *Austin City Limits*. With Scott Newton. Austin: University of Texas Press, 1987.

Escott, Colin. "Road Scholar: Delbert McClinton." In *Tattooed on their Tongues: A Journey Through the Backrooms of American Music*. New York: Schirmer Books, 1996.

Fowler, Gene, and Bill Crawford. *Border Radio*. Austin: University of Texas Press, 2002.

Govenar, Alan. *The Rise of a Contemporary Blues Sound: Texas Blues*. College Station: Texas A&M University Press, 2008.

Guralnick, Peter. *Lost Highway*. Enhanced ed. New York: Little, Brown, 2012. Kindle edition. (The Kindle Edition includes the Delbert McClinton chapter).

Hartman, Gary. *The History of Texas Music*. College Station: Texas A&M University Press, 2008.

Hudson, Kathleen. *Telling Stories Writing Songs: An Album of Texas Songwriters*. Austin: University of Texas Press, 2001.

Jasinski, Laurie, ed. *The Handbook of Texas Music*. 2nd ed. Denton, TX: Texas State Historical Association, 2012.

Lomax, Alan. *The Land Where Blues Began*. New York: The New Press, 2002.

Malone, Bill C. *Country Music, USA*. 2nd rev. ed. Austin: University of Texas Press, 2002.

Mellard, Jason. *Progressive Country: How the 1970s Transformed the Texan in Popular Culture*. Austin: University of Texas Press, 2013.

Meltzer, Richard. *A Whore Just Like the Rest: The Music Writings of Richard Meltzer*. Cambridge, MA: DeCapo Press, 2000.

Nichols, Mike. *Lost Fort Worth*. Charleston, SC: The History Press, 2014.

Patoski, Joe Nick. *An Epic Life*: *Willie Nelson*. New York: Little, Brown and Company, 2008.

Reid, Jan. *The Improbable Rise of Redneck Rock*: *New Edition*. Austin: University of Texas Press, 2004.

Reid, Jan. *Texas Tornado*: *The Times and Music of Doug Sahm*. With Shawn Sahm. Austin: University of Texas Press, 2010.

Rudinow, Joel. "Race, Ethnicity, Expressive Authenticity: Can White People Sing the Blues?" *Journal of Aesthetics and Art Criticism*, 52, no. 1, The Philosophy of Music (Winter, 2004).

Shaver, Billy Joe. *Honky Tonk Hero*. With the assistance of Brad Reagan. Austin: University of Texas Press, 2005.

Shrake, Bud. *Land of the Permanent Wave: An Edwin "Bud" Shrake Reader*. Austin: University of Texas Press, 2008.

Stimeling, Travis D. *Cosmic Cowboys and New Hicks: The Countercultural Sounds of Austin's Progressive Country Music Scene*. New York: Oxford University Press, 2011.

Tipaldi, Art. *Children of the Blues: 49 Musicians Shaping a New Blues Tradition*. New York, Hal Leonard, 2002.

Tosches, Nick. *Country: The Twisted Roots of Rock 'n' Roll*. New York: DaCapo Press, 1996.

Tosches, Nick. *Unsung Heroes of Rock 'n' Roll*. New York: Harmony Books, 1991.

Ward, Brian. *Just My Soul Responding Rhythm and Blues, Race Relations, and Black Consciousness*. Berkeley: University of California Press, 1998.

Index